Winning With the Closed Sicilian

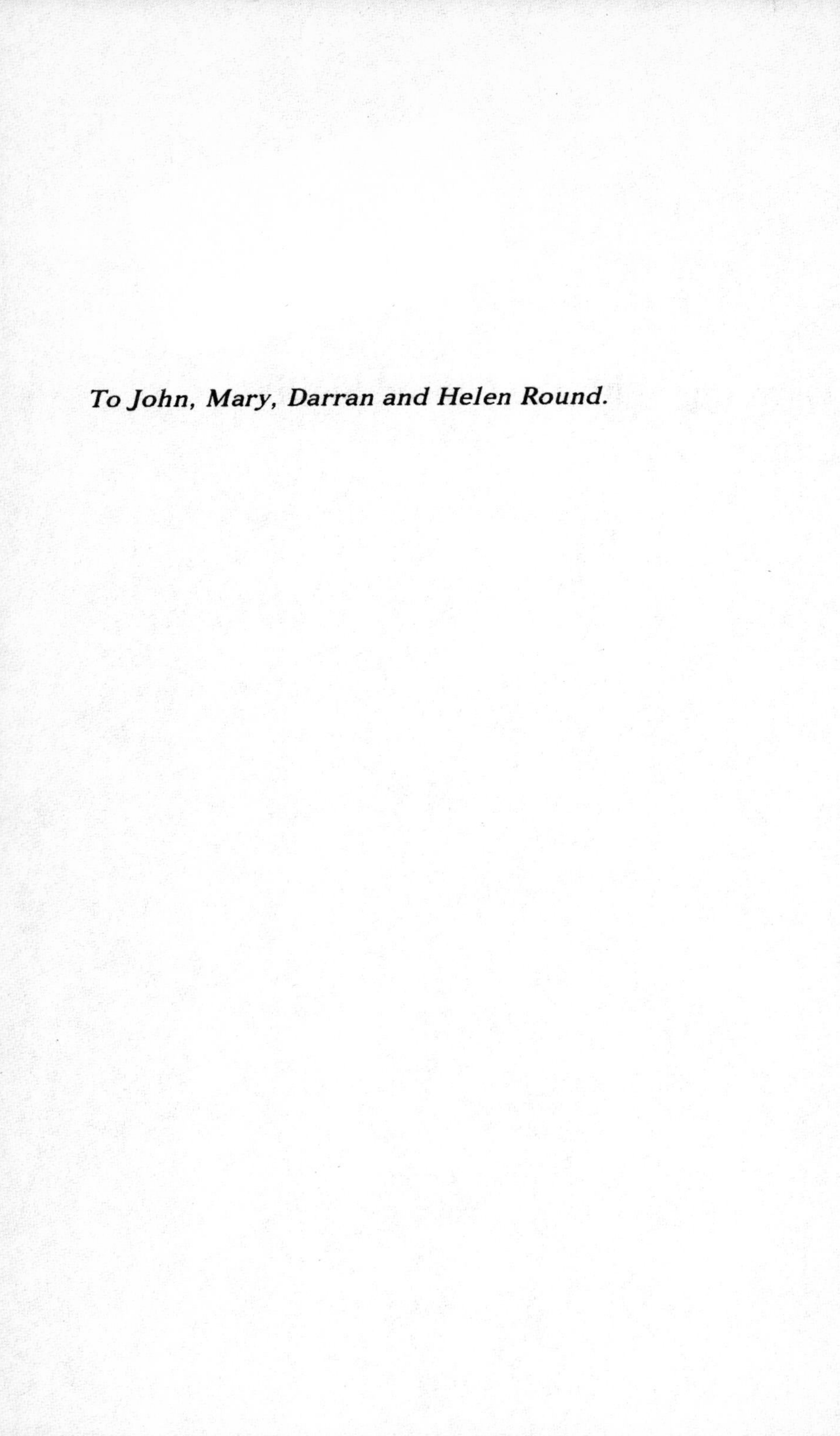

To John, Mary, Darran and Helen Round.

Winning With the Closed Sicilian

Gary Lane

An Owl Book
Henry Holt and Company
New York

Henry Holt and Company, Inc.
Publishers since 1866
115 West 18th Street
New York, New York 10011

Henry Holt® is a registered trademark
of Henry Holt and Company, Inc.

First published in the United States in 1993 by
Henry Holt and Company, Inc.
Originally published in Great Britain in 1992 by
B. T. Batsford Ltd.

Library of Congress Catalog Card Number: 92-56738

ISBN 0-8050-2637-1 (An Owl Book: pbk.)

First American Edition—1993

Printed in the United Kingdom
All first editions are printed on acid-free paper. ∞

10 9 8 7 6 5 4 3 2 1

Adviser: R. D. Keene, GM, OBE
Technical Editor: Andrew Kinsman

Contents

Preface	*7*
Symbols	*8*
Introduction	*9*

1 e4 c5 2 ♘c3 ♘c6 3 g3 g6 4 ♗g2 ♗g7 5 d3 d6

1	6 ♗e3	*13*
2	6 f4 ♘f6	*41*
3	6 f4 e5	*49*
4	6 f4 e6	*59*
5	6 ♘h3 and 5 ... b6	*85*
6	Systems with ... ♖b8	*92*
7	Systems with ♘ge2	*100*
8	Systems with ♘f3	*122*
9	2 ... e6	*135*
10	2 g3	*147*

Index of Variations	*151*

Preface

The recent wave of popularity in the Closed Sicilian (1 e4 c5 2 ♘c3 followed by a kingside fianchetto by White) at Grandmaster level has led to the discovery of many new ways for White to seek an opening advantage. Whilst generally leading to quite blocked positions, this opening is an ideal choice for club and tournament players as the basic strategies are quite simple to master and White is often able to obtain an advantage simply by following logical strategies or exploiting over-optimistic play by his opponent. In addition, the Closed Sicilian avoids the mass of theoretical analysis typical of such variations as the Najdorf and Dragon, which follow the more standard 1 e4 c5 2 ♘f3 and 3 d4.

This book aims to take the reader through the common variations which make up the Closed Sicilian. Emphasis is on the explanation of ideas rather than lists of variations, with the aim of explaining how the positions should be handled. We will discuss games by great exponents of the Closed Sicilian such as former World Champions Anatoly Karpov, Boris Spassky and Vasily Smyslov alongside those of lesser mortals. The author hopes that the reader will not only improve his or her understanding of the opening and the game as a whole, but will be able to successfully apply the ideas in this book in his or her own games.

Gary Lane
April 1992

Symbols

+	Check
++	Double check
mate	Checkmate
!	Good move
!!	Excellent move
?	Bad move
??	Blunder
!?	Interesting move
?!	Dubious move
⩲	Small advantage for White
⩱	Small advantage for Black
±	Clear advantage for White
∓	Clear advantage for Black
+-	Winning advantage for White
-+	Winning advantage for Black
=	The position is equal
1-0	White wins
0-1	Black wins
½-½	Draw
Ol	Olympiad
Ct	Candidates tournament
IZ	Interzonal
Z	Zonal
Ch	Championship
corr.	Correspondence
Jnr	Junior

Introduction

Before we begin to discuss the different variations which comprise the Closed Sicilian, a few words should be said about the layout of the book. The general emphasis is on fashionable variations which the reader is likely to come across in his or her own games. This is supplemented by a discussion of less common variations which have occurred in practice.

The most common position in the Closed Sicilian arises after the sequence **1 e4 c5 2 ♘c3 ♘c6 3 g3 g6 4 ♗g2 ♗g7 5 d3 d6:**

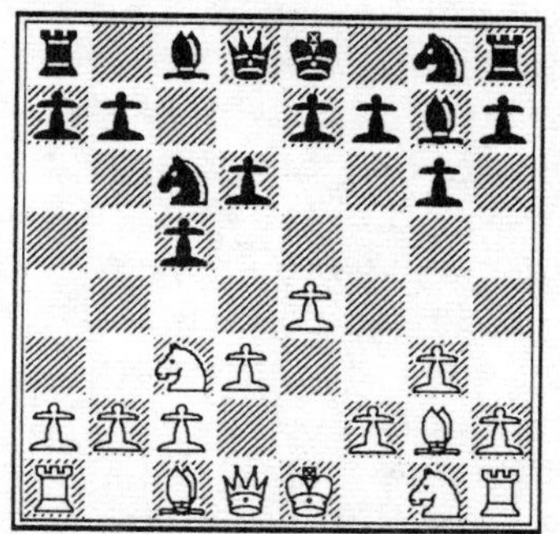

The distinguishing feature of the white strategy is this kingside fianchetto which can be used against almost every Black response.

The first chapter of the book deals with an aggressive line where White plays 6 ♗e3 and then ♕d2, aiming for a rapid attack. This is one of the key variations which have revitalised the Closed Sicilian and is the favourite strategy of Grandmasters Ljubojevic and Romanishin.

In chapter two we move on to the more traditional approach of 6 f4. After 6 ... ♘f6 White concentrates on gaining space on the kingside while Black does the same thing on the other wing. Another approach for Black is 6 f4 e5, known as the Botvinnik System. A related idea in the English opening is discussed for those interested in employing the Reversed Closed Sicilian.

The most common Black strategy after 6 f4 is to play 6 ... e6 and ... ♘ge7, leaving the bishop on g7 unrestricted and exerting a powerful influence on the d4-square and the white queenside. This variation, generally considered to be the main line of the Closed Sicilian, is dealt with in chapter four. Since this variation is so common in practice, the theoretical paths are more well-trodden in this variation than in any of the others so the reader will find slightly more theoretical analysis in this chapter than elsewhere.

Chapter five deals with the unorthodox queenside fianchetto by Black, immediately countering White's powerful kingside fianchetto. In this chapter we also look at the unusual and rather unlikely-looking 6 ♘h3.

One very ambitious and risky venture for Black is to play for an immediate queenside pawn advance by 5 ... ♖b8, reasoning that since White's build-up is rather slow he is ill-equipped to conduct an early breakthrough so Black therefore has time to undertake a counter-attack. Very unclear play results with White trying to utilise his advantage in development to capitalise on Black's lack of respect for his schemes. This system is analysed in chapter six.

The tremendous amount of influence that the young Anatoly Karpov had on the theory and practice of the system with ♘ge2 is evident in chapter seven. This plan tends to lead to a more positional battle in which White tries to accumulate small advantages.

The system with an early ♘f3 is discussed in chapter eight. The idea is to feign the intention of transposing to an Open Sicilian before eventually revealing the true intention by inserting d3. At this stage Black's pieces are usually not ideally placed to deal with the change in circumstances.

Chapter nine deals with a kind of French Defence set-up for Black after 2 ... e6 and 3 ... d5. This has been adopted by Kasparov and Nunn, but should give White a small advantage. Black can also delay playing ... d5 and this possibility is also discussed.

The final chapter looks at the consequences of an immediate kingside fianchetto without 2 ♘c3. This gives White the option of omitting ♘c3 altogether, but allows Black to counter with 2 ... d5.

For those interested in creating a repertoire with the Closed Sicilian, the following alternatives might be considered.

A close scrutiny of either the variation with 6 ♗e3 (chapter 1) or 6 f4 (chapters 2-4), together with a second-string option of either the solid ♘ge2 or ♘f3 systems (chapter 7 or 8). The less-common Black alternatives in chapters 5, 6 and 9 should also be considered.

However, in order to obtain a feel for the typical middlegames which arise in the Closed Sicilian, the reader is recommended to play through each illustrative game in the book.

1) 6 ♗e3

The system with an early ♗e3 from White is one which has helped to revitalise the Closed Sicilian in the last few years. White aims for a rapid mobilisation of his forces with the aim of launching an early kingside attack. As we shall see, it is particularly effective when Black adopts the move 5 ... e6 instead of the normal 5 ... d6.

Spassky - Hjartarson
Belfort 1988

1	**e4**	**c5**
2	**♘c3**	**♘c6**
3	**g3**	**g6**
4	**♗g2**	**♗g7**
5	**d3**	**e6**
6	**♗e3**	

A crafty move which exploits the move-order adopted by Black. The key is that while the c5-pawn is defended, a quick ♕d2, ♗h6 and h4 is possible, leading to a strong attack. This active variation heads for relatively uncharted territory compared to the more standard 6 ♘ge2 or 6 f4. The set-up relies on the fact that a later ... e5 will waste a tempo compared to the situation after 6 f4 e5 7 ♗e3.

6 ... ♘d4?!

The knight occupying the d4-square to curtail a future d4 is such a feature of the Closed Sicilian that it is an automatic choice in this situation by the majority of players. However, in this position it is ill-advised and White can get a comfortable edge. The correct move, 6 ... d6, is considered later in this chapter.

7 ♘ce2! *(1)*

1
B

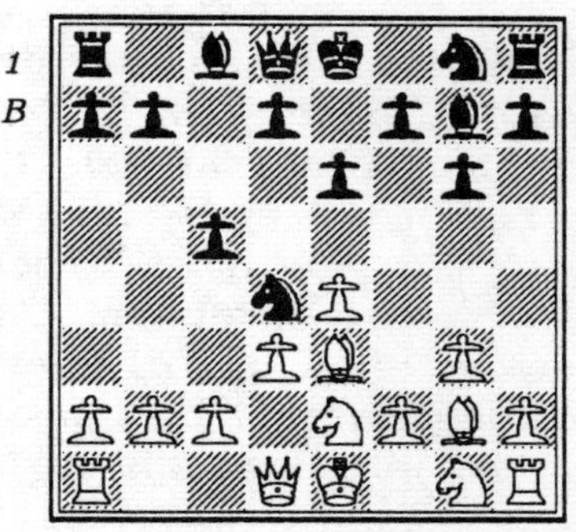

This move often comes

as a shock to Black. The backward knight move is hard for Black to fathom over the board and even more difficult to counter properly. Spassky has made clear his intention to continue with c3 displacing the knight and preparing for a central thrust with d4. If the knights are exhanged then ♘gxe2 continues development and keeps open the options of central or wing-play.

7 ... b6

Faithfully following a traditional continuation which is recommended in all the old books on the opening but is a disastrous choice against the former World Champion. The main alternative, 7 ... d6, is examined in the next illustrative game, but at club level Black often snatches the b-pawn. White has all the fun in the following sharp variations:

a) 7 ... ♘xe2 8 ♘xe2 ♗xb2 9 ♖b1 (9 ... ♕a5+ 10 ♗d2 ♕xa2 11 ♖xb2! ♕xb2 12 ♗c3 with a clear advantage) 9 ... ♗g7 10 ♗xc5 ♕a5+ 11 ♗b4 ♕xa2 12 0-0, when Black has severe problems in getting his king to safety as the powerful bishop on b4 prohibits kingside castling.

b) 7 ... ♘ge7 8 c3 ♘xe2 9 ♘xe2 and now:

b1) 9 ... d6, when White has two promising choices:

b1a) 10 ♕d2 b6 11 ♗h6 0-0 12 h4! ♗xh6 13 ♕xh6 ♔h8 14 h5 ♘g8 15 ♕e3 g5 16 f4! h6 17 e5 ♖b8 18 d4 ♗a6?! (18 ... ♗b7 offers better resistance) 19 0-0-0 ♗xe2 20 ♕xe2 d5 21 ♖hf1 cxd4 22 ♖xd4 ♖c8 23 ♔b1 ♘e7 24 ♗e4! ♘c6 25 ♖dd1 f5 26 exf6 ♕xf6 27 ♗c2 gxf4 28 gxf4 ♘e7 29 ♖de1 ♖c6 30 ♕d3 ♘f5 31 ♖g1 ♖g8 32 ♖xg8+ ♔xg8 33 ♖g1+ ♔f7 34 ♕f3 ♖d6 35 ♖g6 ♕e7 36 ♕g4 ♕h4 37 ♖g7+! ♔f8 38 ♖g8+ ♔e7 39 ♗xf5 ♕e1+ 40 ♔c2 exf5 41 ♕g7+ 1-0 Pribyl - Prodanov, Varna 1976.

b1b) 10 d4 cxd4 11 ♘xd4!? a6 12 ♕d2 ♕c7 13 0-0 e5 14 ♘c2 ♗e6 15 a4 ♖d8?! 16 a5 ♖d7 17 ♗b6 ♕c8 18 ♘b4 0-0 19 ♘d5 ♗xd5 20 exd5 f5 21 f4 ♔h8 22 ♖ac1 ♕e8 23 c4 ♕f7 24 b4, when the queenside pawns are menacingly poised to advance with the protection of the bishops. White had the advantage in Lane - Shutler, West of England Ch 1981.

b2) 9 ... b6 10 d4 cxd4 11 ♗xd4 e5 12 ♗e3 0-0 (12 ... ♗b7 13 0-0 [13 ♕d6!] 13 ... d5 14 exd5 ♗xd5 15 ♕a4+ ♕d7 16 ♕xd7+ ♔xd7 17 ♖ad1 ♔e6 18 ♖fe1= Pichon - Birmingham, Douai 1991) 13 ♕d6! ♗b7 14 0-0 ♖c8 15

♖fd1 ♖c7 16 a4 ♘c6 17 b4 ♖e8 18 ♕d3 ♕a8 19 a5 bxa5 20 b5! ♘e7 21 ♖xa5 f5 22 ♖xa7 ♕c8 23 b6 fxe4 24 ♕d6 ♘c6 25 bxc7 ♘xa7 26 ♗xa7 ♗c6 27 ♗h3 ♗f8 28 ♕xc6 1-0 Kovacevic - Peev, Pancevo 1989.

8 ♗xd4!

This is much better than the routine 8 c3 ♘xe2 9 ♘xe2 ♗b7 10 ♕d2 f5 11 0-0 ♘e7 12 ♖fe1 0-0 13 ♗g5 ♕e8 14 ♘f4 ♘c6= Medina - Mecking, Palma de Mallorca 1969. It is this continuation that most players would expect as it is the standard game in the line. However, Spassky's inspired exchange of his bishop demonstrates that there is no clear route to equality in this variation.

8 ... cxd4
9 e5 ♖b8
10 f4 f6

The only way to avoid the instant loss of the pawn on d4. Not so good is 10 ... d6? 11 ♘xd4 dxe5 12 ♘c6 ♕c7 13 ♘xb8, winning the exchange.

11 ♘f3 fxe5
12 fxe5 ♕c7

Hjartarson prepares to take on e5 to avoid a material deficit.

13 ♘exd4 ♗xe5
14 ♕e2 *(2)*

The situation has become crystal clear: White's lead in development is decisive and should lead to a win as Black's pieces lack any kind of harmony. At the cost of maintaining level material, Hjartarson has dug himself into a positional hole that is difficult to get out of. If the vital bishop returns to g7 then 15 ♘b5 ♕c5 16 d4 ♕e7 17 ♘xa7 or 17 ♘c7+ is very strong. In such extreme circumstances the decision is taken to exchange the main defensive piece in the forlorn hope that White will falter.

2
B

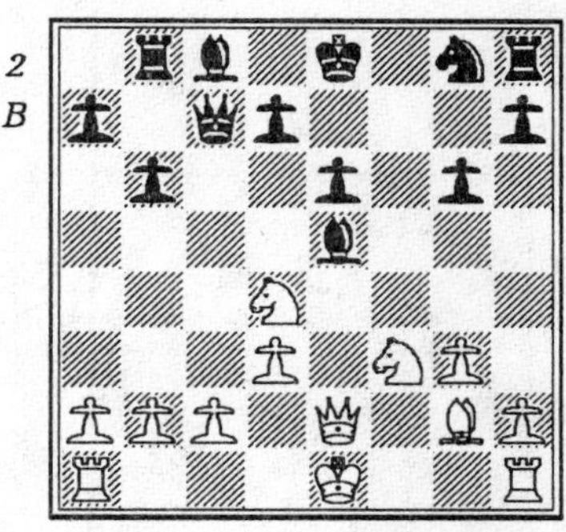

14 ... ♗xd4
15 ♘xd4 ♕c5

It is a reasonable idea to try to get the queen active in an attempt at getting something out of nothing. The main problem for Black is getting the king to safety in the knowledge that when Spassky castles kingside the rook will cut of the escape route. Blocking the open f-file fails to remedy the crisis. 15 ... ♘e7 16 0–0 ♘f5 17 ♘xf5 gxf5 18 ♖xf5 completely wrecks the pawn cover and threatens 19 ♕h5+.

16 ♘b3 ♕g5

An abrupt finish would have resulted after 16 ... ♕e7?? 17 ♕e5, forking the two black rooks.

17 0–0 ♘e7

Hopeless is 17 ... ♘f6? 18 h4, winning the knight.

18 ♖ae1

Sensibly moving the other rook into the action. Now Spassky has all his forces lined up against the king.

18 ... ♖f8
19 ♘d2! *(3)*

3
B

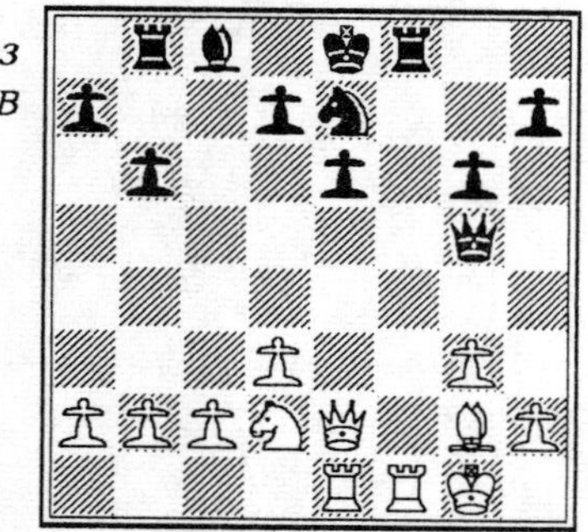

The knight intends to improve its position by taking up a central role on e4 or c4 heading for d6 or f6 which would make life very difficult for Hjartarson. However, there is very litle that he can do about it.

19 ... ♖xf1+
20 ♖xf1 ♘f5

After 20 ... ♗b7 21 ♗xb7 ♖xb7 22 ♕f3! White threatens mate and the capture on b7.

21 ♘c4 ♔e7
22 g4 b5

Desperation, but 22 ... ♘h4 (or 22 ... ♘d6) 23 ♕f2 is hardly pleasant considering the exposed nature of the black king.

23 gxf5 bxc4
24 ♕e5! 1–0

Black resigned in view of the threatened rook and 25 f6+, which would win the queen.

Smyslov – Denker
USSR – USA 1946

1	e4	c5
2	♘c3	♘c6
3	g3	g6
4	♗g2	♗g7
5	d3	e6
6	♗e3	♘d4?!
7	♘ce2!	d6
8	c3	♘c6 *(4)*

4
W

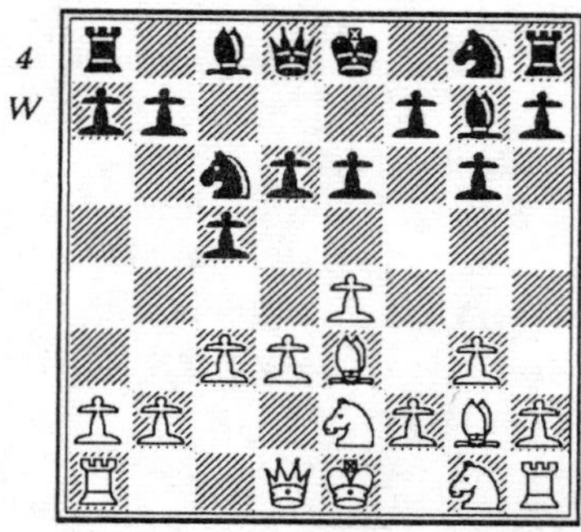

Although this variation has already been discussed

in the previous game, this classic encounter is a model example of how to exploit the accumulated positional advantages which can be derived in the opening.

9 d4 cxd4

10 ♘xd4

The knight recaptures rather than the pawn because White is keen to keep the possibility of opening up the d-file, in order to concentrate operations on the vulnerable d-pawn.

10 ... ♘xd4

11 ♗xd4 e5

Black wants to ease the White dominance of d4 while preparing to counterattack with a future ... d5 or ... f5.

12 ♗e3 ♘ge7

13 ♘e2 0-0

Both sides are happy to complete development.

14 0-0 ♗e6

15 ♕d2!

This connects the rooks and also prevents Black from carrying out his planned 15 ... d5, due to 16 ♗c5 dxe4?? 17 ♕xd8 ♖fxd8 18 ♗xe7.

15 ... ♕c7

16 ♖fc1 *(5)*

A clever idea that seeks to curtail ... d5 by 17 c4 allowing the knight to exert control on the centre via c3. The routine 16 ♖fd1 seems logical but is rather ineffective against 16 ... ♖fd8.

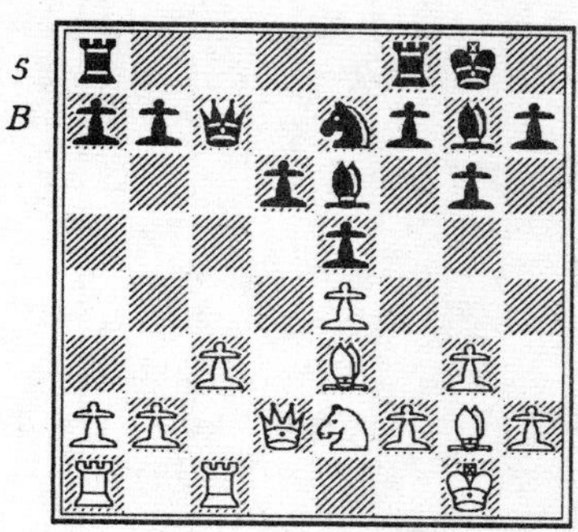

16 ... f5?!

The problem with this active continuation is that the h1-a8 diagonal is now opened primarily to the benefit of White. More testing is 16 ... b5 to prevent c4, although Smyslov can still extract an advantage by 17 a4! a6 18 ♖d1 and now:

a) 18 ... ♖ad8 19 axb5 axb5 20 ♖a7±.

b) 18 ... ♖fd8 19 axb5 axb5 20 ♖xa8 ♖xa8 21 ♕xd6±.

17 c4 fxe4

18 ♘c3 ♘f5

A piece of extensive analysis by Smyslov demonstrates the futility of snatching the pawn: 18 ... ♗xc4 19 ♘xe4 d5 20 ♘g5 d4 21 ♘e6 dxe3 22 ♕xe3 ♕d6 23 ♘xf8 ♗f7 (23 ... ♗d5 24 ♗xd5+ ♘xd5 25 ♕c5 ♗xf8 26 ♕xd6 ♗xd6 27 ♖d1+-) 24 ♖d1 ♘d5 25 ♕b3 ♖d8 26 ♘xg6 hxg6 27 ♗xd5 ♗xd5 28 ♖xd5 ♕xd5 29 ♖d1!+-.

19 Nxe4 Nxe3

It might appear that the knight can take up a central post on d4 but this would be immediately undermined: 19 ... Nd4 20 c5! d5 21 Ng5 Bf7 22 f4!, offering to trade the supporting pawn on e5 to White's advantage.

20 Qxe3 h6
21 Rd1! Rfd8

The pin on the c-file prevents Black from taking on c4 with the bishop: 21 ... Bxc4 22 Rac1 d5 23 Rxd5 Qf7 24 Nd6 winning.

22 Rac1 Rac8
23 b3 b6
24 Nc3 *(6)*

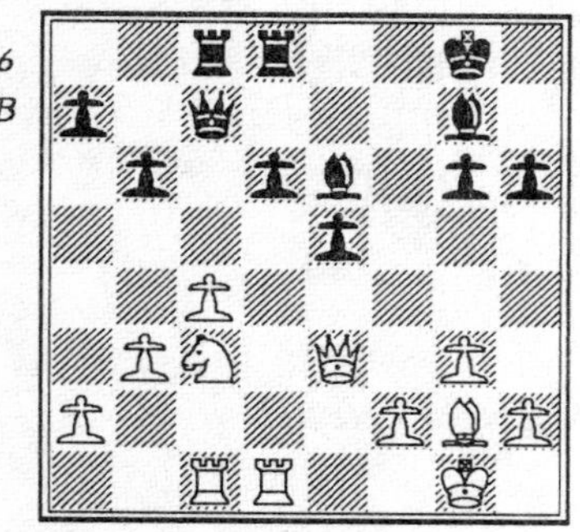

The square d5 is pin-pointed for occupation as Black has feeble control over the white squares. A major drawback of Black's position is the inactivity of the dark-squared bishop which had been barricaded by its own pawns. White is more than happy to exchange Black's other bishop to leave a classic 'good knight' versus 'bad bishop' struggle.

24 ... Qe7
25 Bd5 Kh7
26 Bxe6 Qxe6

Black is on the defensive because the backward pawn on d6 is a cause for concern and the white knight has excellent prospects on d5 or e4.

27 Rd3 Rc7
28 Rcd1 Rf7
29 Ne4 Bf8
30 Rd5

The relentless pressure continues without respite, with White preparing to triple on the d-file with Qd3.

30 ... Qg4
31 R1d3

It is not a good idea to rush things: 31 Nxd6 Bxd6 32 Rxd6 Qxd1+ 33 Rxd1+ Rxd1 34 Kg2 e4! and Black can at least salvage a draw thanks to the pair of rooks. Of course, 31 Qd3 is ruled out by 31 ... Rf3.

31 ... Be7

Black is no longer able to hang on to the pawn due to a tactical combination as White forces a quick win after 31 ... Qe6 32 Qd2 Rfd7 33 c5 bxc5 34 Nxc5, forking the rook and queen.

32 Nxd6 Bxd6
33 Rxd6 Rdf8
34 Qxe5 Rxf2

Black's attack is super-

ficial since his own king is too exposed.

35 ♖d7+ ♖2f7
36 ♖xf7+ ♖xf7
37 ♖d8

White forces Black into a passive position in order to limit any prospects of a counter-attack. Smyslov now managed to secure the point in fine style.

37 ... ♖g7
38 ♕e8 g5
39 ♕h8+ ♔g6
40 ♖d6+ ♔f7
41 ♕xh6 ♕f5
42 ♖d1! ♕c5+
43 ♔g2 ♕e7
44 ♖f1+ ♔g8
45 ♕f6 ♕e8
46 ♕f5 g4
47 ♖f2 ♕e7
48 ♕d3 ♖g5
49 ♖e2 ♕f8
50 ♕e4 ♖g7
51 ♕d5+ ♕f7
52 ♖e6 1-0

Balashov – Shirov
Klaipeda 1988

1 e4 c5
2 ♘c3 ♘c6
3 g3 g6
4 ♗g2 ♗g7
5 d3 e6
6 ♗e3 d6
7 ♕d2

The rather obvious attacking set-up can be quite potent and has been quite successful for White in practice. If Black attempts to castle then White will establish the bishop on h6, castle queenside, and push the h-pawn until eventually exchanging on g7 with excellent chances. The full might of this strategy is examined in the illustrative game Ljubojevic – Quinteros but before this we examine an interesting attempt to prevent White's intended ♗h6 (should the black knight move away from the defence of this square).

7 ... h6!? *(7)*

This is certainly one way of handling White's direct approach but it has the drawback of slightly weakening the kingside in the long-term and fails to contribute to the mobilisation of Black's forces.

8 f4

A quieter approach from an earlier game in the same tournament proved to be just not quite strong enough: 8 ♘ge2 ♘d4 9 0-0

♘e7 10 ♖ae1 ♘ec6 11 a3 ♗d7 12 ♘c1 h5 13 h3 f5 14 exf5 gxf5 15 ♗g5 ♕a5 16 ♘b3 ♘xb3 17 cxb3 ♔f7 18 ♕f4 ♘e5 19 b4 cxb4 20 axb4 ♕b6 21 ♖e3 ♔g6 22 ♖fe1 ♖ae8 23 b5 ♘f7 24 h4 ♗d4 25 ♖3e2 a6 26 ♘a4 ♕a7 27 b6 ♗xb6 28 ♘xb6 ♕xb6 29 d4 e5 30 dxe5 dxe5 31 ♕c1 ♗c6 ½–½ Balashov – Oll, Klaipeda 1988.

8 ... ♘ge7
9 ♘f3 ♘d4
10 0-0 ♘ec6
11 ♘e1 b6
12 ♘d1! *(8)*

8
B

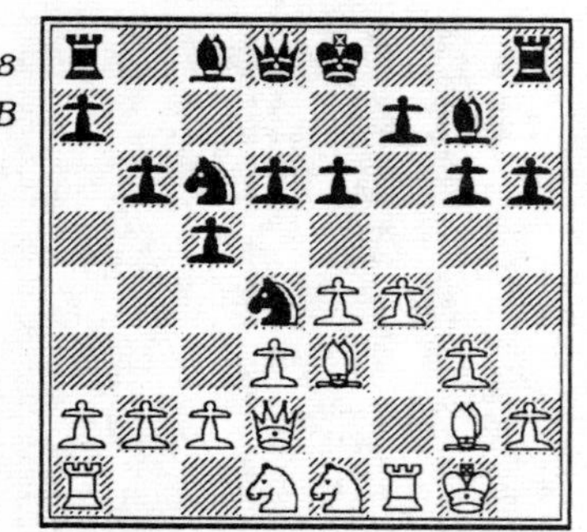

An original idea, planning to oust the knight from the coveted d4-square. Now that Black is unable to exchange on f3, he must make room for the knight to retreat to the active c6-square. The success of Balashov's strategy hinges on the time gained by provoking 7 ... h6.

12 ... ♘e7
13 c3 ♘dc6
14 ♗f2 d5
15 e5

White is eager to create a bulwark centre by closing down the scope of the bishop on g7 and reinforcing the e5-strongpoint with 16 d4. Such a situation can often occur in the opening and the plan of g4, ♗h4, ♘e3, ♘f3, doubled rooks on the f-file and play f5 is White's ideal. If White could carry out his plan it would be very difficult to find a defence so Black decides to mix things up.

15 ... g5!?

Certainly, this is a determined effort to stop Balashov from having everything his own way and this move makes use of 7 ... h6. However, apart from the surprise value this move can hardly be recommended since it worsens the plight of the black king by loosening the pawn cover.

16 ♘e3 ♘g6
17 ♘f3 gxf4
18 gxf4 h5

The f-pawn is poisoned since after its capture Black would get a shattered pawn structure and have a lack of harmony amongst his pieces: 18 ... ♘xf4 19 ♘f5 exf5 20 ♕xf4 ♗e6 21 d4 with the idea of ♘h4 and ♗h3 restoring material equality, with a marked positional plus.

19 h4 ♗h6
20 ♘g5 ♘xf4 *(9)*

9
W

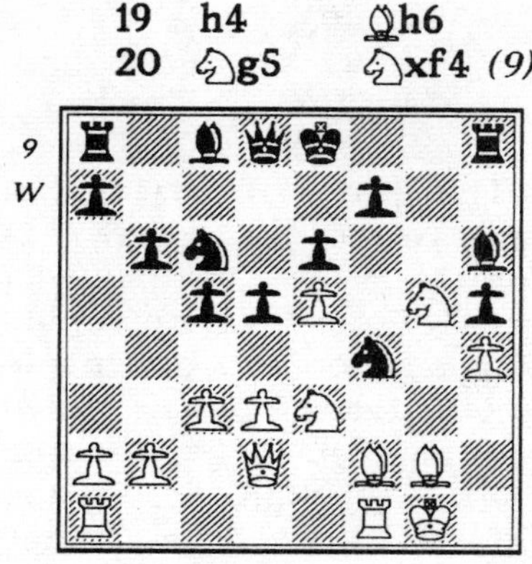

21 ♘xf7!

This strikes a blow in the heart of Shirov's defences. The rampant knight is readily sacrificed as 21 ... ♔xf7 22 ♗g3 ♔g7 23 ♗xf4 keeps the piece count level with an extremely vulnerable black king.

21 ... ♕e7
22 ♘xh6 ♕g7

The best chance because after 22 ... ♖xh6 23 ♗g3 Black has severe problems.

23 ♘f7 ♘xg2
24 ♘xg2 ♕xf7
25 ♗e3 ♕g7
26 ♗g5

After the flurry of exchanges the position has become somewhat calmer. The Soviet Grandmaster has managed to create a sizeable advantage since his bishop is now poised to take up residence on f6 making it difficult for Black to co-ordinate his pieces with his king stuck in the centre.

26 ... ♖h7
27 ♗f6 ♕g6
28 ♕g5

Most club players would rather pursue an attack in this position than exchange queens, but this is the right time to enter a highly favourable ending. Otherwise, a few aimless moves might adversely transform the situation as the White king is on an open file. The strong player must always be prepared to trade his middlegame space advantage into something that is more long-term.

28 ... ♕xg5
29 hxg5 ♗a6
30 g6 ♖h6
31 ♘f4

The pawn on g6 is a monster in terms of its influence. Balashov now threatens 32 ♗g7, cornering the rook, and the monarch cannot come to the rescue as 31 ... ♔f8 32 ♘xe6+ ♔g8 33 ♘f4 leaves Black with another passed pawn to deal with.

31 ... ♘e7
32 ♗g5

When one is just about to play a critical move it often pays to hesitate for a moment. The text is preferred to 32 ♗g7 as Shirov had declared his intention of taking on g6 by his previous move. In these circumstances the bishop on g5 would be better placed than at g7 as it has more room for manoeuvre.

32 ... ♖xg6

There is no point in opting out of the exchange sacrifice: 32 ... ♖h8 33 g7 ♖g8 34 ♘xh5 ♔d8 35 ♖f7, winning.

33 ♘xg6 ♘xg6
34 ♖f6 ♗xd3
35 ♖xe6+ ♔d7
36 ♖d6+ ♔c7
37 ♖xd5

The rook has wreaked havoc in the enemy camp. Now that there are open files for White to exploit, the slim chance that Shirov had of organising some kind of blockade to limit the scope of the rooks is gone.

37 ... ♗e4
38 ♖d2 ♖e8
39 ♖f1 ♖xe5
40 ♗f4!

It is usually a good idea to trade off pieces when you already have a material advantage because then the opponent is less able to organise some desperate tricks. The remainder is a fine display of technique by Balashov, who steadily reduces Shirov's option to the point where he runs out of moves.

40 ... ♘xf4
41 ♖xf4 ♗f5
42 ♔f2 ♗e6
43 a3 ♔c6
44 ♖e2 ♖xe2+
45 ♔xe2 ♗b3

The plan of trying to hang on to the h-pawn is pointless as White will simply ignore it, moving his king over to the queenside to plunder the pawns, aided and abetted by the rook. The only plan for Black here is to try to exchange all the pawns off, leaving a theoretically drawn rook versus bishop ending. Of course in practice, there are no real chances for Black.

46 ♖f5 a5
47 ♖xh5 b5
48 ♔e3 ♔d6
49 ♖h6+ ♔d5
50 ♖a6 a4
51 ♖b6 ♔c4
52 ♔d2 1–0

The finish would have been 52 ... ♗a2 53 ♔c1 ♗b3 54 ♖d6 ♗a2 55 ♔c2 ♗b3+ 56 ♔b1 b4 57 axb4 cxb4 58 ♖d4+, winning the vital pawn.

Ljubojevic – Am. Rodriguez
Biel 1985

1 e4 c5
2 ♘c3 ♘c6
3 g3 g6
4 ♗g2 ♗g7
5 d3 e6
6 ♗e3 d6

7 ♕d2 ♕a5!? *(10)*

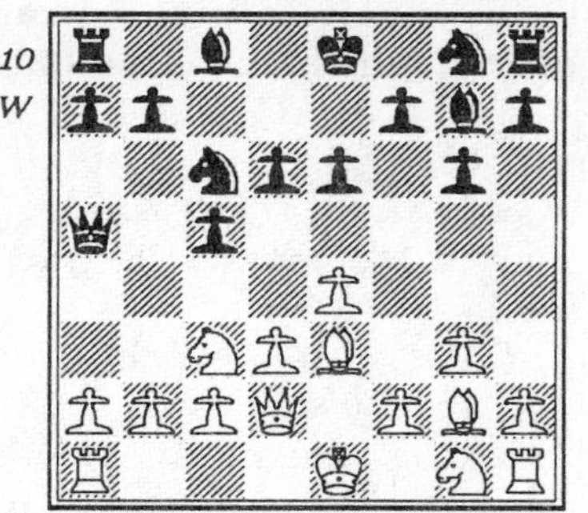

This early queen sortie is designed to curtail any attacking ambitions on the kingside by exerting pressure on c3 and delaying castling until White has adopted less aggressive posts for his pieces. Quite ineffective is 7 ... ♘d4 8 ♘d1 (using the square vacated by the queen) 8 ... e5 (8 ... f5!? 9 c3 ♘c6 10 ♘e2 ♘f6 11 exf5 exf5 12 0-0 0-0 13 h3 ♗d7 14 c4!, when the knight on d1 returns to the game via c3 with a slight spatial edge, Spassky - Ivanovic, Niksic 1983) 9 c3 ♘c6 10 ♘e2 ♗g4 11 0-0 ♘ge7 12 f4 0-0 13 ♘f2 ♗e6 14 ♘h3 ♕c8 15 ♘g5 ♗d7 16 ♖ac1 f6 17 ♘f3 and Black is extremely cramped whilst White is ready to continue with d4 or to prepare for f5, Hort - Kurajica, Zagreb 1969.

The choice of 7 ... ♖b8 invariably transposes to other lines but there is some scope for independent play:

a) 8 ♘h3 ♘d4 9 0-0 ♘e7 10 ♘d1 b6 11 c3 ♘dc6 12 ♗h6 0-0 13 ♗xg7 ♔xg7 14 ♘e3 e5 15 f4 f6 16 ♖f2, preparing to double rooks whilst Black can only wait, Pacis - Shamkovich, Malta Ol 1980.

b) 8 ♘ge2 and now:

b1) 8 ... b5 9 0-0 ♘ge7 10 ♗h6 0-0 11 ♗xg7 ♔xg7 12 f4 b4 13 ♘d1 e5!? 14 f5 f6 15 g4 g5 16 ♘g3 a5 17 ♘h5+ ♔f7 18 ♖f3! h6 19 ♖h3 ♖h8 20 ♘e3 a4 21 a3! bxa3 22 ♖xa3 ♖xb2 23 ♖xa4 ♘g8 24 ♗f1 ♖b1 25 c3 ♔f8 26 ♕a2 ♖b8 27 ♖a8 ♗d7 28 ♖a6 ♗e8 29 ♕d5! ♕c7 30 ♖f3 ♘ge7 31 ♕e6 ♗xh5 32 ♕xf6+ ♔g8 33 gxh5 ♕d7 34 ♘g4 ♖f8 35 ♘xh6+ ♔h7 36 ♘f7 1-0 Romanishin - Ivozchikov, USSR 1979.

b2) 8 .. ♘d4 9 0-0 b5 10 ♘d1 ♘e7 11 ♘c1! b4 12 a3 a5 13 axb4 axb4 14 c3 bxc3 15 bxc3 ♘dc6 16 ♗h6 0-0 17 ♗xg7 ♔xg7 18 ♘e3 d5 19 ♕c2!, when the c5-pawn is a potential target and ♘b3 is now possible, Spassky - Portisch, Mexico (m) 1980.

c) 8 ♘f3 and now:

c1) 8 ... ♘d4 9 ♗xd4! cxd4 10 ♘b5 ♕b6 11 ♕b4 ♔d7 12 e5! dxe5 13 ♘d2 a5 14 ♕a4 ♘e7 15 ♘c4 ♕a6 16 ♕a3 ♘d5 17 ♕c5 ♕c6 18 ♕a7 ♕xb5 19 ♕xb8 ♕b4+ 20 ♔e2 ♕c5 21 ♕a8+- Klinger - Keller, Zurich 1988.

c2) 8 ... ♕b6 9 ♖b1! ♘d4

10 0–0 (10 b4!?) 10 ... ♘ge7 11 b4 ♕d8 12 bxc5 dxc5 13 ♘a4 ♕c7 14 c3 ♘xf3+ 15 ♗xf3 b6 16 d4 ♗d7 17 ♘b2 ♖d8 18 ♘d3 cxd4 19 cxd4 ♗c6 20 ♘b4 ♗b7 (Lane – Dautov, Brussels 1992) 21 d5±.

8 ♘f3

Ljubojevic spurns the usual 8 f4 in favour of keeping the diagonal open for his bishop. This choice is purely a matter of taste and both moves have their adherents.

8 ... ♘d4
9 0–0 ♗d7

An interesting pawn sacrifice gives White the initiative after 9 ... ♘e7, viz. 10 ♗h6 ♗xh6?! 11 ♕xh6 ♘xc2 12 ♖ac1, when the queen will disrupt the kingside via g7 causing considerable damage.

10 ♗f4!

A difficult move to predict as it seems rather simplistic to threaten the pawn that can so easily be defended. However, it manages to expose the drawback of 7 ... ♕a5 (the weak d-pawn) and creates the option of ♘d5 in certain variations. A reliable choice for a solid game is 10 a3 ♖c8 11 ♖ab1 b6, with equal chances: Augustin – D. Byrne, Lugano Ol 1968.

10 ... ♕b6

This retreat is necessary as otherwise White can enter a superior endgame: 10 ... e5 11 ♘xd4! cxd4 (11 ... exf4 12 ♘b3) 12 ♘d5 ♕xd2 13 ♗xd2 ♖c8 14 ♗b4; or 11 ... exd4 12 ♘d5 ♕xd2 13 ♗xd2 ♖c8 14 ♗f4.

11 ♖ab1 ♖c8
12 ♖fe1

Making the most of his lead in development by preparing the e5-advance.

12 ... ♘e7
13 e5 *(11)*

11
B

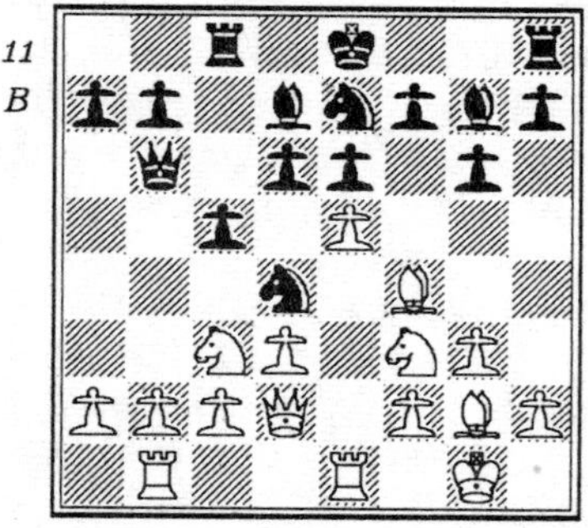

A feature of Ljubojevic's play is his energetic attitude to every position he encounters. Black is forced into making difficult decisions at an early stage of the game. Exchanging bishops no longer has any venom now that White has arranged his pieces for a central push: 13 ♗h6 0–0 14 ♗xg7 ♔xg7 15 ♘xd4 cxd4 16 ♘e2, with equality.

13 ... ♗c6

White has no worries in other continuations.

a) 13 ... ♘xf3+ 14 ♗xf3 dxe5 15 ♗xe5 ♗xe5 16 ♖xe5 0–0 17 b4! cxb4 18 ♘e4 f6 19 ♖xb4, when the rook will seek shelter on c5 whilst giving up the queen is unpromising for Black as his pawns are easy targets and the rooks will have difficulty in working effectively together.

b) 13 ... d5 14 ♘e2 ♘xf3+ 15 ♗xf3 d4!? (otherwise 16 d4 blocks the centre in preparation for a kingside pawn storm) 16 c3, seeking to undermine d4, which may come under further pressure by a timely b4.

14 ♘e4 ♗xe4

The powerful knight has to be removed from the board to avoid instant ruin.

15 ♖xe4 ♘xf3+
16 ♗xf3 dxe5

If Black seeks to form a blockade with 16 ... d5 then White's greater space makes the job of manoeuvring his pieces a lot easier. One possible plan could be to play c3 and d4 to increase support of e5 so that the bishop on g7 labours against a rock-solid formation and White is free to probe for kingside weaknesses.

17 ♗xe5 ♗xe5
18 ♖xe5 0–0

At long last Rodriguez has found time to allow the king to reach sanctuary. However, there is cause for concern in the absence of the dark-squared bishop, which is traditionally a fine defensive piece in the particular system.

19 h4!

An excellent way of adding life to such positions, undermining the fianchetto pawn structure. White can afford to make his own king slightly more vulnerable because Black lacks open lines to create counterplay.

19 ... ♘f5
20 c3 h5

It is prudent to take measures to avoid the irritating 21 h5, albeit at the cost of compromising the pawn shield. If White had managed to carry out his plan then there would be the pleasant choice of keeping the status quo until the time was right to exchange on g6 or to proceed with h6, aiming for complications exploiting the threat of back-rank mates and ♕f6.

21 ♖be1 ♖fd8
22 a3 ♕c7? *(12)*

With the assumption that there is nothing to fear, Black embarks upon a course of action which involves putting pressure on e5, so that when he doubles his rooks on the d-file the option of Rd1 would be ruled out. Not so clear is 22 ... Rd7 (22 ... Qd6 23 Bxb7 Rb8 24 Bg2 Qxd3 25 Qxd3 Rxd3 26 R1e2 with a slight edge due to the active bishop and chances against the loose a- and c-pawns) 23 Qg5 Qxb2 24 Bxh5 Qxc3 25 Bg4, when the odds are in White's favour and he can try to break through with h5. For example, 25 ... Qxd3 26 h5 Kg7 (26 ... Ne7 27 Qf6 gxh5 [otherwise 28 h6 with mate on g7] 28 Rg5+ Ng6 29 Bxe6! wins) 27 hxg6 fxg6 28 Rxe6 with a massive advantage.

12
W

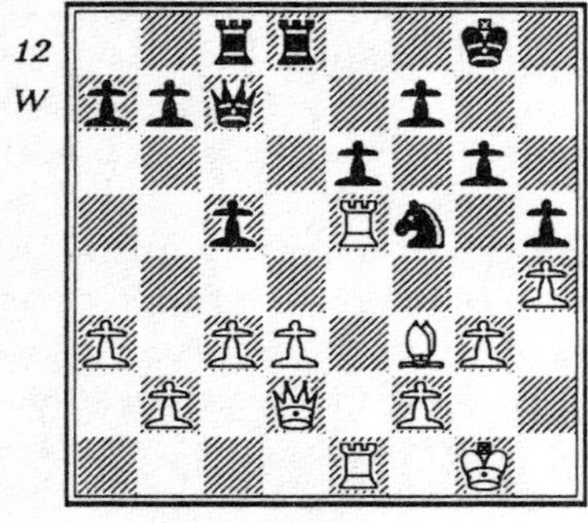

23 Bxh5!

An astonishing sacrifice. This combination is made feasible by White having his forces on central squares where they are poised to turn their attention to an onslaught against the black monarch at the slightest opportunity. The calculation involved in making this difficult sacrificial decision to shed material is eased by the fact that there are a series of forcing moves.

23 ... f6

The full weight of Ljubojevic's opportunism is revealed after 23 ... gxh5 24 Rxf5! exf5 25 Qg5+ Kf8 26 Qxh5 Kg7 27 Qg5+ Kf8 28 Qf6 Kg8 29 Re7 Qxe7 30 Qxe7 when two rooks for a queen is scant compensation as White can leisurely pick of the black pawns and a future h6 will be troublesome.

24 Rxf5

Clinically destroying any lingering hopes of survival.

24 ... gxf5

Not much better is 24 ... exf5 25 Bxg6 Rd5 (intending ... Kg7) 26 Qh6 Qg7 27 Qh5, when the bishop can be re-routed via f5 to e6 with a lethal check.

25 Rxe6 Rd6
26 Qe2 Rcd8
27 Re7 R8d7
28 Bf7+

It is hardly surprising that with the black kingside standing in ruins a mating web can be quickly created.

28 ... Kf8

Similar play to the game results from 28 ... Kg7 29 Qh5.

29 Re8+ Kg7

There is no escape after

29 ... ♔xf7 30 ♕h5+ ♔g7 31 ♕h8+ ♔g6 32 h5+ ♔g5 33 ♖g8+ winning.

30 ♖g8+ 1–0

Ljubojevic – Quinteros
Mar del Plata 1981

1	**e4**	**c5**
2	**♘c3**	**♘c6**
3	**g3**	**g6**
4	**♗g2**	**♗g7**
5	**d3**	**e6**
6	**♗e3**	**d6**
7	**♕d2**	**♘ge7?!**

This natural developing move allows White to unleash a violent attack that has claimed many victims over the years. However, even very strong masters as Black often get caught out by assuming that White's relatively strange move-order will transpose back into the main lines. Such careless play can cost the game.

8 ♗h6 *(13)*

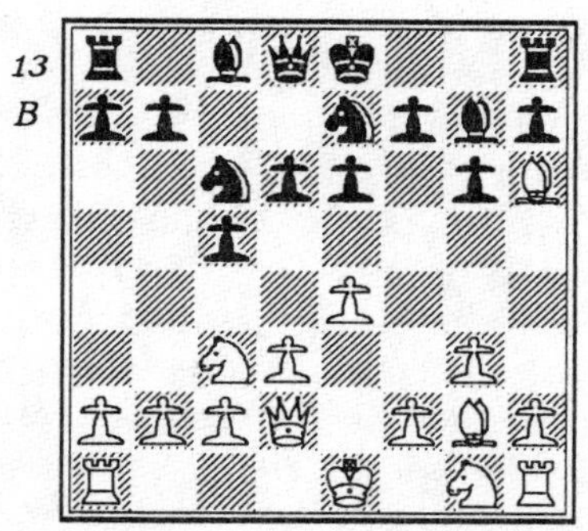

8 ... ♗xh6

If Black decides to castle he faces a violent attack. Even if mate is avoided, the costs incurred by awkward defensive measures eventually bring the game to a quick finish, i.e. 8 ... 0–0 9 h4 and now:

a) 9 ... ♕e8 10 0–0–0 ♘b4? 11 a3 ♘bc6 12 h5 f5 13 ♗xg7 ♔xg7 14 ♘b5 ♕d8 15 ♘f3 a6 16 hxg6 hxg6 17 ♕h6+ ♔f7 18 ♘c3 ♔e8 19 d4 cxd4 20 ♘xd4 e5 21 ♘xc6 bxc6 22 f4 exf4 23 exf5 ♗xf5 24 g4 ♗d7 25 ♘e4 ♕c7 26 ♘xd6+ 1–0 Szakolczai – Gombocz, Kecskemet II 1989.

b) 9 ... f6 10 ♗xg7 (10 h5? ♗xh6 11 ♕xh6 g5 intending ♔h8 and ♘g8, which traps the queen) 10 ... ♔xg7 11 h5 ♖h8 12 ♘ge2 ♗d7 13 d4 cxd4 14 ♘xd4 ♘xd4 15 ♕xd4 ♗c6 16 0–0–0 e5 17 h6+ ♔f7 18 ♕c4+ ♔f8 19 f4 ♘c8 20 fxe5 ♘b6 21 ♕f1 f5 22 exf5 ♕g5+ 23 ♔b1 ♕xf5 24 ♗xc6 bxc6 25 ♕g2 ♕c8 26 ♖xd6 1–0 Jones – Harwar, London 1988.

9 ♕xh6 ♘d4
10 0–0–0

This is one of the special cases in the Closed Sicilian where White is happy to castle queenside. In this instance, it facilitates getting the king to safety, bringing the rook into play and defending c2. Of course, White might be more cautious if the black bishop on g7 was still bearing down on the queenside.

10 ... ♘ec6
11 ♘ge2 ♗d7

The Argentinian Grandmaster has no choice but to prepare to castle queenside before the state of his kingside deteriorates to such an extent that the king is trapped in the centre of the board.

12 ♕g7 *(14)*

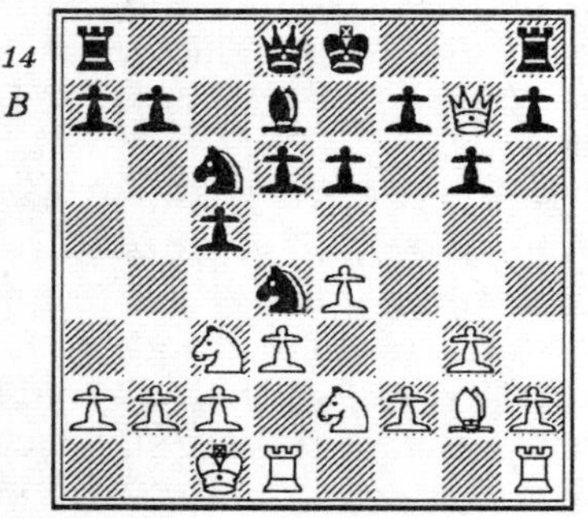

14
B

The rich tactical nature of the position allows plenty of room for deviations from the text, but the theme of invading with the queen is always the same. Exchanging knights is one alternative attempt to expose the inadequacies of Black's set-up: 12 ♘xd4 cxd4 13 ♘e2 ♕a5 14 ♔b1 ♕a4 15 c3 dxc3 16 ♘xc3 ♕b4 17 d4 ♖c8 18 ♕g7 ♖f8 19 ♖he1 ♘a5 20 ♘d5 ♕a4 21 ♕f6 ♘c6, Hort - Hodgson, Wijk aan Zee 1986, when White could have won by 22 ♕h4 h6 (22 ... exd5 23 exd5+ ♘e5 24 ♕f6!+-) 23 ♘f6+ ♔e7 24 e5! g5 25 exd6+ ♔xd6 26 ♘e4+, followed by ♕xh6 winning.

12 ... ♖f8

An off-beat alternative suggested by Parma is 12 ... ♔e7?!. Upon closer scrutiny, 13 ♘f4, with the threat of ♘d5+, is just one example of how the king can be swiftly persecuted.

13 ♔b1

Capturing the pawn on h7 immediately causes White some problems after 13 ♕xh7 ♕f6 since, unlike in the game, the capture on e2 would be check, e.g. 14 ♕h6 ♕xf2 15 ♖df1 ♕xg2 16 ♖hg1 ♘xe2+.

13 ... ♕e7

Good or bad, 13 ... h5!? should be played to postpone the crisis.

14 ♕xh7 ♕f6
15 ♕h6 ♕xf2

A curious decision as the queen has been left with no escape for the sake of capturing a lone pawn. Quinteros probably assumed that he could escape with three pieces for the queen but the lack of harmony amongst his pieces should have set off warning bells in his head. There is little to be gained by 15 ... ♘xe2 16 ♘xe2 ♕xf2 17 ♖hf1 ♕xg2 18 ♘f4, or 17 ... ♕xe2 18 ♗f3, when the queen is trapped.

16 ♖df1 ♕xg2
17 ♖hg1 ♕xe2
18 ♘xe2 ♘xe2
19 ♖g2

If White adopts a passive attitude then his opponent will castle to co-ordinate his rooks. Then Black would shuffle his other pieces around to prevent any open files which might permit White's rooks into the game. However, Ljubojevic stays alert.

19 ... ♘ed4
20 c3 ♘b5
21 a4 ♘c7
22 ♖gf2 *(15)*

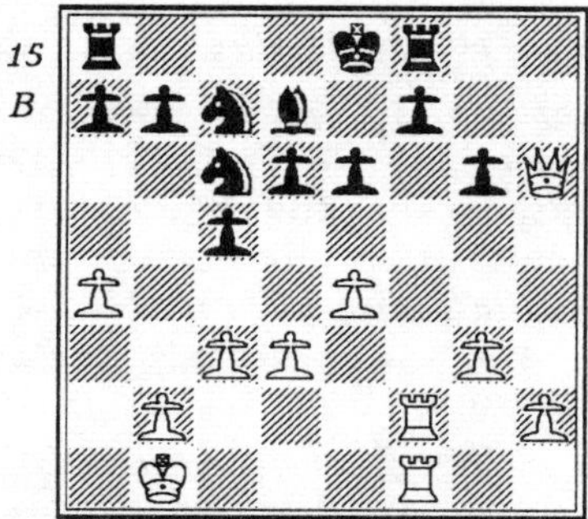
15
B

Ljubojevic hassles his opponent as much as possible to prevent him from consolidating. The weak point on f7 is pinpointed, shattering any plans for Black to castle queenside as the f7 pawn would then fall.

22 ... ♘e5
23 d4! cxd4
24 cxd4 ♘c6

Black recognises his grim plight. Black had hoped that the threat to fork queen and rook would allow him some time to reorganise. However, White had a nice combination planned: 24 ... ♘g4 25 ♕xf8+! ♔xf8 26 ♖xf7+ ♔g8 (26 ... ♔e8? 27 ♖f8+ ♔e7 28 ♖1f7 mate) 27 ♖xd7 with a won position since the rooks take up residence on the seventh rank and simply start taking all the black pawns.

25 ♕xf8+! ♔xf8
26 ♖xf7+ ♔g8
27 ♖xd7 ♘e8
28 ♖df7

A clever little ploy to make the most of the dominant rooks. The intention is 29 ♖f8+ ♔h7 30 ♖1f7+ ♔h6 31 ♖h8+ ♔g5 32 ♖7f8, winning a piece.

28 ... ♘g7
29 ♖xb7 a5
30 ♖f6 ♔h7
31 d5 exd5
32 ♖xd6 1-0

Rohde - Dlugy
USA Ch 1986

1 e4 c5
2 ♘c3 ♘c6
3 g3 g6
4 ♗g2 ♗g7
5 d3 d6

This is probably more accurate than 5 ... e6 as it

gives Black extra flexibility.

6 ♗e3 e5

This plan to contest the centre is perfectly reasonable, whilst 6 ... e6 transposes to the earlier games in this chapter. The more passive double fianchetto should yield White a slight initiative: 6 ... b6 7 ♕d2 ♗b7 8 ♘h3!? ♘f6 9 ♗h6 ♗xh6 10 ♕xh6 e6 11 0-0-0 ♕e7 12 ♖he1±.

7 ♕d2 *(16)*

The launch of the by now familiar idea of gearing up to ♗h6 to trade the bishops.

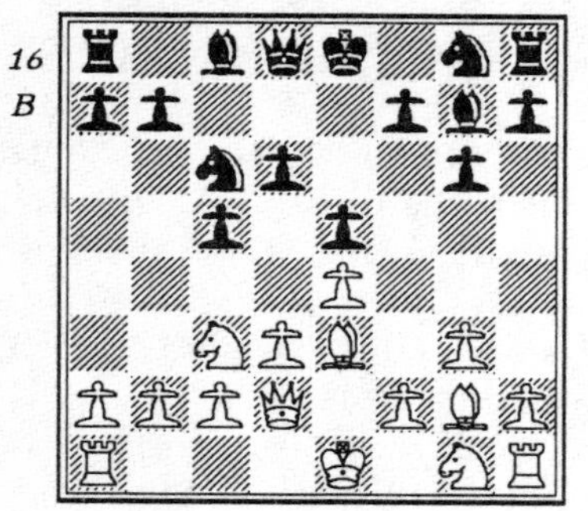

16
B

7 ... ♘ge7

Less confrontational measures are more common here, since White's attack has something of a formidable reputation. Black has a choice of alternatives:

a) 7 ... ♗e6 8 f4 exf4 (better is 8 ... ♘ge7 9 ♘f3 ♘d4 10 0-0 0-0 11 ♖ae1 ♘xf3+ 12 ♗xf3 ♕d7= Hort – Tal, Wijk aan Zee 1968) 9 ♗xf4 ♘d4 10 ♘f3 ♕d7 11 0-0 ♘e7 12 ♘g5 h6 13 ♘xe6 fxe6 14 ♗h3 ♘ec6 15 ♘d5 g5 16 ♗e3 ♕d8 17 c3 exd5 18 cxd4 ♘e7 19 dxc5 dxc5 20 ♕d1 ♕a5 21 ♕g4 ♕c7 22 ♖ae1 ♘c6 23 ♕h5+ ♔d8 24 ♖f7 1-0 La Rota – Birnboim, Saint John Open 1988.

b) 7 ... ♖b8 8 ♘ge2 ♘ge7 9 0-0 0-0 10 ♖ae1 b5 11 ♔h1 b4 12 ♘d1 ♘d4 13 f4 ♗e6 14 ♘c1± Suttles – Minic, Palma de Mallorca IZ 1970.

c) 7 ... ♘d4 8 ♘ce2 (8 ♘d1!? ♗d7 9 c3 ♘e6 10 f4 ♘ge7 11 ♘f3 0-0 12 0-0= Hawkes – Murray, Canada 1981) 8 ... ♘e7 9 c3 ♘e6 10 f4 f5 11 ♘f3 ♗d7 12 fxe5 dxe5 13 ♗h6 ♗f6 14 d4! exd4 15 e5 dxc3 16 ♘xc3 ♗g7 17 ♗xg7 ♘xg7 18 0-0-0 ♘e6 19 ♘g5 h6 20 ♘b5! ♗xb5 21 ♘xe6 ♕b6 22 ♕d6 ♖c8 23 ♖he1, when the black king is caught in the centre and the endgame favours White, Al. Karpov – Kallai, Budapest 1989.

8 ♗h6

Certainly the most popular choice in contemporary practice, but White can follow a different path:

a) 8 h4 h5 9 ♘h3 ♘d4 10 0-0-0 (10 f4!? exf4 11 ♘xf4 ♗g4 12 0-0 0-0 13 ♖ae1= Fedorowicz) 10 ... ♕a5 11 ♖df1 b5 12 ♔b1 b4 13 ♗xd4 cxd4 14 ♘e2 ♖b8 15 f4 ♗e6 16 ♘c1= Chiburdanidze – Pamuk, Kusadasi 1990.

b) 8 ♘f3 0-0 9 0-0 ♘d4

10 ♗h6 f6 11 ♗xg7 ♔xg7 12 h4 ♗e6 13 ♘h2 ♕d7 14 f4 ♖ae8 15 ♖f2 exf4 16 ♖xf4± Vorotnikov – Novikov, USSR 1981.

c) 8 f4 ♘d4 9 ♘f3 ♗h3 10 0–0 ♗xg2 11 ♔xg2 0–0 12 ♖ae1 ♕d7 13 ♘e2 b6 14 ♘eg1 ♘ec6 15 c3 ♘xf3 16 ♘xf3 d5 17 fxe5 dxe4 18 dxe4 ♕xd2 19 ♗xd2 ♘xe5 20 ♘xe5 ♗xe5 21 ♗f4 ♖fe8 22 ♔f3 ♖ad8 23 ♖d1 and White has a superior position, Hort – Johansson, Czechoslovakia 1968.

8 ... ♗xh6

Dlugy follows the critical line to try to exploit White's simple strategy which, to a certain extent, has neglected the routine development of his pieces. Of course, the king is now destined to castle queenside, a plan which Rohde appreciates and tries to prevent. Black has problems after 8 ... 0–0 9 ♗xg7 (9 h4 f6 10 ♗xg7 ♔xg7 11 h5 g5 12 h6+ ♔h8 13 0–0–0 ♘g6 14 ♘ge2 ♘d4 15 ♖df1= La Rota – Smejkal, New York 1988) 9 ... ♔xg7 10 f4 ♘d4 11 ♘f3 ♗g4 12 0–0 ♕d7?, Ljubojevic – van der Wiel, Tilburg 1983, 13 fxe5! ♘xf3+ (13 ... ♗xf3 14 exd6 ♗xg2 15 dxe7+–) 14 ♗xf3 dxe5 15 ♗xg4 ♕xg4 16 ♕f2, intending 17 ♕xc5 or 17 ♕f6+–, analysis by van der Wiel.

9 ♕xh6 ♘d4

10 ♖c1 *(17)*

17
B

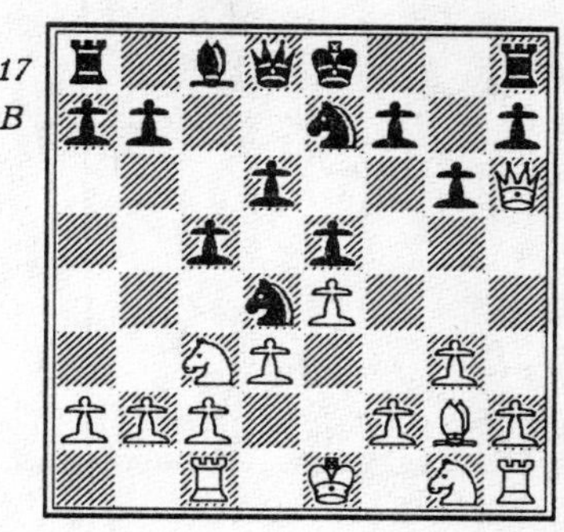

Not the only move but probably the best. 10 ♕d2 is quite playable; Korolev – Minasian, USSR 1984, reached equality after 10 ... ♕a5! 11 h3 ♘ec6 12 ♖c1 ♗e6 13 a3 ♖c8 14 ♘d5 ♗xd5 15 exd5 ♕xd2+ 16 ♔xd2 ♘e7. Still awaiting practical tests is 10 0–0–0!? which is rather risky here in view of Black marching the b-pawn forward with a rapid queenside initiative.

10 ... ♗e6
11 ♘f3

Nothing much is gained from 11 ♕g7 ♔d7! (Minic), when Black has the threat of trapping the queen with 12 ... ♘ef5 13 exf5 ♘xf5.

11 ... ♕b6
12 ♘d1 ♕a5+

Dlugy decides to snatch an extra pawn and then try to hold off the White initiative.

13 c3 ♘xf3+
14 ♗xf3 ♕xa2
15 0–0 *(18)*

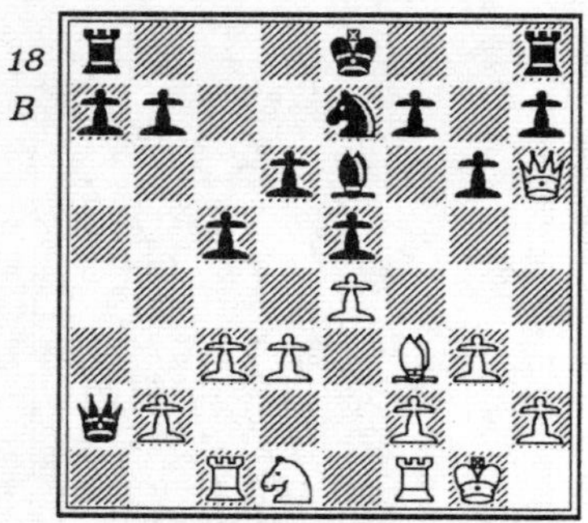

Although White has a material deficit, he already has an open line on the queenside where the black king is bound to head for and can also gain time by harassing the queen. The position is highly complex with Black trying to make up for the time used by his wandering queen.

15 ... ♘c6
16 ♘e3 0-0-0

At last the king seeks shelter, now that the knight on c6 protects a7 after 17 ♖a1.

17 ♘d5 ♔b8
18 ♖a1 ♕b3
19 ♖a3! ♕b5

Resisting the temptation to snatch another pawn. Instinctively one can tell that after 19 ... ♕xb2 Black is asking for trouble as the two white rooks would quickly swoop on the open a- and b-files.

20 ♕d2

Now that the queen has done its job on the kingside, it is switched to the other flank to join in the dangerous attack.

20 ... ♗xd5
21 exd5 ♘e7
22 ♖fa1

Systematically softening up the last line of defence, the black pawn chain.

22 ... a6

After the plausible 22 ... ♘c8 23 b4 cxb4 24 c4 ♕b6 25 ♖a4 b3 26 ♖b4 ♕d4 27 ♖a3, White is in control.

23 ♖a5 ♕d7

If Black opts for 23 ... ♕b6 24 b4 cxb4 25 cxb4 and then 26 b5 leaves Black in a critical situation.

24 b4 cxb4
25 c4!

By rejecting the obvious recapture White manages to bring the queen into the game and will soon be able to exploit the power of the open lines around the king.

25 ... ♕c7
26 ♕xb4 ♔a7

There is no escape if the king flees to the other side 26 ... ♔c8 27 c5!, intending c6, wins for White.

27 ♕a3

Lining up an obvious sacrifice on a6 but Dlugy must compromise his pieces even to defend against such blatant threats.

27 ... ♕b6
28 ♖b5 ♕d4

White breaks through

after 28 ... Qc7 29 c5 dxc5 30 d6, when the bishop adds it considerable weight against b7.

29 c5! Ra8

Everything is bleak for Black: 29 ... dxc5 30 Rxb7+ Kxb7 31 Qxa6+ Kc7 32 d6+ Kd7 (32 ... Qxd6 33 Qb7 mate; 32 ... Rxd6 33 Qb7+) 33 Qb7+ Ke6 (33 ... Kxd6 34 Ra6+) 34 Qxe7+ Kf5 35 g4+ Kf4 36 Qf6 mate.

30 c6 1–0

Hodgson – Crouch
Scotland 1987

1	**e4**	**c5**
2	**Nc3**	**Nc6**
3	**g3**	**g6**
4	**Bg2**	**Bg7**
5	**d3**	**d6**
6	**Be3**	**Nf6**

The set-up is designed to facilitate quick castling and to harass the bishop.

7 h3 *(19)*

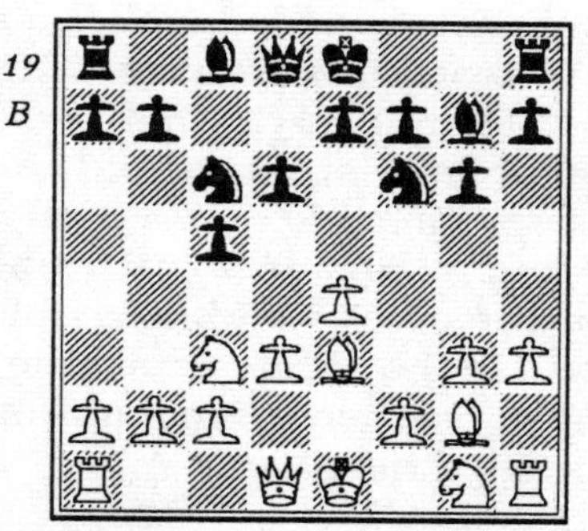

This natural response cuts out ... Ng4 and is useful for a later pawn push.

Certainly not the co-operative 7 Qd2?! Ng4 8 Bf4 e5 9 Bg5 f6 10 Be3 Nxe3 11 fxe3 0-0 12 Nge2 Ne7∓ Nikolic – Smejkal, Varna 1971.

Pachman has experimented with the unlikely-looking 7 Qc1!? which had a flurry of activity in the 1950s and has now been largely forgotten:

a) 7 ... 0-0 8 Bh6 Nd4 9 Bxg7 Kxg7 10 f4!± Pachman.

b) 7 ... h5 8 h3 and now:

b1) 8 ... e5 9 f4 Be6 10 Nf3 Nd4 11 Ng5 Bd7 12 0-0 0-0 13 Qd2 b5 14 Nd1 Qe7 15 c3 gives White a spatial advantage, whilst the threat of f5 is strong, Pachman – Toran, 1955.

b2) 8 ... Rb8 9 f4 Nd7 10 a4 a6 11 Nf3 Nd4 12 Qd2 b5 13 axb5 axb5± Pachman – Najdorf, 1954.

b3) 8 ... Bd7 9 f4 Qb6 10 Nf3 Nd4 11 Nh4! Bc6 12 0-0 Nd7 13 Kh2 0-0-0 14 Nd1 and the prospect of c3, b4 offers White good attacking chances, Pachman – Ciocaltea, Bucharest 1952.

c) 7 ... Nd4!? and now:

c1) 8 Nd1 e5 9 c3 Ne6 10 Bh6 0-0 11 Bxg7 Nxg7 12 Ne2 (Pachman – Olafsson, Portoroz IZ 1958) 12 ... d5 13 exd5 Nxd5 14 0-0 Be6= (*ECO*).

c2) 8 h3 Bd7 9 Nge2 Qb6 10 Rb1= Berensen – Najdorf,

Mar del Plata 1956.

7 ... ♕b6!?

Crouch is renowned for his opening innovations and this unusual approach aims to hit b2 while lending support to the control of d4. From an objective point of view, it is far from clear that this is an improvement on other lines since an integral part of the system for Black is the advance of his b-pawn, which is now blocked. There is a wide choice of moves available:

a) 7 ... 0–0 8 ♕d2 and now:

a1) 8 ... ♖b8 9 ♗h6 ♗e6 10 ♗xg7 ♔xg7 11 ♘ge2 b5 12 f4 b4 13 ♘d1 ♘d4 14 0–0 ♕c8 15 ♔h2 ♘xe2 16 ♕xe2 c4 17 d4 d5 18 e5 ♘e4 19 ♗xe4 dxe4 20 g4 h5 21 ♘e3 White is poised for f5 with a crushing victory in sight, Dunworth - Tardio Fran, Andorra 1991.

a2) 8 ... ♘d4 9 ♘ce2 e5 10 c3 ♘c6 11 f4 b6 12 ♘f3 exf4 13 ♗xf4 ♗a6 14 0–0 ♖e8 15 c4 b5 16 cxb5 ♗xb5 17 ♖f2!± Ljubojevic - Sunye, Brasilia 1981.

b) 7 ... ♗d7 8 ♕d2 h6 9 ♘ge2 ♕c8 10 g4 ♖b8 11 d4 cxd4 12 ♘xd4 ♘xd4 13 ♗xd4 b5 14 ♗xa7 b4 15 ♘e2 ♖b7 16 ♗d4, when the extra pawn swings the balance in White's favour, Lombardy - Ungureanu, Siegen Ol 1970.

c) 7 ... ♖b8 8 f4 (8 ♕d2 b5 9 ♗h6 0–0 10 ♗xg7±) 8 ... ♗d7 9 ♘f3 0–0 10 0–0 b5 11 ♕e1 b4 12 ♘d1 ♘e8 13 g4 ♘d4 14 ♕g3 ♘xf3+ 15 ♗xf3+± Knaak - Malich, East Germany 1974.

8 ♖b1 0–0

9 ♘ge2

A matter of taste. Also possible is 9 f4, ♘f3, 0–0 with a good game.

9 ... ♘d4

10 0–0 e5 *(20)*

20
W

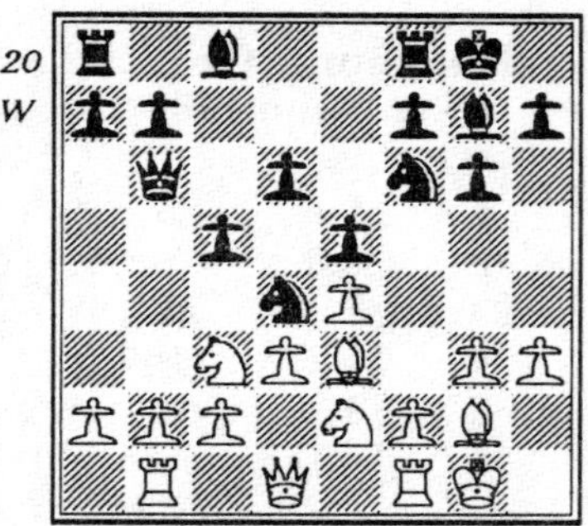

Firmly securing d4. When, as here, the knight is on f6 rather than e7, the inclusion of ... e5 encourages White to beaver away with f4, f5 and g4 trying for a complete stranglehold on the kingside. Normally, when White gets in f5 one of the black knights is able to use the vacant e5 stronghold, but here this option is ruled out.

11 f4 ♗e6

12 ♔h2 ♘xe2

13 ♕xe2

A general evaluation of

this position shows that White is clearly on top: White's pieces are well placed to get things going on the kingside, and Black will have a hard job meeting this; furthermore, Black is unable to organise any effective counterplay.

13 ... exf4

Sensing that 14 f5 will be the start of a major offensive, Crouch decides to put White off by clearing e5 for the knight. Having admitted that 10 ... e5 was an error, this attempt at making up for it is not quite good enough as now the g-file is open for further operations.

14 gxf4 ♖fe8
15 ♕f2

The queen side-steps any potential pin on the e-file which might be possible after f5 and feigns a shift of emphasis to the possibility of a further transfer of the queen to h4.

15 ... ♖ad8

Black is in a desperate state of affairs. He has no immediate counter chances and even his intended ... d5 will take some time to organise as the c-pawn is vulnerable.

16 ♔h1

Hodgson can afford this luxury as time is not pressing. This prophylactic move aims to avoid any desperate tactics based upon ♘h5 or ♗e5+ once the f5-pawn is advanced.

16 ... ♘h5

Black is not happy that White can indulge in fancy moves to prove his advantage and goes on the offensive. However, Hodgson has created such a powerful position that he can really do anything he likes until the moment is right for the crunching advance of the f-pawn.

17 ♗f3 f5

Not surprisingly, Black is not content with meekly retreating and stops the threat of the surging f-pawn once and for all, although he had to accept his pawns becoming a bit ragged. His idea is that some play might be drummed up by exploiting the pair of bishops and fighting for control of the g-file.

18 ♗xh5 gxh5
19 ♖g1 ♔h8 *(21)*

This all looks quite natural and it the next step is for White to double his rooks with much the better chances. However ...

20 ♖xg7!

Black is busted. The shattered black defences suffer a terrible blow with the removal of the main protector of the king. After

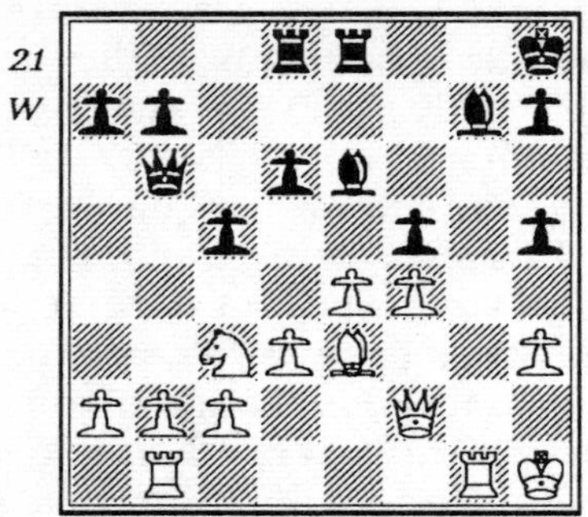

21
W

this finely calculated sacrifice the white pieces pour into Black's position.

20 ... ♔xg7
21 ♖g1+ ♔h8

Upon 21 ... ♔f7 (21 ... ♔f8) 22 ♕h4 is very uncomfortable, so Black seeks safety in the corner where queen intrusions appear easier to fend off.

22 ♘a4 1-0

Scintillating stuff. The delicate knight move prepares for a killer check on d4: 22 ... ♕b4 23 c3 ♕xa4 24 b3 ♕c6 25 ♗d4+ cxd4 26 ♕xd4 mate.

Romanishin – Torre
Indonesia 1983

1	**e4**	**c5**
2	**♘c3**	**♘c6**
3	**g3**	**g6**
4	**♗g2**	**♗g7**
5	**d3**	**d6**
6	**♗e3**	**b5** *(22)*

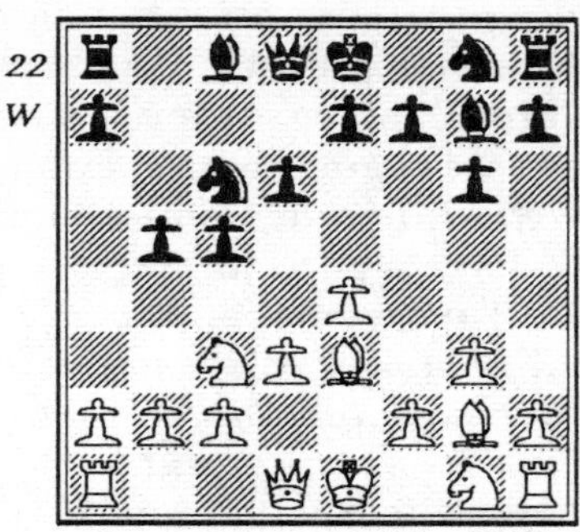

22
W

A number of other moves have been tried.

a) 6 ... ♘d4 7 ♕d2 ♕a5 8 f4 ♖b8 9 ♘ge2 ♘xe2 (Radovici – Suba, Rumania 1983) 10 ♔xe2!±.

b) 6 ... ♗d7 7 ♕d2 ♖c8 (7 ... ♘d4 8 ♘d1 ♗c6 9 c3 ♘f5 10 f4 ♘xe3 11 ♘xe3 ♘f6 12 ♘f3 0–0 13 0–0± Ignjatev – Shamkovich, USSR 1962) 8 ♘ge2 ♘d4 9 0–0 e6 10 ♘d1 ♘ge7 11 ♘c1 0–0 12 c3 ♘dc6 13 ♗h6 e5 14 ♗xg7 ♔xg7 15 ♘e2 ♗e6 16 f4 f6 17 ♘e3 d5 18 f5 with a spatial advantage, Dunworth – van Dongen, Clichy 1991.

c) 6 ... ♘h6 7 ♕c1 ♘g4 8 ♗d2 ♘d4 9 h3 ♘e5 10 ♘ce2 ♕b6 11 f4 ♘xc2+?! 12 ♕xc2 ♕xb2 13 ♕xb2 ♘xd3+ 14 ♔f1 ♗xb2 15 ♖b1 ♗e6 16 ♗c3 and White's extra piece is stronger than the opposing pawns, Smyslov – Bronstein, USSR Ch 1951.

d) 6 ... ♖b8!? 7 ♕d2 and now:

d1) 7 ... e6 is considered earlier in the chapter with the sequence 6 ... e6 7 ♕d2 ♖b8.

d2) 7 ... b5 and now:

d21) 8 ♘f3 b4 9 ♘d1 ♗g4 10 h3 ♗xf3 11 ♗xf3 ♘d4 12 ♗g2 ♘f6 13 0–0 0–0 14 c3 bxc3 15 bxc3 ♘b5 16 a4 ♕a5 17 ♖a2 ♘c7 18 ♘b2 ♘d7, Camilleri - Riza, Novi Sad Ol 1990.

d22) 8 ♘ge2 b4 9 ♘d1 ♘d4 10 0–0 e6 11 ♘c1 ♘e7 12 c3 bxc3 13 bxc3 ♘dc6 14 ♗h6 0–0 15 ♗xg7 ♔xg7 16 ♘e3 ♗b7 17 ♘b3 a5 18 a4 ♗a6 19 ♖fb1= Ljubojevic - Tringov, Lucerne Ol 1982.

d23) 8 f4 b4 9 ♘d1 e6 10 f5 exf5 11 exf5 ♘e5 12 fxg6 hxg6 13 ♘f3= Lamford - Schmidt, Thessaloniki Ol 1988.

Of all these variations, clearly only 6 ... ♖b8, preparing ... b5, is a significant alternative to 6 ... e5/e6.

7 e5

Black's temporary weakening of the long diagonal meets with a natural reaction from White.

7 ... ♕d7

Safeguarding the knight. Torre springs a double-edged variation on his opponent to see if Romanishin is ready for a rapid confrontation, rather than settling for a more patient manoeuvring game. Unclear is 7 ... ♗b7 8 exd6 exd6 9 ♘xb5 ♘ge7! 10 ♘c3 ♕b6 11 ♖b1 ♘e5 (Ljubojevic - Miles, London 1982) 12 ♘e4 0–0.

8 exd6

Ljubojevic - Miles, Plovdiv 1983, continued 8 ♘f3 ♘h6 9 exd6 exd6 10 ♘e4 ♘f5 11 ♗g5 (11 ♗f4!?) 11 ... 0–0 12 0–0 with equal chances. The text is an attempt to improve upon this line by keeping the long diagonal open.

8 ... exd6

9 ♘ge2 ♘ge7

It would be foolish for Black to push his luck by grabbing the b-pawn and giving up the valuable d5-square: 9 ... b4?! 10 ♘d5 ♗xb2 11 ♖b1 ♗g7 12 0–0 ♗b7 13 c3 with tremendous play.

10 d4!

While Black's control over d4 is lax; White seizes his chance to launch a central push, relying on the disharmonious state of the opposing pieces.

10 ... b4

Out of the question is 10 ... cxd4 11 ♘xd4 when the b5 and d6 pawns are weak and the pressure on c6 is mounting. White also has the brighter prospects after 10 ... ♘f5 11 dxc5 ♘xe3 12 fxe3 dxc5 13 ♘xb5, remaining at least one pawn ahead.

11 ♘e4 0–0

Flicking the knight away fails to a cheeky reply: 11 ... f5 12 ♗h6! 0–0 (12 ... ♗xh6?? 13 ♘f6+) 13 ♗xg7 ♔xg7 14 ♘g5 h6 15 ♘f3, when White has managed to remove the valuable dark-squared bishop.

12 ♗h6

Keeping faith with the plan revealed on move six.

12 ... c4?! *(23)*

23
W

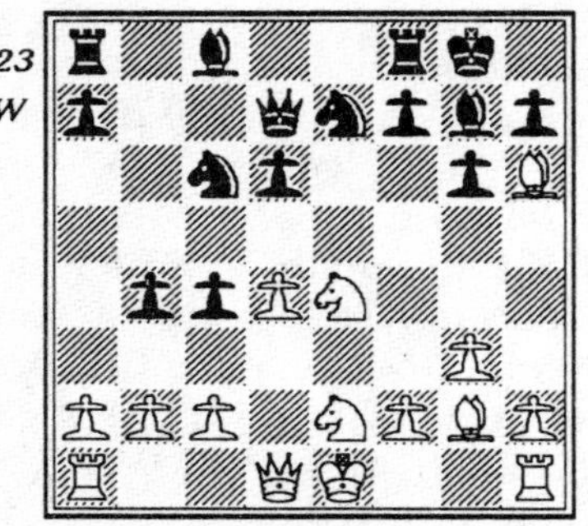

A more stubborn approach is required to cope with Black's pressing problems and the key square on d4 should be left covered now that the bishops are about to be swopped off. the best line is 12 ... ♗a6! 13 ♗xg7 ♔xg7 14 d5 (14 dxc5?! d5! 15 ♘d6 ♕e6∓) 14 ... ♘e5 15 0-0 ♕f5 (15 ... ♘xd5 16 ♕xd5 ♗xe2 17 ♘xc5 ♕f5 18 ♖fe1 ♘f3+ 19 ♗xf3 ♕xf3 20 ♕d4+, intending ♘d7 with the better chances; 19 ... ♗xf3 20 ♕xf5 gxf5 21 ♘d3 a5 22 ♖e3 and White is better; 15 ... h6 16 ♖e1 f5 17 ♘xc5 dxc5 18 ♘f4 ♕d6 19 ♘e6+ ♔h7 20 ♘xf8+ ♖xf8 21 f4 ♘g4 22 ♖e6) 16 ♘xd6 ♘f3+ 17 ♗xf3 ♕xf3 18 ♘f4 ♕xd1 19 ♖fxd1±, according to an analysis by Romanishin and Stetsko.

13 ♗xg7 ♔xg7
14 d5 ♘e5
15 f4 ♘g4
16 h3

This chance to chase the knight to a poor square on the edge of the board is made possible by 16 ... ♘e3 17 ♕d4+ and 16 ... ♘f6 17 ♘xf6 ♔xf6 18 ♕d4+. Both these variations utilise the d4-square neglected by Black on his twelfth move.

16 ... ♘h6
17 g4 f5!?

The cramped conditions are not to Torre's liking so before White is able to consolidate he takes a calculated gamble to try to shake off the shackles on his position.

18 ♕d4+ ♔g8
19 ♘f6+ ♖xf6
20 ♕xf6 fxg4 *(24)*

24
W

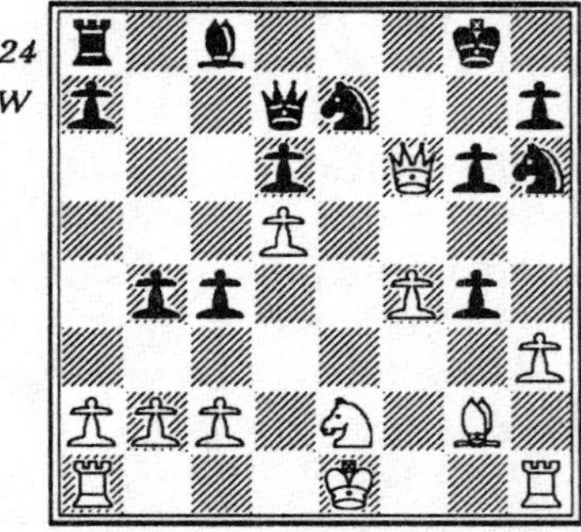

In return for giving up the exchange Black has an extra pawn and has left White with a difficult decision. If he recaptures on g4

then the knight captures on this square with a troublesome initiative, whilst castling queenside is met by ... ♗b7 with a complicated game.

21 ♕e6+!

Sealing Black's fate by opening another line so that his rooks are able to exert their influence more freely. The endgame is certainly not the end of the matter but by trading in favourable circumstances Romanishin emerges with much the better chances. Of course, a swift decision on the merits of the ending was required since if Torre had managed to insert ... ♗b7 then the pin against g2 would make ♕e6+ impossible.

21 ... ♕xe6
22 dxe6 d5
23 ♘d4

White holds on to the e6 pawn, of course, as otherwise Black would roughly have material equality.

23 ... ♖b8
24 0-0-0 ♖b6
25 ♖he1 ♔g7
26 ♖e5!

Safe and steady. The rash tactical flourish backfires after 26 ♗xd5 ♘xd5 27 e7 ♗d7 28 ♘e6+ ♔f6 29 ♖xd5 ♖xe6, with counterplay.

26 ... ♗b7
27 ♖de1 ♖d6
28 ♖g5 gxh3
29 ♗xh3

White has managed to force Black into taking on h3, which allows the bishop to reinforce e6. This will free the rooks from the burden of merely defending the weak pawn.

29 ... ♖d8
30 ♖g3 ♔f6
31 ♔d2

The standard principle that the king should take an active role in the ending is followed. It would have been wiser to delay this venture, however, by 31 a3! a5 32 ♔d2 ♖a8 33 ♖a1, removing all Black's hopes of confusing the issue.

31 ... ♖d6
32 a3 c3+!

This is the difference to the last note.

33 bxc3 bxa3
34 ♖a1 ♖a6
35 ♗f1 ♖a4

Useless is 35 ... ♖a5 36 ♘b3 ♖a4 37 ♘c5+-.

36 ♗b5 ♖a5
37 ♗d3 a2
38 ♖h3 ♔g7
39 ♘b3 ♖a3
40 ♖ah1?!

A calmer approach is 40 ♔c1 intending 41 ♔b2, winning the pawn.

40 ... ♘eg8
41 ♖a1 ♘g4
42 f5 g5
43 ♘d4

Missing a wonderful opportunity to finish the game in style: 43 ♖xh7+! ♔xh7 44 f6+ ♔h8 45 ♖h1+ ♘4h6 46 e7 ♘xf6 (47 ... ♗c6 48 f7!) 47 ♖xh6+ ♔g7 48 ♖xf6 ♖xb3 49 e8(♕)+-.

43 ... ♘4f6

44 e7 ♔f7

The end is not in doubt after 44 ... ♘xe7 45 ♘e6+, followed by taking on g5.

45 ♘b5 1-0

Black resigned in view of 45 ... ♖a6 46 ♘c7 ♖c6 47 ♖xh7+!+-.

2) 6 f4 ♘f6

In the next three chapters we shall consider the various possibilities after 6 f4. The system involving 6 ... ♘f6 is not ideally equipped to deal with the expansionist plan conducted by White on the kingside. Usually there are no problems for him in advancing a pawn to f5 which can then be supported by the g- and h-pawns. Black has to rely on queenside pressure to restore the balance but this is often just not good enough, particularly since the knight on f6 blocks the g7-bishop from the game.

Spassky – Geller
Suhumi (6) 1968

1	**e4**	**c5**
2	**♘c3**	**d6**
3	**g3**	**♘c6**
4	**♗g2**	**g6**
5	**d3**	**♗g7**
6	**f4**	**♘f6** *(25)*

Bold attempts to oppose White's strategy by advancing the f-pawn make little impression against straight

25
W

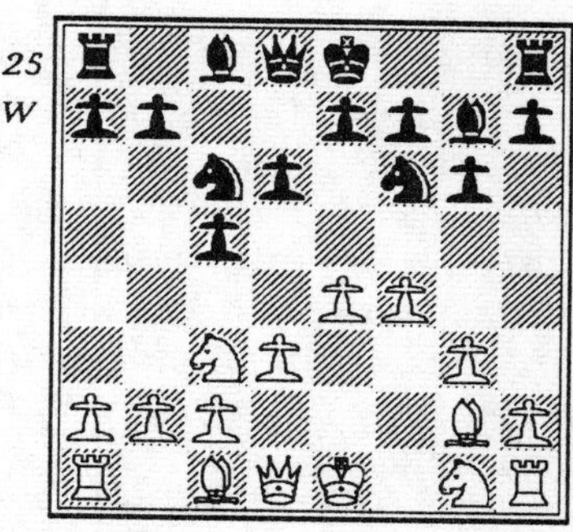

forward play.

a) 6 ... f5 7 ♘f3 ♘f6 8 0–0 0–0 9 ♔h1 ♔h8 (9 ... ♗d7 10 ♗e3 ♖b8 11 ♕e2 b5 12 ♗g1 b4 13 ♘d1 ♘e8 14 c3 ♘c7 15 ♖c1 ♘e6 16 ♘e3± Smyslov – Larsen, Munich Ol 1958) 10 ♗e3 ♗e6 11 ♗g1 ♕d7 12 exf5 ♗xf5 13 d4 b6 14 d5 ♘b4 15 a3 ♘a6 16 ♖e1 ♘c7 17 ♘h4 ♗g4 18 ♕d3± Raicevic – Martinovic, Vrnjacka Banja 1978.

b) 6 ... b6 7 ♘f3 ♗b7 8 0–0 ♕d7 9 ♗e3 f5 10 ♕d2 ♘f6 11 ♔h1 0–0–0, Bernstein – Fischer, Netanya 1968, and now 12 a3 gives White the better chances.

7 ♘f3 0–0

Alternatives are nothing special:

a) 7 ... ♖b8 8 0-0 ♗d7 (not 8 ... b5?! 9 e5! dxe5 10 fxe5 ♘g4 11 e6 ♗xe6 12 ♘g5± Wade - R. Byrne, Hastings 1971/2) 9 h3 ♘d4 10 ♗e3 ♘xf3+ 11 ♕xf3 0-0 12 ♕f2 ♗c6 13 ♖ad1 ♕c7 14 d4 cxd4 15 ♗xd4± Bhend - Attard, Kecskemet 1964.

b) 7 ... ♗d7 8 h3 h5 9 ♗e3 ♕b6 10 ♕c1 ♘d4 11 ♘h4 ♗h6 12 ♘d1 ♖g8 13 c3 ♘c6 14 ♕d2 e5 15 fxe5 ♗xe3 16 ♘xe3 ♘xe5 17 0-0, when White has tremendous play on the f-file and possibilities of sticking a knight on d5, Minev - Dimitrov, Bulgaria 1961.

8 0-0 ♖b8

The only way to generate any real counterplay is to push forward the b-pawn. White took advantage of a clumsy strategy in the game Hickl - Nemet, Chiasso 1991, after 8 ... a6?! (8 ... d5 9 e5 ♘e8 10 d4 cxd4 11 ♘xd4 ♘c7 12 ♗e3 favours White; 8 ... ♘e8 9 h3 ♘c7 10 ♗e3 b6 11 ♕d2 ♗b7 12 f5 b5 13 ♗h6! exchanging the key defensive piece, Smyslov - Ilivitsky, USSR 1952) 9 h3 ♗d7 10 ♗e3 ♖c8 11 ♕d2 b5 12 a3 ♕c7 13 g4 ♕b8 14 ♔h1 a5 15 f5 b4 16 axb4 axb4 17 ♘e2 c4 18 ♘f4 ♕b5 19 g5 ♘e8 20 ♘d5 c3 21 bxc3 ♗xc3 22 ♘xc3 bxc3 23 ♕f2 ♖b8 24 ♘h4 ♘g7 25 ♖a3 ♕b2 26 ♖aa1 ♘b4 27 ♖a7 ♗b5 28 f6! exf6 29 gxf6 ♘h5 30 ♘f5! ♕xc2 31 ♕h4 ♗xd3 32 ♖g1 ♘c6 33 ♕xh5 ♗xe4 (33 ... gxh5 34 ♗f3+ ♔h8 35 ♗h6 ♖g8 36 ♗g7+ ♖xg7 37 fxg7+ ♔g8 38 ♘h6 mate) 34 ♕h6 1-0.

9 h3

Another way of forcing through f5 by 9 ♘h4 is perfectly acceptable but lacks the bite of the text move:

a) 9 ... ♗d7 10 f5 b5 11 ♗g5! b4 12 ♘d5 a5 (12 ... ♘xd5 13 exd5 ♘d4 14 ♕d2!±) 13 ♔h1 ♘e5 14 ♕d2 ♗c6 15 ♖ae1 and White has a slight edge. Spassky - Petrosian, World Ch (17) 1966.

b) 9 ... ♘d4 10 f5 b5 11 ♗g5 b4 12 ♘e2 ♘xe2+ 12 ♕xe2 ♘d7 14 ♖ab1 ♘e5 (14 ... ♖b6?! 15 ♕d2 ♖a6 16 ♗h6 ♖xa2 17 fxg6 fxg6 [17 ... hxg6 18 ♗xg7 ♔xg7 19 ♘f5+] 18 e5± Medina - Korchnoi, Parma de Mallorca 1968) 15 ♕d2 a5 16 ♗h6 ♗d7 17 ♘f3 ♕b6 18 ♘xe5 dxe5 19 ♗e3± Lein - Saharov, USSR Ch 1968.

9 ... b5

The logical step. Spassky - Benko, Palma de Mallorca 1968, continued: 9 ... ♘e8 10 ♗d2 b5 11 ♖b1 e6 12 ♕e1 ♘d4 13 ♘xd4 cxd4 14 ♘e2 ♕b6 15 a3 e5 16 ♔h2 f5 17 exf5 gxf5 18 ♗a5 ♕a6 19 b4, threatening to ruin the black pawn structure by taking on e5.

10 a3 *(26)*

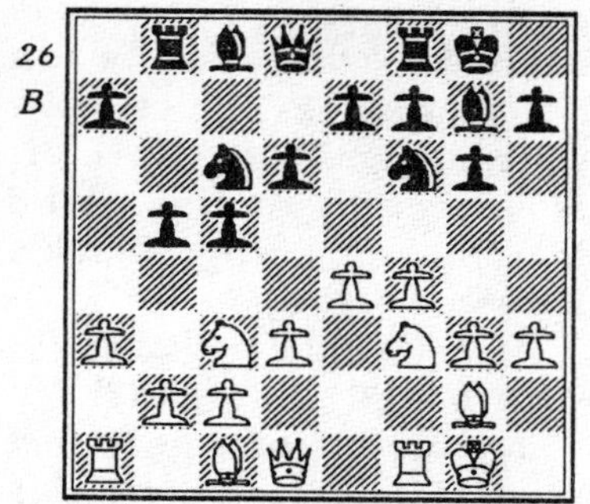

White has scored a high percentage of wins by following Spassky's plan in this position but there may even be an improvement which has been suggested by Kasparov. A very similar position can arise when the Closed strategy is employed by Black to counter the English (which involves being a move down), after 1 c4 g6 2 ♘c3 ♗g7 3 g3 ♘c6 4 ♗g2 d6 5 ♘f3 e5 6 d3 f5 7 0-0 ♘f6 8 ♖b1 h6 9 b4 0-0 10 b5 ♘e7 11 a4 ♗e6! Returning to the text, if it is possible to dispense with 10 a3, then 10 ♗e3 comes into consideration. For example: 10 ... b4 11 ♘e2 c4?! 12 dxc4 ♘xe4 13 ♘e1+-. This is a marked improvement on 10 g4 b4 11 ♘e2 c4 12 ♗e3 (12 dxc4?! ♘xe4 13 ♘e1 ♕b6+) 12 ... ♗a6 13 ♘ed4 ♘xd4 14 ♗xd4 ♕c7 15 ♖f2= Smyslov - Taimanov, USSR 1959.

To get a grasp of how to handle the position with the pawn on a2 it is worth nothing how the World Champion handled it in the English: 12 ♗a3 ♖c8! 13 ♘d2 b6 14 e3 g5 15 d4 exd4 16 exd4 f4 17 ♖e1 ♗g4 18 ♘f3 ♕d7 19 c5 ♖ce8 20 ♖c1 ♘f5 21 ♕d3 ♔h8 22 cxd6 cxd6 23 ♖xe8 ♕xe8 24 ♖f1 ♕h5 25 ♘e4 ♘xe4 26 ♕xe4 ♗h3 27 ♘e5?! ♗xg2 28 ♔xg2 g4 29 ♗xd6 ♖f6 30 ♗b8 ♕h3+ 0-1 Psakhis - Kasparov, La Manga 1990.

Using the Closed against the English saves a lot of time studying a seperate defensive system. A good example is how a world class player benefitted from the lesson given in the main game under discussion: 1 c4 e5 2 ♘c3 ♘c6 3 g3 g6 4 ♗g2 ♗g7 5 ♘f3 f5 6 d3 ♘f6 7 0-0 d6 8 ♖b1 0-0 9 b4 a6 10 a4 h6 11 b5 axb5 12 axb5 ♘e7 13 ♗b2 ♗e6 14 ♖a1 ♖c8 15 ♖a7 b6 16 ♕c2 g5 17 ♖fa1 f4 18 ♘d2 fxg3 19 hxg3 ♕e8 20 ♘ce4 ♘g4 21 ♘f1 ♘f5 22 e3 ♕g6 23 ♖b7 ♘h4 24 gxh4 gxh4 25 f3 ♖xf3 26 ♕e2 ♖f7 27 ♘h2 ♖cf8 28 ♖aa7 h3 29 ♖xc7 ♖xc7 30 ♖xc7 ♘f2 0-1 Schneider - Short, Solingen 1986. Black freely attributed his entire strategy to having seen Spassky - Geller.

10 ... a5

11 ♗e3 b4
12 axb4 axb4
13 ♘e2 ♗b7

Black's alternatives here are discussed in the next game, Reshevsky - Korchnoi.

14 b3!

Up to this game there had been conflicting views on how to cope with the defence of the queenside pawns. Indeed, only two games earlier in this match, Spassky had played 14 ♕d2 ♖a8 15 ♖ab1 ♕a5 16 b3 ♖fc8 17 f5! ♕b6 18 g4 ♖a2 19 ♘c1 ♖a5 20 ♕f2 ♕c7?! 21 ♘e2 ♖a2 22 ♖bc1 ♕d8 23 ♘f4 ♕e8 24 ♘g5 ♘d4! 25 fxg6 hxg6 26 ♘d5 with an edge but there was plenty of room for improvement by Black, for example: 16 ... d5! 17 e5 d4= (Vorotnikov). The immediate kingside advance only leads to equality: 14 g4 ♖a8 15 ♖b1 ♖a2 16 ♘c1 ♖a6 17 ♕e1 ♕c7 18 ♘e2 ♖a2 19 ♕h4= Bakulin - Sax, USSR 1970.

14 ... ♖a8

Whatever Black opts to do, White can follow a similar attacking path: 14 ... ♕c7 15 g4 ♖a8 16 ♖c1 ♖a2 17 ♕e1!? ♘d7 18 ♕h4±, Marjanovic - Hernandez, Vrsac 1977.

15 ♖c1

This is Spassky's clever idea. The rook is given the job of defending the c-pawn, which releases the queen to roam freely on the kingside. White has now managed to remove all his pieces from the a1-h8 diagonal, nullifying Black's powerful bishop.

15 ... ♖a2
16 g4 ♕a8?!

The queen soon gets left out of the action after this faulty plan takes it to the wrong side of the board. Geller suggests 16 ... e6 which can be met by 17 ♘g3 ♖e8 18 f5!±, according to *ECO*.

17 ♕e1 ♕a6
18 ♕f2

Carefully avoiding 18 ♕h4? ♘xe4 19 dxe4 ♕xe2.

18 ... ♘a7
19 f5 ♘b5
20 fxg6 hxg6

Black refrains from 20 ... fxg6 because the white knights would hop into e6 via f4 or g5.

21 ♘g5 ♘a3

Geller is obsessed with his time-consuming plan to win a pawn. Spassky is happy to go along with this since it allows him to continue with his plan to storm the black king's fortress.

22 ♕h4 ♖c8

To give the king an escape square.

23 ♖xf6!

Removing the main defensive piece by the exchange sacrifice which allows the queen to gain access to the heart of the black position.

23 ... exf6
24 ♕h7+ ♔f8
25 ♘xf7! *(27)*

27
B

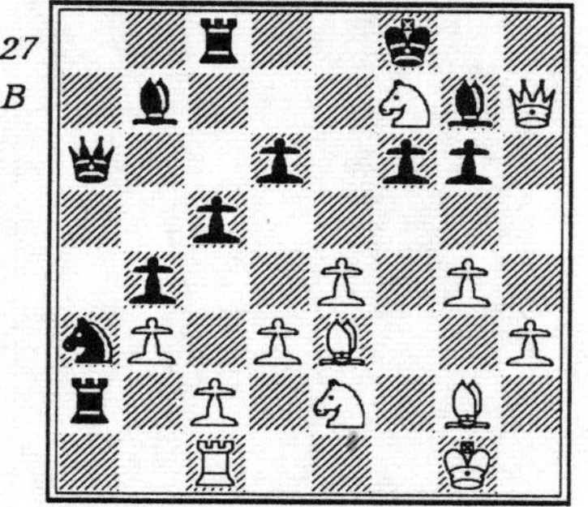

The key to a powerful combination ripping apart the pawn barrier: 25 ... ♔xf7 26 ♗h6 ♖g8 27 ♘f4 ♖xc2 28 ♖f1 ♔f8 29 ♘xg6+ ♔f7 30 ♘f4 ♔f8 31 ♘h5 ♗xh6 32 ♕xh6+ ♔e7 33 ♕h7+ ♔d8 34 ♘xf6+-.

25 ... ♖xc2
26 ♗h6! ♖xc1+

The relentless pressure cannot be abated: 26 ... ♖xe2 27 ♕xg7+ ♔e8 (27 ... ♔e7 28 ♘g5+) 28 ♘g5! fxg5 29 ♗xg5+-; 26 ... ♕xd3 27 ♕xg7+ ♔e8 28 ♖xc2 ♘xc2 29 ♘f4, with a crushing win in prospect.

27 ♘xc1 ♔xf7

Black continues to suffer after 27 ... ♗xh6 28 ♘xh6 ♔e8 29 ♘g8 ♔f8 30 ♘e7, intending to take on g6 with mate to follow.

28 ♕xg7+ ♔e8

The king can flee in another direction but the result remains the same: 28 ... ♔e6 29 g5 fxg5 30 ♗xg5 ♖e8 31 h4 (32 ♗h3+) 31 ... d5 32 exd5+ ♔d6 (32 ... ♗xd5 33 ♕xg6+ and ♕xa6) 33 ♗f4+ ♖e5 34 ♗xe5 mate.

29 g5

Winning by force. Spassky could also have tried for a flashier finish with 29 e5! ♗xg2 30 e6, mating.

29 ... f5
30 ♕xg6+ ♔d7

There is no respite after 30 ... ♔d8 31 ♕f7 (intending 32 g6 and 33 g7) 31 ... ♖c7 32 ♕f8+ ♔d7 33 g6 ♖c8 34 g7 ♕a1 35 g8(♕)+-.

31 ♕f7+ ♔c6
32 exf5+ 1-0

Reshevsky – Korchnoi
Amsterdam (5) 1968

1	**e4**	**c5**
2	**♘c3**	**d6**
3	**g3**	**♘c6**
4	**♗g2**	**g6**
5	**d3**	**♗g7**
6	**f4**	**♘f6**
7	**♘f3**	**0-0**
8	**0-0**	**♖b8** *(28)*
9	**h3**	**b5**
10	**a3**	**a5**
11	**♗e3**	**b4**
12	**axb4**	**axb4**
13	**♘e2**	**♘e8**

Releasing the bishop to

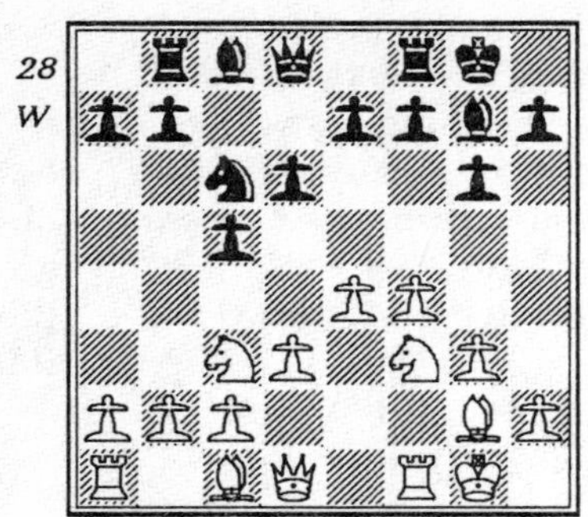

28
W

control the a1–h8 diagonal and starting the slow process of manoeuvring this knight to d4. The question is whether White can do much in the meantime to exploit Black's laborious plan. Other tries have not emerged with much credit:

a) 13 ... ♗d7 14 g4 ♘e8 15 ♖b1 ♘c7 16 ♕e1 ♘b5 17 ♕f2 ♖a8 18 f5 ♖a2 19 ♕h4 ♘e5 20 ♘xe5 ♗xe5 21 ♗h6 with excellent prospects, Lazarev – Smit, USSR 1963.

b) 13 ... ♕c7 14 b3 ♗b7 15 g4 ♖a8 16 ♖c1 ♖a2 17 ♘g3, generating an attack with 18 f5, Tarve – Karasev, USSR 1972.

14 ♖b1

Moving the rook off the a-file to protect the b-pawn and leaving White free to concentrate on his kingside ambitions.

14 ... ♘c7
15 f5 ♘b5 *(29)*

Korchnoi keeps faith with his plan and is wise not to rise to the f-pawn bait. White can use h5 as a launch-pad for the queen after 15 ... gxf5?! 16 ♘g5! h6 (16 ... fxe4 17 ♗xe4) 17 exf5 with a discovered attack on c6 and good play on the light squares around the black king.

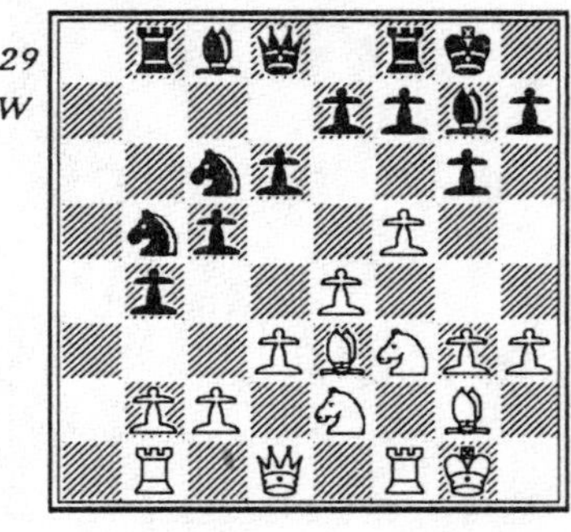

29
W

16 ♕d2 ♘bd4
17 ♘h4

Based upon the need to support f5. Also coming into consideration was 17 g4 (17 ♗h6?? ♘xe2+ 18 ♕xe2 ♗xh6) 17 ... ♘xe2+ 18 ♕xe2 ♘e5 merely allows White to gain a move on the game, whilst 18 ... ♔h8 19 ♕f2, intending ♕h4, looks difficult to handle.

17 ... ♘xe2+
18 ♕xe2 ♘e5

Now that White has stretched his pawn formation, Black adopts the well-known scheme of planting a knight on e5 to curtail any direct advances on the king. On this square it is sometimes difficult to dislodge and helps Black to create some breathing-space to reorganise his pieces. However, in this case White can easily exchange it.

19 ♘f3

The main defensive piece is removed. After the more obvious 20 ♕f2 and 21 g4, the knight obstructs the h-pawn which is required to act as a battering-ram to storm the black citadel.

19 ... ♘xf3+
20 ♕xf3 ♗b7

Black embarks on a scheme to hold White at bay and decides to put the bishop on the long diagonal where it creates the possibility of ... d5 or ... e6 in certain circumstances and at least gives White something to think about.

21 h4 ♔h8 *(30)*

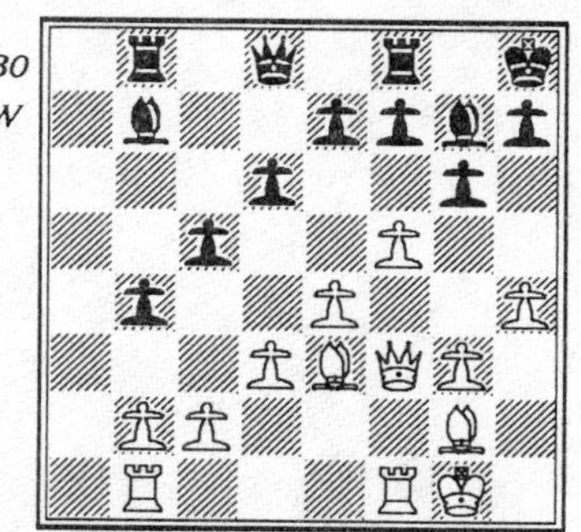

22 ♕e2?!

Logical and good is 22 g4!, when White has much the better chances with a territorial advantage and threatens dangerous pawn breaks on the kingside.

22 ... ♗e5
23 g4

Back on the right path but Black has now been given an extra move to construct a defence.

23 ... e6
24 g5

If the queen were still on f3 then 24 f6 would be possible and White could aim for an invasion on the vulnerable h6 square.

24 ... exf5
25 exf5 ♗xg2

This ploy of eliminating potential attacking pieces is the simplest way out of such situations.

26 ♕xg2 ♕d7
27 fxg6?

The tension is released and with it any real thoughts of winning the game. Worth consideration was 27 ♖f3, delaying the exchange of pawns in the hope that Black may be forced to compromise his position.

27 ... fxg6
28 b3

Otherwise the rook must remain on a passive square to protect the b2-pawn.

28 ... ♔g7
29 ♖xf8 ♖xf8
30 ♖f1 ♖xf1+
31 ♔xf1 ♕e6

The game now drifts towards a draw with both

players quietly testing each other before admitting the inevitable.

32	**♔g1**	**♗c3**
33	**♗f2**	**h5**

Satisfied that White has no intention to wreck his own pawns by capturing on h6 and leaving the h4-pawn vulnerable, Korchnoi decides to speed up the draw by eliminating his last pawn weakness.

34	**♕b7+**	**♔f8**
35	**♕b8+**	**♔e7**
36	**♕b7+**	**♕d7**
37	**♕e4+**	

If White is content to have a perpetual check then Black can do little about it.

37	**...**	**♕e6**
38	**♕b7+**	**♕d7**
39	**♕e4+**	**♕e6**
40	**♕b7+**	**½–½**

3) 6 f4 e5

One of the most popular ideas for Black in the Closed Sicilian is the Botvinnik System reversed, which is characterised by 6 ... e5. What it lacks in flexibility it makes up for by immediately fighting for control of the centre. The temporary drawback of closing in the dark-squared bishop is countered here by having the option of exchanging on f4. This line was originally developed in the English after, for example, 1 c4 g6 2 ♘c3 ♗g7 3 g3 e5 4 ♗g2 ♘c6 5 e4. The question posed for White in the Closed Sicilian is whether his extra move is of any consequence. Theory concentrates on a tricky line that allows White to utilise his extra tempo in the critical variations in an effort to pose Black serious problems early on.

Balashov – Ilic
Kusadasi 1990

1	**e4**	**c5**
2	**♘c3**	**♘c6**
3	**g3**	**g6**
4	**♗g2**	**♗g7**
5	**d3**	**d6**
6	**f4**	**e5**
7	**♘h3!?** *(31)*	

31
B

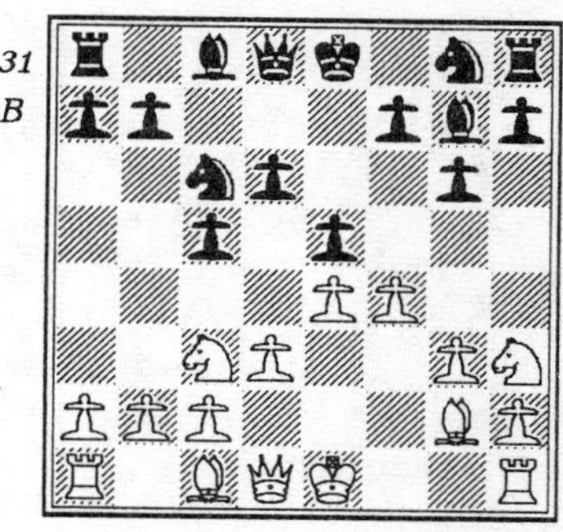

This is the crucial response, aiming to keep the f-line free for the rook to take a positive stance. It also keeps the d1-h5 diagonal clear to allow the queen to enter the fray at an appropriate moment. The more cautious 7 ♘f3 is not without some bite but usually results in a more patient manoeuvring game, after 7 ... ♘ge7 8 0-0 0-0 and now:

a) 9 h3!? ♘d4 10 g4 f5 11 gxf5 exf4 12 ♗xf4 gxf5 13

♗g5 ♕e8 14 ♗xe7 ♕xe7 15 ♘d5 ♘xf3+ 16 ♕xf3 ♕g5 17 exf5 ♗xf5 18 c3 ♖ae8 19 ♖ae1 ♗e5 20 ♘c7 ♖e7 21 ♕d5+ ♔g7 22 d4 cxd4 23 cxd4 ♖xc7 24 ♖xe5 ♖c2 25 ♖exf5 ♖xf5 26 ♖xf5 ♖c1+ 27 ♔h2 ♕e3 28 ♕f7+ 1–0 Baecke – Mongeay, Novi Sad Ol 1990.

b) 9 ♗e3

b1) 9 ... ♘d4 10 ♕d2 ♗g4 (10 ... ♗e6 transposes to a variation considered in chapter one after 6 ♗e3 e5 7 ♕d2 ♗e6 8 f4 ♘ge7 9 ♘f3 ♘d4 10 0–0 0–0) 11 ♘h4 exf4 12 ♖xf4 ♗e6 (13 ... g5) 13 ♖f2 d5 14 ♗h6 ♖c8 15 ♗xg7 ♔xg7 16 ♖af1 f6 17 exd5 ♘xd5 18 ♘e4 ♘xc2?! 19 ♕xc2 ♘e3 20 ♕c3 ♘xf1 21 ♗xf1 b6 22 ♘f3 and White is better, Lijedahl – Spassky, Gothenburg 1973.

b2) 9 ... exf4 10 gxf4 (10 ♗xf4!?) 10 ... ♘d4 11 ♕d2 ♘ec6 12 ♖ab1 ♗g4 13 ♘d5 ♘xf3+ 14 ♗xf3 ♗xf3 15 ♖xf3 f5= Bastian – Ribli, Baden-Baden 1981.

7 ... ♘ge7

The alternative is 7 ... exf4, which is examined in the game Roos – Stoica later in this chapter.

8 0–0 0–0

The most natural reply but one which allows White a crushing onslaught against the king. It is hardly surprising that Black is often caught out by making such a standard move in the opening, as it would appear to the casual observer that both sides are merely completing their development. A better move is 8 ... ♘d4, which is examined in the next game (Spassky – Hort).

9 f5! *(32)*

32
B

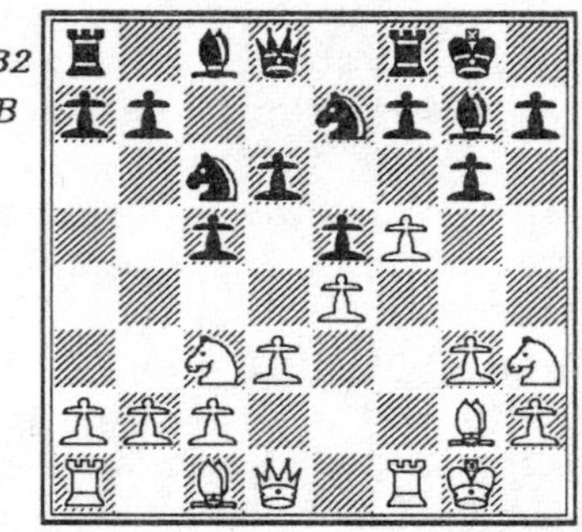

This is the difference between the Botvinnik System as it is employed in the English and the Closed Sicilian and is the main reason for numerous Black defeats. The idea is to use the light squares on e4 and h5 to gain entry to the heart of Black's kingside fortress.

9 ... f6

A typically passive attempt at putting up the shutters in a futile attempt to keep White out. White storms through in fine style if the pawn is taken: 9 ... gxf5 10 exf5, and now:

a) 10 ... ♘xf5 (10 ... f6 11

♕h5 d5 12 g4 with a bind) 11 ♕h5 (12 ♗e4 or ♘g5 is very strong in all lines) 11 ... ♘fd4 12 ♗e4 f5 13 ♗d5+ ♔h8 (13 ... ♗e6 14 ♘g5 h6 15 ♘xe6+-) 14 ♘g5 h6 15 ♕g6! hxg5 16 ♕h5+ ♗h6 17 ♕xh6 mate.

b) 10 ... ♗xf5 11 ♖xf5! ♘xf5 12 ♗e4 and Black is in trouble however the knight is moved or defended:

b1) 12 ... ♘fd4 13 ♕h5 ♖e8 (13 ... f5 14 ♗d5+ ♔h8 15 ♘g5 h6 16 ♕g6!+-) 14 ♕xh7+ ♔f8 15 ♗g5 ♕d7 16 ♘d5 ♖e6 17 ♖f1 ♘xc2 18 ♗g6 ♘2d4 19 ♗h6 1-0 Bilek – Gheorghiu, Bucharest 1968.

b2) 12 ... ♘fe7 13 ♗xh7+! ♔xh7 14 ♕h5+ ♔g8 15 ♘g5+-.

b3) 12 ... ♘h4 13 gxh4 ♕xh4 14 ♔g2 h6 15 ♗e3 f5 16 ♗f3 ♘d4 17 ♗f2 ♕e7 18 ♘d5 ♕d7 19 ♗h5 ♕c6 20 c4, when the two pieces for the rook give White a lasting advantage – L. Pickett and A. K. Swift.

b4) 14 ... ♘cd4 13 ♕h5 ♕f6 14 ♘d5 ♕e6 15 c3 h6 16 cxd4 ♘xd4 17 ♘g5 ♘f3+ 18 ♘xf3 ♖ac8 19 ♘h4 c4 20 ♘f5 cxd3 21 ♗xh6 d2 22 ♘de7+ ♔h8 23 ♗xg7 mate Ipek – Stefansson, European Jnr Ch 1973.

10 g4

Supporting f5 and vacating g3 for the queen's knight to transfer to the kingside via e2.

10 ... ♗d7
11 ♘f2

Releasing the h-pawn to add to Black's discomfort. This is an essential component of Balashov's plan to break through on the kingside since otherwise his pieces are blunted by the opposing pawns.

11 ... ♔h8

Black has severe problems in activating his pieces so he reluctantly plays a waiting move. He plans to see exactly how White intends to handle the forthcoming attack and to respond accordingly.

12 ♘e2 ♗e8
13 ♘g3 d5

Now that the knight is no longer controlling d5, Ilic seeks some counterplay in the centre.

14 h4 *(33)*

33
B

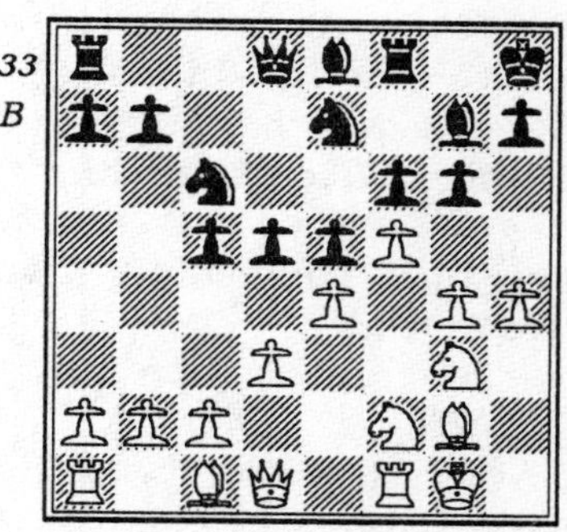

With the attack at its height, the decision to allow the exchange of queens may appear surprising. In fact, White has such total domination of the kingside, that his initiative is sufficient to be a real menace even in a queenless middlegame. Not so good is 14 ♕e1 ♘d4, when the threat to the c-pawn means that the queen must return to its original square.

14 ... dxe4
15 dxe4 ♕xd1
16 ♖xd1 b6
17 c3

A precautionary measure to prevent the bothersome ... ♘d4 at a later date.

17 ... ♗f7
18 ♗e3 ♖fd8
19 ♖e1!

This decision not to exchange rooks explains why Balashov was quite content to exchange the queens. With all the entry squares on the d-file under his control, there is no need for him to indulge in any exchanges, which would make it more difficult for him to convert his spatial advantage into something more substantial.

19 ... h6
20 g5

After a short break to re-position, the attack is back on course.

20 ... hxg5
21 hxg5 fxg5
22 ♗xg5 ♖d6 *(34)*

This guards against the threat of 23 f6, forking two pieces.

34
W

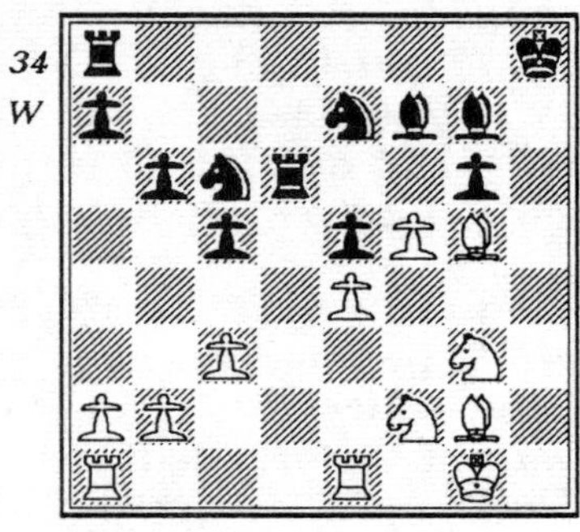

23 ♘g4

It is easy for White to play this stage of the game because all the earlier measures to shift his pieces to the kingside have enabled total co-ordination.

23 ... ♗f8
24 ♔f2

Suddenly the rooks are poised to utilise the h-file and a mating net is not far away. It has been impossible for Black to unravel his pieces in the face of the constant pressure which has been the theme of this whole game.

24 ... gxf5
25 exf5 ♘d5

Black is now only trying to survive and has yet to produce any real threat in the whole game, a sure sign of faulty opening play.

26 ♘e4 ♖dd8
27 ♖h1+

With so many pieces swarming around the king a

swift end is inevitable.

27	...	Kg7
28	Bh6+	1–0

Spassky – Hort
Bugojno 1978

1	e4	c5
2	Nc3	Nc6
3	g3	g6
4	Bg2	Bg7
5	d3	d6
6	f4	e5
7	Nh3	Nge7
8	0–0	Nd4

Hort is not interested in arguing the dubious theoretical merits of castling and decides to increase his control over f5 by using a more central post for the knight.

9 f5!?

A surprising continuation but one that is justified on positional grounds. Euwe recommended 9 Nd5 but so far there have been few practical tests. Opting out of the myriad of complications in the hope of building a small plus is also possible: 9 Rf2 h6 (better is the immediate 9 ... exf4) 10 Be3 exf4 11 Nxf4 0–0 12 Qd2 f5 13 Raf1 Kh7 14 Ncd5 fxe4 15 Bxe4 Bf5 16 c3 Ndc6 17 Bxf5 Rxf5 18 Nxe7 Nxe7 19 g4 Rf6 20 d4 Qc8 21 h3 b5 22 Qd3 Qc6 23 d5 Qb7 24 b3 Rxf4 25 Bxf4 Nxd5 26 Bxd6 Qc6 27 Bf8 Bf6 28 c4? (28 Rxf6!) ½–½ Spassky – Timman, Buenos Aires Ol 1978.

9	...	gxf5
10	Qh5 *(35)*	

35
B

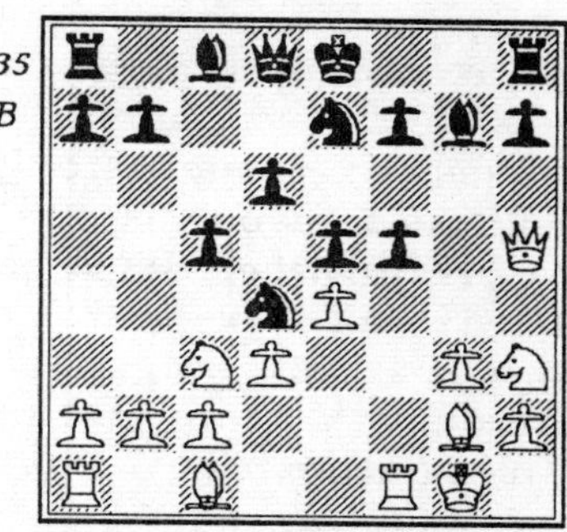

A swashbuckling style is necessary if White wishes to undertake a lightning charge against the king.

a) 10 Bg5!? f6! 11 Qh5+ Kd7 12 exf5 Nxc2 13 Rac1 Nd4 14 Ne4 Qf8 15 Be3 Nec6 16 Nhf2?! (16 Nhg5!) 16 ... Kc7 17 Bxd4 exd4 18 Nxd6!? Qxd6 19 Ne4 Qf8 20 Rxc5 Bd7 21 b4 Kb8? 22 b5 Ne5 23 Rxe5! fxe5 24 f6 Bh6 25 Qxe5+ Kc8 26 Nd6+ Kc7 27 b6+ 1–0 Trapl – Pribyl, Czech Ch 1972.

b) 10 Ng5!? h6 11 exf5 hxg5 (11 ... Ndxf5 12 Nxf7 Kxf7 13 g4 is unclear) 12 f6 Bf8 (12 ... Bxf6 13 Rxf6 d5 14 Bxg5 Be6 15 Rf2 and White is in control) 13 fxe7 Bxe7 14 Nd5 Be6 15 c3 Nc6 16 Qa4 Kf8 (16 ... 0–0 17 b4! with promising play) 17 b4! cxb4 18 d4! exd4 (18 ... bxc3 19 Nxe7 Nxe7 20 Bxg5 Qb6

21 ♖ab1 ♕xd4+ 22 ♕xd4 exd4 23 ♗f6±) 19 cxb4 ♘e5 20 ♗b2 ♕d7 21 ♕xd7! ♗xd7 22 ♗xd4 g4 (Seret - Birnboim, Malta Ol 1980) 23 ♖ae1 gives White the advantage according to Seret.

10 ... h6

Generally thought to be in White's favour is 10 ... ♘xc2 11 ♖b1 when Black has gained an insignificant pawn, but his knight has moved away from its excellent outpost.

11 ♖f2

This has the dual purpose of preparing to double rooks on the f-file while guarding c2.

11 ... ♗e6
12 ♗e3 ♕d7

Black is careful to avoid stirring up trouble by taking on e4 which would merely give the opposing forces greater access to f7 along the open file.

13 ♖af1 0-0-0

Whisking the king to safety now that White has apparently congested his pieces on the other side of the board.

14 ♘d5!

The best way to make progress, addding to the struggle of f5 by offering an exchange on d5 and making way for the c3-advance.

14 ... fxe4
15 ♘xe7+ ♕xe7
16 ♗xd4 cxd4 *(36)*

36
W

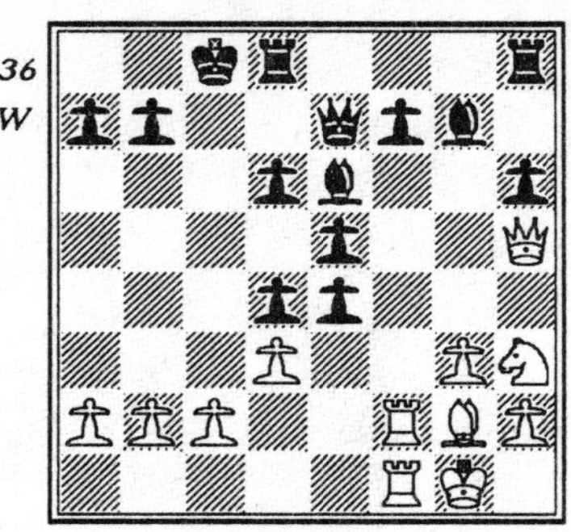

17 ♖xf7!

The reasoning behind the series of exhanges now becomes abundantly apparent. White has finally managed to extract something from the relentless pressure piled on f7, as 17 ... ♗xf7 18 ♖xf7 ♕e8 19 ♕g4+ ♔b8 20 ♕xg7 wins two bishops for the rook and leaves White in an overwhelming position.

17 ... ♕e8

The bishop is now immune since the rook is pinned.

18 ♗xe4 ♖f8

It would appear that suddenly the situation has become rather desperate for White who cannot move the rook on f7 without incurring a material loss.

19 ♗f5!

This elegant riposte is what Spassky had in mind before entering the complications. Another pin is introduced and it becomes clear that White has everything under control because the bishop can be exchanged on e6 with check, ruling out any loss on f7.

19 ... ♕xf7
20 ♕xf7 ♖xf7
21 ♗xe6+ ♖fd7
22 ♖f7

Although Black can easily sidestep any ambitions of a lengthy pin on the rook, his position is critical. In fact, Spassky has set his sights on the long-term goal of exchanging all the rooks off to reach a possibly favourable 'good knight' versus 'bad bishop' ending.

22 ... ♔c7
23 ♗xd7 ♖xd7
24 ♖xd7+ ♔xd7 *(37)*

37
W

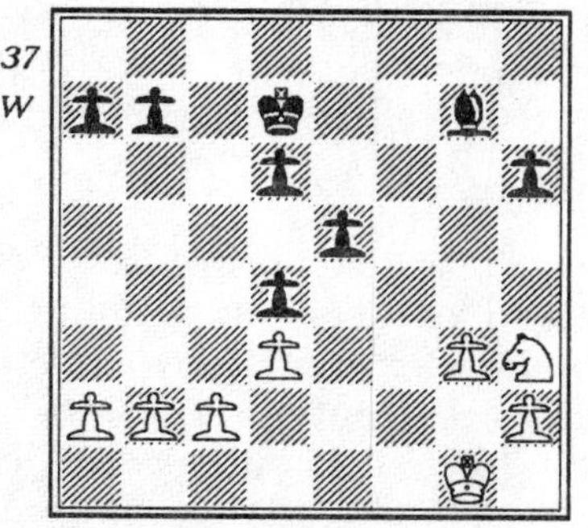

25 ♔g2

White has chances of an advantage if his king is able to gain entry amongst the opposing pawns since Black has no control over the light squares. Another key factor is that Black has his pawns split into three islands, which means that they cannot easily defend one another if the black forces become tied down by a timely creation of a white passed pawn on the kingside.

25 ... ♔e6
26 ♔f3 d5

Black pins his hopes on creating a passed pawn but the white knight can easily blockade, leaving the king to probe the weakened black pawns. 26 ... ♔f5 would have kept the white king out.

27 ♔g4 ♔f6
28 ♔h5 ♗f8
29 ♘g1

More astute was 29 a4, forestalling any plans to close down the queenside.

29 ... b5!
30 ♘e2 a5
31 g4 a4
32 h4

White prepares to create a passed pawn.

32 ... b4
33 b3 a3
34 ♘g3 e4!

Now that Black has established a pawn on a3 he has some chances of making a fight-back since White has to be wary of a black king infiltration.

35 g5+

Certainly not 35 dxe4 dxe4 36 ♘xe4+ ♔e5, intending ... d3, ... ♔d4-c3-b2, when it is Black who is on the verge of victory.

35 ... hxg5
36 hxg5+ ♔e5
37 ♔g4 ♗g7?

Now White gains a vital tempo and the game; 37 ... e3! would have held the balance.

38 ♘h5 ♗f8
39 g6 e3
40 ♔f3 ♔f5
41 g7 1-0

Roos - Stoica
Bagneux 1979

1 e4 c5
2 ♘c3 ♘c6
3 g3 g6
4 ♗g2 ♗g7
5 d3 d6
6 f4

White can also try 6 ♘h3 after which 6 ... e5 7 f4 simply transposes to the text. However, Black can also play 6 ... h5, 6 ... ♘f6, or 6 ... e6 as discussed in chapter five.

6 ... e5
7 ♘h3 exf4

This avoids all the possibilities associated with a future f5.

8 ♗xf4 *(38)*

After 8 ♘xf4 White tends to enjoy a slight edge. There are a couple of examples of this plan which continued: 8 ... ♘ge7 9 0-0 0-0 and now:

a) 10 ♗e3 ♖b8 11 a3 ♘e5 12 ♔h1 b6 13 ♕e2 ♗b7 14 g4 ♘7c6 15 h3 ♕d7 16 ♕f2 ♘e7 17 ♕g3 ♔h8 18 ♖f2 b5 19 ♖af1 a5 20 ♗c1 b4 21 axb4 axb4 22 ♘cd5 ♘xd5 23 exd5 ♖fe8 24 ♗e4 b3 25 c3 c4 26 dxc4 ♘xc4 27 ♗g2 ♗a6 28 ♖d1 ♖e7 ½-½ Spassky - Andersson, Reykjavik 1988.

b) 10 ♘fd5 ♘xd5 11 ♘xd5 ♗e6 12 ♘f4 ♗d7 13 c3 b5 14 a3 a5 15 ♗e3 ♘e5 16 h3= Bilek - Evans, Lugano Ol 1968.

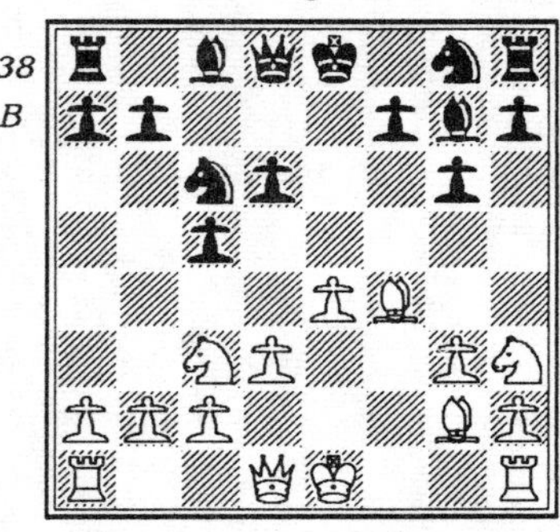
38
B

8 ... ♘ge7
9 ♕d2

White is preparing to swap off the strong black bishop after 10 ♗h6. A reliable alternative is 9 0-0 h6 10 ♖b1 0-0 11 a3 ♗e6 12 ♗e3 ♘e5 13 ♘f4 with a double-edged position, Spassky - Portisch, Geneva (13) 1977.

9 ... h6

Probably the best way to counter White's direct action. However, now Stoica is unable to castle kingside and must decide at what point to lash out with the inevitable ... g5.

10 0-0 Ne5

The possibility of advancing the g-pawn immediately has also been tested: 10 ... g5 11 Be3 Ne5 12 Nf2 0-0 13 h4!?, with an unbalanced position, Hodgson - Kudrin, Hastings 1986/87.

11 Kh1 Bd7

Black becomes obsessed with the old-fashioned plan of creating play on the queenside, at the cost of letting the state of affairs on the other wing become critical. This strategy is very risky, bearing in mind active roles taken by White's forces in this particular position.

12 Rae1

Although there is no definite threat attached to the text, it signals that White's stranglehold on the centre is reaching significant proportions. He is now able to gradually form a formidable power base without fear of a counter-attack.

12 ... b5
13 Nd5 Nxd5
14 exd5

At the small cost of doubling d-pawns White has managed to open up the e-file, making use of his rook. Black suddenly finds himself in a tangle as he still cannot castle kingside due to the loose h-pawn.

14 ... g5
15 Bxe5 Bxe5 *(39)*

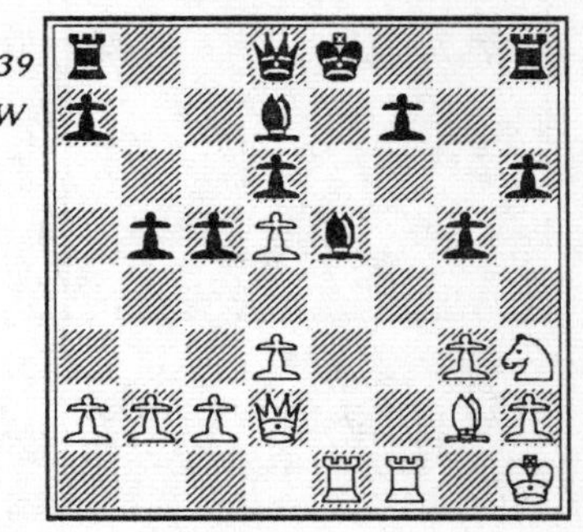

16 b4!

The start of an energetic scheme to exploit the exposed monarch, seizing the opportunity to shake the foundations of the black pawn structure.

16 ... 0-0

White would be happy with 16 ... Rc8 (16 ... cxb4? 17 d4) 17 bxc5 Rxc5 18 d4.

17 bxc5 Qc8

This is the point of Black's plan since now he hits the knight and h3 and prepares to recapture on c5.

18 Nxg5!

In hot pursuit of the king! This fine sacrifice is made possible by White's formidable pair of rooks which are poised for a decisive entry into the heart of Black's kingside fortress.

18 ... hxg5 *(40)*

40
W

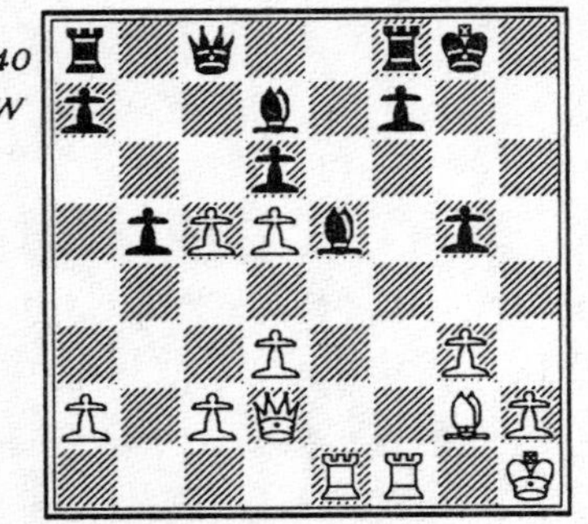

19 ♖xe5!

This ingenious idea of giving up another piece justifies the whole combination. Now Stoica can no longer rely on the bishop retreat to counter the queen check on g5.

19 ... f6

Not even worth considering was 19 ... dxe5 20 ♕xg5+ ♔h7 21 ♖f6 mating.

20 ♖e7

Lining up yet another threat: 21 ♖xf6 ♖xf6 22 ♕xg5+.

20 ... ♕d8
21 cxd6 ♗e8
22 ♗h3

Black is completely busted and now it is only a matter of finding the *coup de grâce*.

22 ... ♕xd6
23 ♗e6+ ♔h8
24 ♕xg5! 1–0

Black resigned, in view of 24 ... ♕xe7 25 ♕h6+ ♕h7 26 ♕xf8+ ♕g8 27 ♕xg8 mate and 24 ... fxg5 25 ♖xf8 mate.

4) 6 f4 e6

The games in this chapter deal with the main battleground of the Closed Sicilian. Over the years, numerous attempts have been made to introduce new ideas against the system which is generally regarded as the most robust defence available to Black. Most commonly White will use his spatial advantage for the transfer of forces to the kingside. Black normally prevents an early d4 by occupying that square with a knight, and can fend off carefully laid plans to play f5 with ... f5 himself.

Currently, the most important line is 10 e5 which is such a new and complicated idea that it fails to get even a mention in most reference books. Other moves lead to a middlegame typified by positional manoeuvring to try to develop an advantage.

In order to develop a feel for these positions we shall first examine model games by Karpov and Spassky before moving on to a discussion of the critical 10 e5 and various other alternatives for White and Black.

Karpov – Quinteros
Buenos Aires 1980

1 e4 c5
2 ♘c3 d6
3 g3 g6
4 ♗g2 ♗g7
5 d3 ♘c6
6 f4 e6
7 ♘f3 ♘ge7
8 0–0 0–0
9 ♗e3 *(41)*

41
B

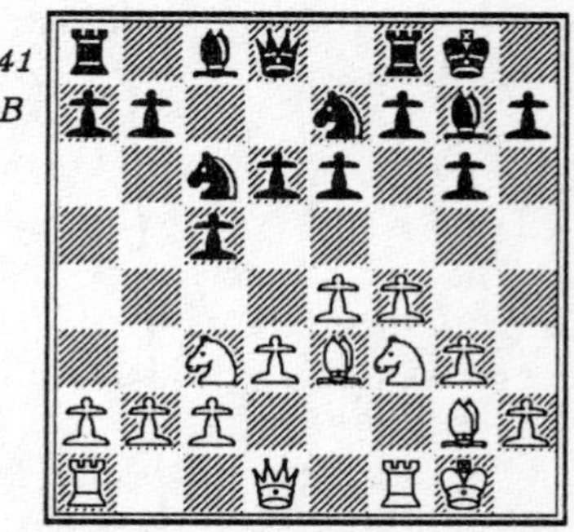

White prepares an advance in the centre with 10 d4. The main alternative, 9 ♗d2, is considered later in the chapter (Spassky –

Beikert). Other possibilities are harmless:

a) 9 ♔h1 (making room on g1 for the bishop which will eventually be played to e3) 9 ... ♖b8 10 a4 ♘d4 11 ♘h4 f5 12 ♘b1 a6 13 c3 ♘dc6 14 ♗e3 b5 15 axb5 axb5 16 ♘d2 ♗d7= Larsen - Pavlov, Halle 1963.

b) 9 ♕e2 ♖b8 10 ♗d2 b5 11 ♖fe1 b4 12 ♘d1 a5 13 ♖b1 a4 14 ♘e3 ♖e8 15 ♕f2 ♘d4 16 c3 ♘xf3+ 17 ♗xf3 ♗a6 18 ♗e2 a3 19 cxb4 cxb4∓ Marjan - Kirov, Novi Sad 1974.

c) 9 g4?! (premature) 9 ... f5 10 h3 d5?! (10 ... ♘d4!) 11 gxf5 gxf5 12 e5 d4 13 ♘b5 ♗d7 14 ♘d6 ♖b8 15 ♘d2 b5 16 a4 a6 17 axb4 axb4 18 ♕h5 ♘c8 18 ♘2e4! gives White a potent attack, Seredenko - Kot, 1962.

9 ... ♘d4

This move is the standard reply, to block White's central advance.

10 ♖b1

Karpov's aim is to play ♘e2 and c3 to force through d4. The rook move is a precaution against the discovered attack on b2 after 10 ♘e2 ♘xe2+ 11 ♕xe2 ♗xb2.

10 ... ♘ec6

This method of reinforcing d4 is one of the most popular ways of treating the position. A variety of other moves have been tested:

a) 10 ... ♗d7 11 ♘e2 ♘xf3+ (11 ... ♘xe2+ 12 ♕xe2 ♗b5 13 ♘h4 ♘c6 14 f5!? exf5 15 exf5 ♕e7 16 ♕d2 ♕xe3+ 17 ♕xe3 ♗d4 18 ♕xd4 ♘xd4= Saeed - de Bruycker, Malta Ol 1980) 12 ♗xf3 ♕c7 13 ♕d2 ♖ad8 14 c4 b6 15 g4 f5 16 gxf5 exf5 17 ♘c3 ♖de8 18 ♖be1 ♕b8 19 ♖e2 ♘c6 20 ♔h1 ♘d4 21 ♗xd4 ♗xd4 22 ♘d5 ♔h8 23 ♖fe1 fxe4 24 ♖xe4 ♗c6 25 ♖e7 ♕d8 26 ♖xa7 ♖xe1+ 27 ♕xe1 ♗xb2 28 ♕e6 ♗g7 29 ♔g2 ♗xd5 ½–½ Christiansen - Andersson, Mar del Plata 1981.

b) 10 ... b6 11 ♘e2 ♘xf3+ 12 ♗xf3 ♗b7 13 ♗g2 ♕d7 14 c3 f5 15 ♖e1 ♖ad8 16 ♕c2 ♔h8 17 ♖bd1 ♕c8 18 c4 ♕a8 19 ♗d2 ♘c6 20 ♗c3 e5 21 ♖f1 ♘d4 22 ♘xd4 exd4 23 ♗d2 ♖de8 24 ♖de1 ♖e7 25 ♖e2 ♖fe8 26 ♖ef1 ♔g8 27 ♗c1 ½–½ Casper - Kosten, Jurmala 1987.

c) 10 ... ♖b8 11 ♘e2 ♘xf3+ 12 ♗xf3 and now:

c1) 12 ... ♕a5 13 a3 ♗d7 14 d4 ♕c7 15 ♕d2 ♖fd8 16 g4± Koskela - Lumongdong, Novi Sad Ol 1990.

c2) 12 ... b6 13 c3 (13 g4 f5 14 ♘g3 ♗b7 15 c3 ♕d7= Nicevski - Bukic, Yugoslav Ch 1981) 13 ... ♗b7 14 d4 ♕c7 15 ♕d2 f5 16 e5 ♗xf3 17 ♖xf3 cxd4 18 exd6 ♕xd6 19 ♗xd4 ♘c6 20 ♖d3 ♘xd4 21 ♘xd4 e5 22 fxe5 ♕xe5 23 ♖e1 ♕c5 24 b4 ♕c4 25 ♘e6 ♖fe8 26

♖de3 ♗h6 27 ♘f4 ♖xe3 28 ♖xe3 ♗g5 29 ♕d7 ♕xa2 30 ♖e8+ ♖xe8 31 ♕xe8+ ♔g7 32 ♘e6+ ♔h6 33 ♘xg5 ♔xg5 34 ♕d8+= Lane - Condie, Manchester 1983.

d) 10 ... d5 11 ♘e2 dxe4?! 12 dxe4 ♘ec6 13 e5 ♘xe2+ 14 ♕xe2 ♕a5 15 ♘d2 ♘d4 16 ♕c4 ♖d8 17 ♘e4 b6 18 b4 ♕a4, McLaren - Ree, Canadian Open 1971, and now 19 ♘xc5! bxc5 20 ♗xd4 is winning thanks to the discovered attack in a8.

11 ♘e2 ♘xf3+
12 ♗xf3 b6
13 c3

It is wise to resist the temptation to try to exploit the control of the h1-a8 diagonal by 13 e5?! ♗b7 (13 ... d5?! 14 c3!, intending d4) 14 d4 cxd4 15 ♘xd4 ♘xd4 16 ♗xb7 ♘f5!, giving Black the edge.

13 ... ♗b7
14 ♕d2 d5 *(42)*

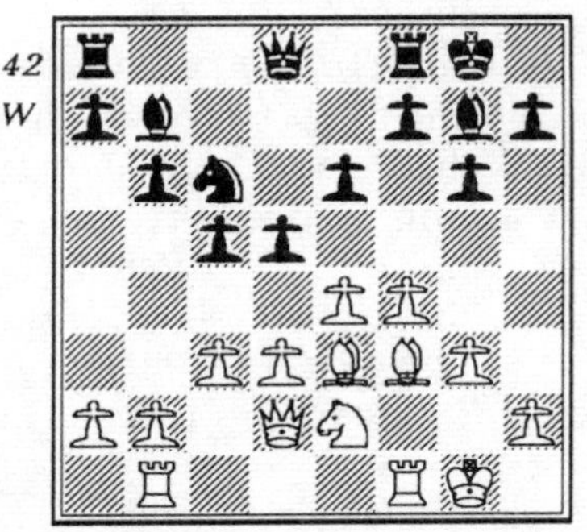

42
W

Now the centre will become closed, benefitting White, whose spatial advantage enables him to manoeuvre the pieces better. Quinteros realises the inherent dangers in such a scheme, but believes that a draw can be extracted from the game by his policy. A slower idea is 14 ... ♘e7, intending ... b5-b4, but this is not in keeping with the solid set-up introduced by 11 ... b6.

15 e5 a5

It would be a mistake to allow White to make use of a pin: 15 ... d4?! 16 cxd4 cxd4 17 ♘xd4, winning a whole pawn.

16 d4 ♕e7
17 ♗f2 ♗a6

The bishop seeks out a more active post now that ... d5 has limited its scope on b7.

18 ♖fe1 h5?!

In his efforts to hinder support for the advance f5 Black merely induces his opponent to switch attention to opening the h-file for attacking operation. Much safer was 18 ... ♖ac8 with the intention of ... cxd4 to bring the knight to b4 if the pawn recaptures.

19 h3 ♖ac8
20 ♔g2 f5

Another measure to prevent g4, which also allows the queen a chance to cover h7 once the bishop moves.

21 ♕e3 ♖f7

22 a3!

Now the intrusion of the knight on b4 has been eliminated the white forces can be rearranged without hindrance. Not so good was 22 dxc5? bxc5 23 ♕xc5 ♕xc5 24 ♗xc5 ♘xe5!, when it is Black who has excellent prospects.

22 ... a4
23 g4 cxd4
24 cxd4 hxg4
25 hxg4 ♘a5

Although the knight heading for c4 may become influential it needs the help of the other pieces. Black's plan is rather slow, however, and White has chances to organise a lightning breakthrough on the kingside.

26 gxf5 ♖xf5

This capture by the rook is indicative of something wrong with Black's strategy: the g-pawn is now weak and the open h-file will soon be occupied by the white rooks. It is clear that 26 ... gxf5 27 ♗h5 and 28 ♗g6 was too dangerous.

27 ♗g4 ♖ff8
28 ♖h1

White is in control of the situation and plans to construct a mating net.

28 ... ♔f7
29 ♖h7 ♖h8
30 ♖bh1 ♘c4 *(43)*

In a conclusive piece of analysis, Cebalo refutes a frantic try to avoid the inevitable: 30 ... ♖xh7 31 ♖xh7 ♖h8 32 ♕h3 ♖xh7 33 ♕xh7 ♕e8 34 f5! exf5 (34 ... gxf5 35 ♗h5++-) 35 ♘f4 fxg4 36 e6+! ♔f6 37 ♗h4+ ♔f5 (37 ... g5 38 ♘h5+) 38 ♕xg7 ♘c6 39 ♕f7+-; 33 ... ♕f8 34 f5! exf5 (34 ... gxf5 35 ♗h5+ ♔e7 36 ♗h4+ ♔d7 37 ♗f6+-) 35 ♘f4 fxg4 36 e6+ ♔e8 (36 ... ♔e7 37 ♘xg6++-; 36 ... ♔f6 37 ♕xg6+ ♔e7 38 ♗h4+ ♔c7 39 e7+-) 37 ♕xg6+ ♔d8 38 ♗h4+ ♔c7 39 e7+-.

43
W

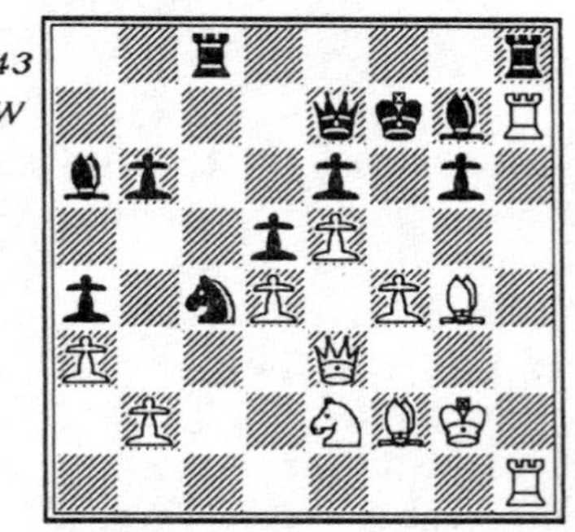

31 ♕g3 ♘xb2
32 f5!

It is fitting that the decisive move is the one that Black has spent much effort trying to prevent.

32 ... ♖xh7
33 fxg6+ ♔g8
34 gxh7+ ♔h8
35 ♘f4 1-0

Spassky – Gufeld
Wellington 1988

1 e4 c5

2	♘c3	♘c6
3	g3	g6
4	♗g2	♗g7
5	d3	d6
6	f4	e6
7	♘f3	♘ge7
8	0-0	0-0
9	♗e3	♘d4
10	♗f2 *(44)*	

44
B

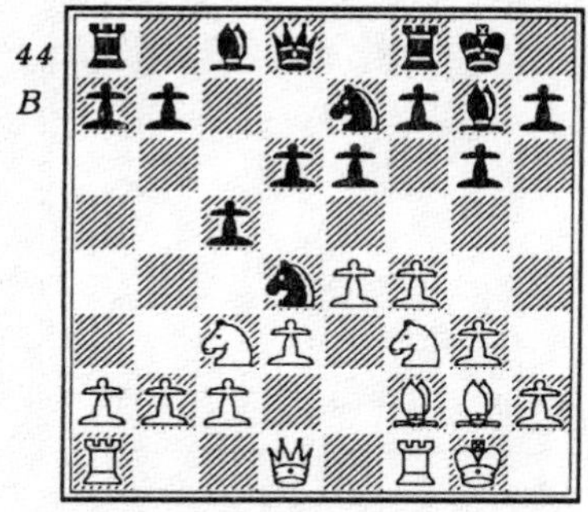

The bishop moves to a safer square to prepare a future e5 or ♘xd4

10 ... ♘xf3+

Black has a number of moves to choose from:

a) 10 ... ♘ec6 and now:

a1) 11 ♘xd4 ♘xd4 (11 .. cxd4 12 ♘e2 f5 13 c3 dxc3 14 bxc3 ♗d7 15 ♖b1 b6= Roos - Benjamin, New York 1984) 12 ♖b1 (12 e5!? dxe5 13 fxe5 ♗xe5 14 ♘e4 f5 15 ♘xc5 ♕d6 16 b4! ♘c6 17 ♖b1 ♗d4 18 ♕d2 ♗xf2+ 19 ♕xf2 ♖b8 20 a3= Spassky - Hjartarson, Munich 1991) 12 ... ♗d7 13 ♘e2 ♕a5! 14 ♘c1 (14 c3 ♘xe2+ 15 ♕xe2 ♕xa2 16 e5 ♕b3 17 exd6 ♖fc8 18 f5 gxf5 19 g4 is unclear, Spassky - Miles, Gjovik 1983) 14 ... ♗a4 15 b3 ♗c6 16 ♗e1 ♕a3 17 c3 ♘b5 18 ♘e2 f5 19 ♕c2 ♖ae8 20 ♖d1 ♖f7 ½-½ Spassky - Adorjan, Gjovik 1983.

a2) 11 ♘d2 ♖b8 12 ♘cb1 ♘e7 13 c3 ♘dc6 14 a4! b6 15 ♘f3 e5 16 ♘bd2 ♗a6 17 ♕e2 exf4 18 gxf4 ♖e8 19 ♖fe1 ♘d5 20 ♗g3= Todorcevic - Portisch, Szirak IZ 1987.

a3) 11 e5!? dxe5 12 ♘xe5 ♘b4 13 a3 ♘d5 14 ♘e4 f6 15 ♘c4 b6 16 c3 ♘f5 17 ♕e2 ♗b7 18 b4 cxb4 19 axb4 ♕d7 20 ♖a3 ♗c6 21 ♖fa1 ♖fd8 22 ♘cd2 ♘fe7 23 b5 ♗b7 24 d4 ♘c8 25 c4 ♘b4 26 ♘b3 e5 27 ♘ec5 bxc5 28 ♘xc5 ♕f7 29 ♘xb7+-, McLaren - Hassapis, British Ch 1990.

b) 10 ... ♖b8 11 ♕d2 ♕a5 12 a3 ♗d7 13 ♖fd1 ♖fc8 14 ♖ab1 b5 15 ♘d5 ♕d8 16 ♘xe7+ ♕xe7 17 c3 ♘b3 18 ♕c2 ♘a5 19 d4 cxd4 20 ♗xd4 ♗xd4 21 ♖xd4 gives White good chances against d6, Fernandes - Mossong, Haifa 1989.

c) 10 ... ♗d7 and now:

c1) 11 ♕d2 ♕a5 12 ♔h1 ♘ec6 13 a3 ♘xf3 14 ♗xf3 ♘d4 15 ♗g2 ♘b5 16 ♗e1 ♘xc3 17 bxc3 ♗c6 18 f5 exf5 19 exf5 ♗e5 20 ♗xc6 bxc6 21 f6 with excellent attacking prospects, Kornasiewicz - Georges, Zurich 1988.

c2) 11 ♖b1 ♕a5 12 ♘d2 ♖d8 13 ♘e2 ♕xa2?! (13 ... ♘xe2+ 14 ♕xe2 ♕xa2 15 ♘c4 ♕a4

16 e5 d5 17 ♗xc5!) 14 ♘c4 ♕a6 15 ♖a1 ♕c6 16 ♘xd4 ♗xd4 17 ♖xa7 b5 18 e5 d5 19 ♘e3 ♖a8 20 ♖xa8 ♖xa8 21 c3 ♗xe3 22 ♗xe3 ♖a2 23 ♕b3 ♖a4 24 ♖c1 ♘f5 25 ♗f2 c4 26 dxc4 ♕xc4 27 ♕c2 ♖a2 28 ♗f1 ♕a4 29 ♕xa4 bxa4 30 ♖b1 h5 31 ♗c5 ♗c6 32 ♗d3 ♔g7 33 ♔f2 f6 34 ♗xf5 gxf5 35 exf6+ ♔xf6 36 ♗a3, when the black rook remains a spectator for the rest of the game giving White the advantage, Berend - Groszpeter, Cannes 1991.

d) 10 ... f5 11 ♘xd4 cxd4 12 ♘e2 e5 13 c3 dxc3 14 bxc3 exf4 15 ♘xf4 ♔h8 16 ♕b3, occupying e6, looks promising for White, whilst the isolated black d-pawn is a long-term weakness, Abramovic - Vuruna, Vrnjacka Banja 1989.

e) 10 ... b6 11 ♘xd4 cxd4 12 ♘e2 e5 13 c3 dxc3 14 ♘xc3 ♗e6! (14 ... ♗b7 15 d4±) 15 d4 exf4 16 gxf4 (Abramovic - Stohl, Vrnjacka Banja 1989) 16 ... ♕d7 17 ♗h4 f6!? (17 ... d5? 18 f5 gxf5 19 ♗xe7+-) 18 d5 ♗h3 is unclear, according to Stohl.

11 ♗xf3 ♘c6
12 ♗g2 ♘d4

Black is ready to confront White by allowing him some active play in a bid to lure him to overstretch his forces. After 12 ... ♖b8 play might continue quietly in the following fashion: 13 ♖b1 b6 14 ♕d2 ♗d7 15 a3 ♖c8 16 ♘e2 ♘d4 17 c3 ♘xe2+ 18 ♕xe2 ½-½ Spassky - Karpov, Linares 1983.

13 e5!? *(45)*

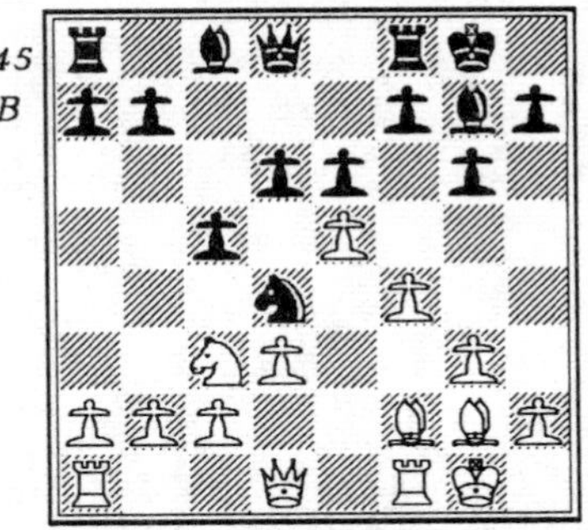

An enterprising approach to the situation. This pawn thrust breaks up the black pawn structure and opens the position up for the two white bishops. As we shall see, this position might also arise after the move order 10 e5 ♘ef5 11 ♗f2 ♘xf3+ 12 ♕xf3 ♘d4 13 ♕d1.

13 ... dxe5

After the meek 13 ... d5 14 ♘a4 b6 15 c3, White has a comfortable edge, whilst 13 ... ♖b8 and 13 ... f5 are considered later, by transposition, in the illustrative game Donev - Zagrebelni.

14 fxe5 ♗xe5

White has a good game if Black refrains from taking the pawn: 14 ... ♖b8?! 15 ♘e4 b6 16 c3 ♘f5 17 ♘f6+

♔h8 (17 ... ♗xf6 18 exf6 ♕xf6 19 g4+-) 18 g4 ♘e7 19 ♕f3 ♗b7 20 ♕h3 ♗xf6 21 exf6 ♘g8 22 ♗g3 ♗xg2 23 ♕xg2 ♖c8 24 ♕e4 ♕d7 25 ♗e5 ♖fd8 26 ♖f3 ♕d5 27 ♕f4 ♖d7 28 ♖h3 ♖cd8 29 ♖xh7+! ♔xh7 30 g5 1-0 Rogulj - Paunovic, Belgrade 1987.

15 ♘e4

The intended response to regain the pawn.

15 ... f5

White is on top in every line:

a) 15 ... ♕c7 16 c3 ♘c6 17 ♗xc5 ♖d8 18 d4 (18 ♗e3!?) 18 ... b6 19 ♗a3 ♗b7 20 ♕f3 ♗g7 21 ♘d6! ♖xd6? 22 ♗xd6 ♕xd6 23 ♕xf7+ ♔h8 24 ♕xb7+-.

b) 15 ... ♗d7 16 c3 ♘f5 17 ♗xc5 ♖e8 18 ♕f3 ♗c6 19 d4 ♗g7 20 ♖ad1±, Campora - Oblitas, Buenos Aires 1991.

c) 15 ... ♗g7 16 c3 ♘f5 17 ♗xc5 ♖e8 18 ♕f3 ♕c7 19 d4 a5 20 g4 ♘h6 21 ♖ae1, Balashov - Groszpeter, Biel 1989.

16 ♘xc5 ♕d6?!

It is difficult to decide which is the best square for the the queen to try to oust the white knight. The prudent 16 ... ♕c7 would have been much more appropriate according to most commentators. However, the same white plan is suitable even against this improvement.

After 17 b4 play might continue:

a) 17 ... ♗g7 18 c3 and now:

a1) 18 ... ♘b5 19 ♕b3 ♘xc3 20 ♖ae1 ♕f7 21 ♘xe6 ♗xe6 22 ♖xe6 with the initiative, Balashov - Karpman, Moscow 1989.

a2) 18 ... ♘c6 19 ♕b3 ♔h8 20 d4 ♖e8 21 ♖ad1 b6 22 ♕a4!+- Koslesar - Lechtynsky, Czech Ch 1990.

b) 17 ... ♘b5? 18 a4 ♗xa1 19 ♕xa1 ♘d6 20 ♗d4±.

c) 17 ... ♘c6 18 d4 ♗f6 19 c3 ♖b8 20 ♕b3 ♘d8 21 ♗e3!? ♔g7 (21 ... ♗e7 22 d5 exd5 23 ♕xd5 ♘f7 24 ♗f4 ♗d6 25 ♗xd6 ♕xd6 26 ♖ad1 ♕c7 27 ♖fe1± Abramovic - Damljanovic, New York 1988) 22 ♗f4 e5 23 dxe5 ♗xe5 24 ♗xe5 ♕xe5 25 ♖fe1 ♕c7 (Abramovic - Am. Rodriguez, New York 1988) 26 ♖ad1!±.

d) 17 ... f4!? (Gufeld) 18 gxf4 ♖xf4 19 c3 ♘b5 20 d4 ♗d6 21 ♕e1±.

e) 17 ... a5?! 18 c3 ♘b5 19 d4 ♗f6 (19 ... ♘xc3 dxe5+-) 20 ♕d3 ♘d6 21 b5 with a clear advantage, Campora - Correa, Sao Paulo 1989.

17 b4 ♖b8

Of course, White had seen the tricky 17 ... ♘b5?! 18 a4! ♗xa1 19 ♕xa1 ♘c7 20 ♘xb7 ♗xb7 21 ♗xb7 ♕xb4 22 ♗xa8 ♖xa8 23 ♕e5 with enormous presence on the dark squares around the king.

The host of alternatives also ensure White the better chances:

a) 17 ... ♘c6 18 ♖b1 b6 19 d4 ♗xd4 20 ♗xd4 ♕xd4 21 ♕xd4 ♘xd4 22 ♗xa8 bxc5 23 ♖f2± Panno - Cifuentes, Santiago 1989.

b) 17 ... ♗g7 and now:

b1) 18 a4 e5 19 c3 ♘c6 20 a5± Gufeld.

b2) 18 ♖b1 a5! 19 ♘xb7 ♗xb7 20 ♗xb7 axb4 21 ♗xa8 ♖xa8∞ Lane - Al. Schneider, Cappelle la Grande 1992.

18 c3 ♘b5

19 d4 *(46)*

46

B

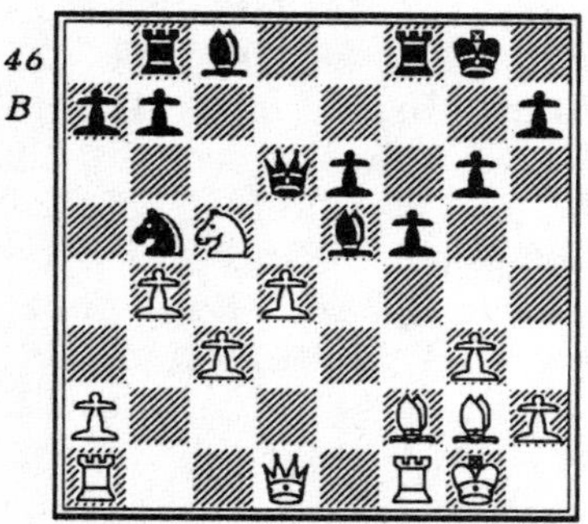

A tactical device which guards the knight and exerts pressure on the centre. The point is that 19 ... ♘xc3 is strongly met by 20 dxe5, winning a piece.

19 ... ♗f6

20 ♕b3

The e-pawn comes under fire from the queen, which also protects the c-pawn.

20 ... b6

21 ♘d3 ♗b7

22 ♗xb7 ♖xb7

23 a4

A neat measure to temporarily reduce the effectiveness of the rook on b7.

23 ... ♘c7

24 ♖fe1 ♘d5

25 c4

It is time to roll the pawns forward on a dual mission to control key squares and create a passed pawn. Gufeld encouraged these advances with the provocative knight in the centre, but it was a faulty plan and the weakness of the black e-pawn makes up for the d-pawn being difficult to defend.

25 ... ♘e7

26 ♘f4!

There is no need to be anxious about the fate of d4 now that White can home in on the e6-pawn.

26 ... ♘c6

Not advisable is 26 ... ♗xd4 27 ♖ad1 ♗xf2+ 28 ♔xf2 ♕b8 (28 ... ♕c6 29 ♘xe6+-) 29 ♘xe6 ♖c8 30 c5+-.

27 ♖xe6

White now has nothing to fear from 27 ... ♘xd4 28 ♖xd6 ♘xb3 29 ♖b1, when the knight is trapped.

27 ... ♕xb4

28 ♕d3 ♘e7

29 ♗e1

Suddenly the black queen is under threat, which allows White to move his bishop to a more potent position.

29 ... ♕b2
30 ♗c3 ♕b3 *(47)*

47
W

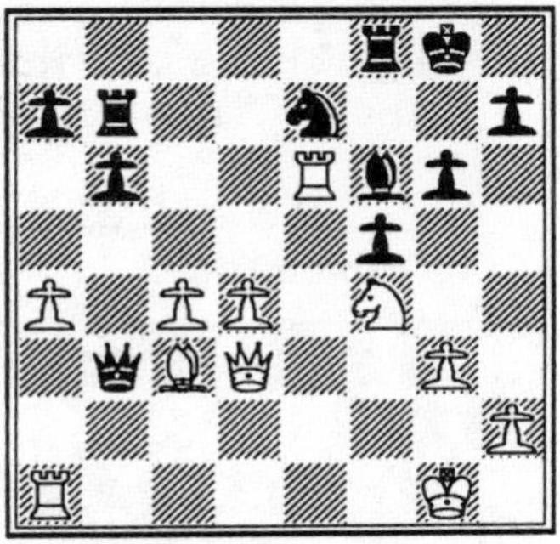

31 ♖xf6!

The former World Champion finds a remarkable exchange sacrifice that utilises the new location of his bishop, which is now ready to dominate the a1-h8 diagonal.

31 ... ♖xf6
32 d5 ♔f7

After 32 ... ♖d6 33 ♕d4 the king is trapped.

33 ♘e6

An excellent move. The knight not only threatens 34 ♘d8+ but also 34 ♘d4, which actually wins the queen. Not so forcing is 33 ♕d4 ♘g8! when Black is still in the game.

33 ... ♖xe6
34 dxe6+ ♔xe6
35 ♖e1+ ♔f7
36 ♕d4

Now the queen is ready to join in the hunt for the king and the lack of harmony amongst the black pieces makes it impossible to mount a defence.

36 ... ♕xa4
37 ♕g7+ ♔e8
38 ♗f6

White really hammers home the advantage by converging on the hapless monarch.

38 ... ♔d8
39 ♕f8+ ♕e8
40 ♖d1+ ♖d7
41 ♗xe7+

A nice touch: the queen and rook are pinned.

41 ... ♔c7
42 ♕xe8 1-0

Balashov - Pigusov
USSR 1990

1	**e4**	**c5**
2	**♘c3**	**♘c6**
3	**g3**	**g6**
4	**♗g2**	**♗g7**
5	**d3**	**d6**
6	**f4**	**e6**
7	**♘f3**	**♘ge7**
8	**0-0**	**0-0**
9	**♗e3**	**♘d4**
10	**e5**	**♕b6!?**

This is widely regarded as the antidote to 10 e5 but, the way Balashov tackles it, this assessment must be doubtful. The idea is to threaten b2 whilst being in a position to defend c5 after the pawn exchanges in the centre.

11 ♖b1 *(48)*

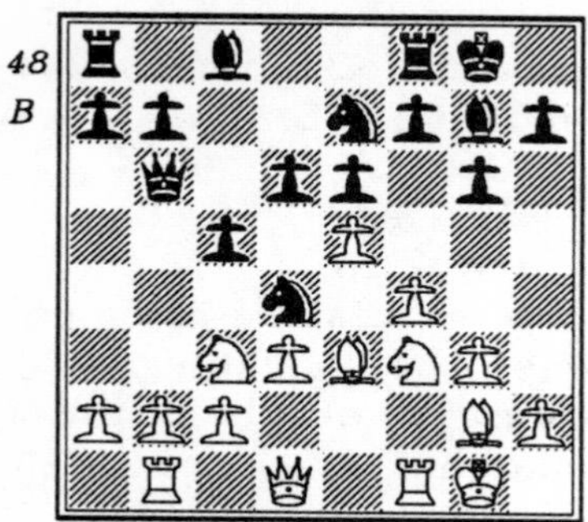

This sensible move is the correct choice. Optimistic play in the centre fails to yield White any advantage in this position: 11 ♘e4 ♘ef5 12 ♗f2 ♕xb2 13 ♘xd4 cxd4 14 g4 ♘e3 (14 ... dxe6 15 gxf5 exf5 16 ♘d6±) 15 ♗xe3 dxe3 16 ♘xd6 f6! (16 ... g5?! 17 ♕e2 gxf4 18 ♘c4 ♕d4 19 ♖ac1! b5 20 c3 ♕d7 21 ♗xa8 bxc4 22 d4+- Adorjan, Vegh) 17 ♕e2 fxe5 18 ♘c4 ♕d4 19 fxe5 ♖f2 20 ♕xe3 ♖xf1+ 21 ♖xf1 ♗xe5 22 ♕xd4 ♗xd4+ 23 ♔h1 ♖b8 24 ♖b1 ½–½ Spassky - Horvath, Rotterdam 1988.

11 ... ♘ef5
12 ♗f2 ♘xf3+
13 ♕xf3

The best policy is to keep faith with the normal plan and, to a certain extent, ignore the addition of ♖b1 and ... ♕b6. Grandmaster Abramovic once tried to inject some originality to the situation with unfortunate consequences: 13 ♗xf3 dxe5 14 fxe5 ♗xe5 15 ♘a4 ♕c7 16 ♗xc5 (16 ♘xc5 ♘d4!) 16 ... ♗d7! 17 ♗xf8 ♖xf8 18 ♘c3 ♘e3 19 ♕d2 ♘xf1 20 ♔xf1 ♖c8 21 ♗d1 ♕a5 22 d4 ♗g7 23 a3 ♖c4 24 d5 exd5 25 ♕xd5 ♗h3+ 0–1 Abramovic - Cebalo, Yugoslav Ch 1989.

13 ... dxe5
14 fxe5 *(49)*

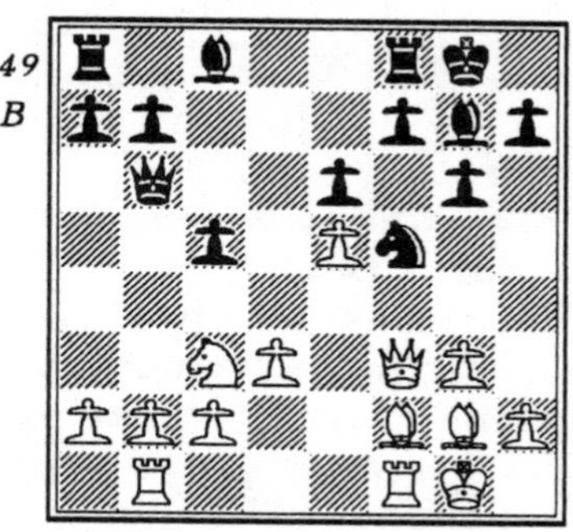

The text improves on the game Bastian - Mueller, Germany 1988, where 14 ♘a4?! ♕c7 15 fxe5 ♗xe5 16 ♗xc5 ♗d7! 17 ♗xf8 ♖xf8 18 ♘c3 ♗d4+ 19 ♔h1 ♘e3 20 ♕e4? (20 ♕f4) 20 ... ♕b6 21 ♖f4 e5 22 ♘e2 ♗c6 23 ♘xd4 ♗xe4 24 ♖xe4 exd4 25 ♗f3 ♖c8 26 ♖e7 ♕f6 0–1 frightened off many devotees to the line.

In fact, the real mistake is the plan to put the knight on a4, to stake a claim against the c5-pawn. This only manages to disrupt the harmony of the white pieces, allowing Black to create significant counterplay. The white knight belongs in the centre, where it can contribute to the kingside activity while maintaining the pressure on c5.

14 ... ♗xe5
15 ♘e4! ♘d4

An amusing finish occurs after 15 ... ♗d7? (15 ... ♗d4 16 g4!) 16 ♗xc5 ♗d4+ 17 ♔h1+-, if the bishops are exchanged then ♘f6+ and ♘xd7 is fatal; Balashov - Kiselev, Moscow 1989.

16 ♕d1 f5
17 ♘d2 ♕c7
18 c3 ♘b5
19 ♕e2

For the price of a pawn White has a considerable initiative which, coupled with the disarray of Black's forces, gives him an edge. Now the obvious threat is 20 d4, revealing a discovered attack on b5, amd White can also gain time by molesting the black knight with his a-pawn.

19 ... a6
20 a4 ♘a7
21 ♘c4 ♗f6 *(50)*
22 b4!

Balashov insists on maintaining the tension with this excellent confrontational move. The key to White's play is the lamentable lack of development of the black queenside, which seems to cast

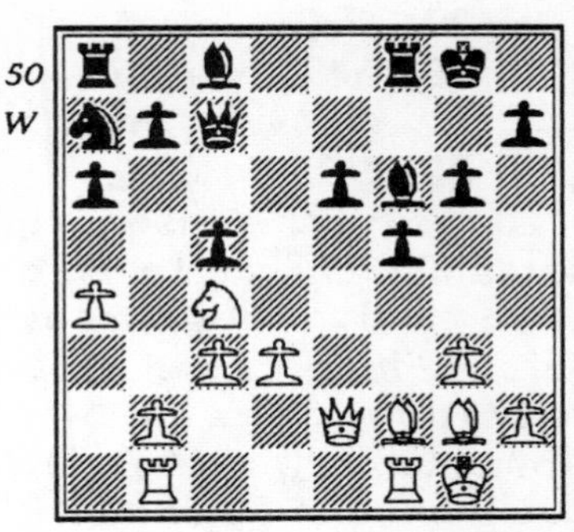

doubt on the whole concept of 10 ... ♕b6.

22 ... cxb4
23 ♘b6 ♖b8
24 ♘xc8 ♘xc8
25 ♕xe6+

Material equilibrium is restored, with interest. Now the full power of the pair of bishops on an open board is revealed and it is very difficult for Black to restrict their effectiveness.

25 ... ♔g7
26 cxb4 ♕d6
27 ♕xd6 ♘xd6
28 ♖bc1

The rook takes up a position on the c-file and would like to move to the seventh rank. Black can meet the basic threats, but only at the cost of further reducing the co-ordination of his own pieces.

28 ... ♖f7

White would maintain a distinct edge after 28 ... ♖bc8 29 ♖c5!, since the rook cannot be taken else the b-pawn falls.

29 ♖c5 ♗g5
30 h4 ♗d2
31 ♗d4+ ♔h6
32 ♖d5 ♖d7

Here Black wisely ignores the chance to take a pawn and simultaneously defend d6 because of the refutation: 32 ... ♗xb4 33 ♖b1 a5 (33 ... ♗a3 34 ♖b3) 34 ♖xb4 ♖xb4 35 ♖xd6+-.

33 ♗f3! ♖bd8

The pawn is still immune from capture as Krasenkov shows in his analysis: 33 ... ♗xb4? 34 g4! fxg4 35 ♗xg4 ♖dd8 (35 ... ♖f7 36 ♖b1!) 36 ♗b6 and ♗c7 wins.

34 ♗b6 ♖e8
35 ♗c5 ♖ed8
36 g4!

The threat of 37 ♗d4 and 38 g5 mate forces Black to jettison a significant amount of material.

36 ... fxg4
37 ♗xg4 ♘f5
38 ♖xd7 1–0

Donev – Zagrebelni
Ruse 1989

1 e4 c5
2 ♘c3 ♘c6
3 g3 g6
4 ♗g2 ♗g7
5 d3 d6
6 f4 e6
7 ♘f3 ♘ge7
8 0–0 0–0
9 ♗e3 ♘d4
10 e5 ♘ef5
11 ♗f2 ♘xf3+

Not to be trusted is the decision to refuse to take up the gauntlet: 11 ... d5?! 12 ♘xd4 ♘xd4 13 ♘a4 b6 14 b4 ♗d7 15 bxc5 ♗xa4 16 ♗xd4 ♖c8 17 cxb6 ♖xc2 18 ♕b1 axb6 19 ♗xb6 ♕d7 20 ♖f2 ♖fc8 21 ♖xc2 ♗xc2 22 ♕b4 ♗xd3 23 a4 ♗f8 24 ♕d4 ♗a6 25 a5 ♕b7 26 h4 h5 27 ♕e3 ♖c2 28 ♖c1 ♖xc1+ 29 ♕xc1 ♗c4 30 ♕xc4 1–0 Le Blancq – Raymaekers, Guernsey 1988.

12 ♕xf3 ♘d4

A radical solution to the position flounders against accurate play: 12 ... ♖b8 13 ♘e4 b6 14 g4 ♗b7 15 ♕h3 ♗xe4 16 dxe4 ♘d4 17 ♗h4 ♘e2+ 18 ♔h1 ♘xf4 19 ♗xd8 ♘xh3 20 ♗e7 ♗xe5 21 ♗xf8 ♔xf8 22 ♗xh3 ♗xb2 23 ♖ab1 ♗e5 24 ♖f3 b5 25 g5 ♔e8 26 ♗f1 b4 27 ♖h3 ♔f8 28 ♖xh7 a5 29 ♗c4 ♔g8 30 ♖h3 ♗f4 31 ♖f1 ♗xg5 32 ♖hf3 ♖d8 33 ♖xf7 d5 34 exd5 exd5 35 ♗xd5 1–0 Thorhallsson – Petursson, Reykjavik 1989. Those players who have sought more independent lines have speculated with 12 ... ♗d7!? a move which has attracted some attention: 13 ♕xb7 ♖b8 14 ♕xa7 ♖xb2 15 ♖ac1 (15 ♘e4!?) 15 ... dxe5 16 fxe5 ♗xe5 17 ♘e4 ♗c6 18 ♕xc5 ♗xe4, Kindermann – Spassov, Novi Sad Ol 1990, and now 19 ♗xe4

♗d4! 20 ♗xd4 ♘xd4 is unclear, according to Spassov.

13 ♕d1 f5 *(51)*

51
W

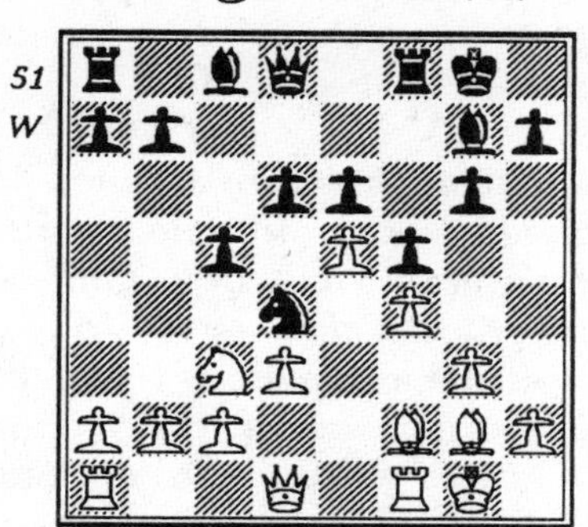

This is one of the most searching tests of White's plan, forcing open the f-file before ♘e4 can be played.

It is extremely important to note that 13 ... dxe5 14 fxe5 ♗xe5 transposes to the illustrative game Spassky - Gufeld. Often Black has drifted at this point having been confronted with a position in which he is unfamiliar with the theoretical recommendations, and highly complex: 13 ... ♖b8 14 ♘e4 dxe5 15 c3 ♘f5 16 ♗xc5 ♖e8 17 fxe5 b6 18 ♗d6 ♖b7 19 ♕e2 ♖d7 20 d4 ♗b7 21 ♗a3 ♕c8 22 g4 ♗a6 23 ♕f2 ♗xf1 24 ♖xf1 ♘e7 1-0 Martin - Britton, Barnsdale 1989.

14 exf6 ♕xf6
15 ♘e4 ♕e7
16 c3 ♘c6
17 ♕b3! *(52)*

The queen is now ideally

52
B

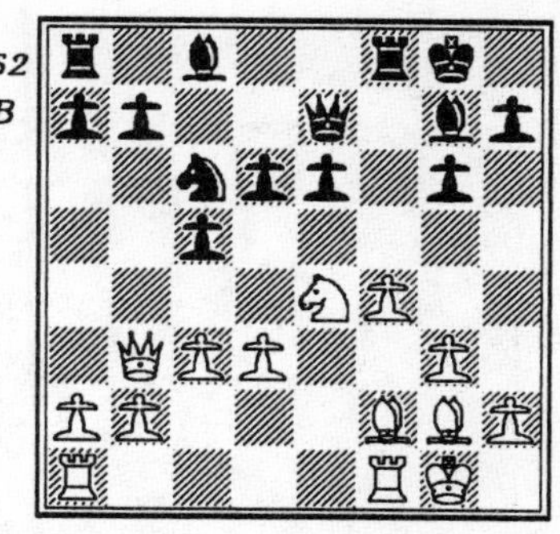

situated to add its influence against e6 and the queen's rook is able to move to the centre. White maintains only a slight plus after the more routine 17 ♕d2 e5 18 ♖ae1, Balashov - Arnason, Reykjavik 1989.

17 ... ♘d8
18 ♖ae1

Now that the control of d4 has slackened there is a possibililty that a change in plan might have had desirable consequences: 18 d4!? cxd4 19 ♗xd4 ♗xd4 20 cxd4 and Donev suggests that White should proceed with ♕a3, d5 and ♖ae1 with the advantage.

18 ... ♕c7
19 d4 c4
20 ♕c2 ♘f7
21 h4 *(53)*

Even in this relatively calm position White has managed to engineer a spatial advantage with good attacking chances. Black will have difficulty transferring his pieces to the kingside to form an adequate defence.

53
B

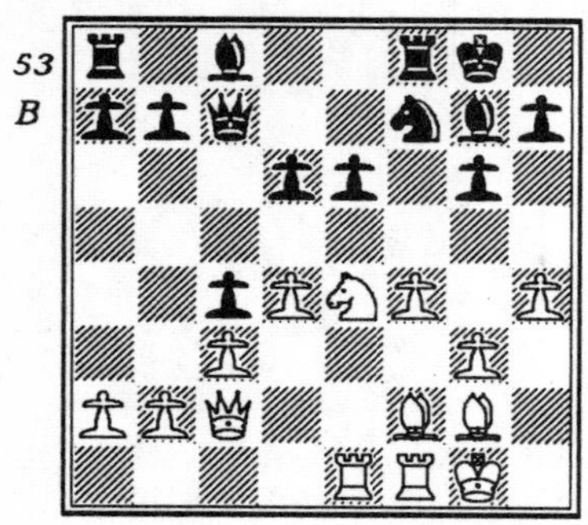

21 ... ♗d7
22 h5 gxh5
23 ♕e2 ♕a5
24 d5!

A crafty ploy to cut off the queen from the protection h5, since 24 ... ♕xd5?? 25 ♘f6+ picks up the queen.

24 ... exd5
25 ♕xh5 ♕b5
26 ♘g5?!

It is here Donev falters just when he could tip the balance heavily in his favour. A little more precision was required: 26 a4! ♕xb2 (26 ... ♕a5 27 ♗d4!) 27 ♕xd5 ♗c6 28 ♕e6, with ♘f6+ as a potent threat.

26 ... ♘xg5
27 ♕xg5 ♖f5
28 ♕e7 ♕c6
29 ♕e2 ♖e8
30 ♕d2?!

It is clear that White can still exert considerable pressure on d5, especially as the rook on f5 can always be nudged away by g4 at the right moment. Even so, the right move was 30 ♕c2, so that the e-file cannot be blocked.

30 ... ♖e4!

After this move Black is clearly back in the game. Although the rook can be taken, Black's extra pawn would have a new lease of life, restricting the scope of the white rooks, and Black's white-squared bishop would be very powerful.

31 ♖d1 ♗f8
32 ♗d4 ♖h5
33 ♗f3 ♖h3

Black is being rather carefree, putting both his rooks in a precarious position, but this is the only way to make an impact against the tough defensive structure.

34 ♔g2 ♖h6
35 ♖h1 ♖g6
36 ♗h5 ♖h6
37 f5! ♗xf5
38 ♕g5+

Once again the attack could have been delayed slightly, with devastating consequences: 38 ♖df1! ♗g6 39 ♕g5, intending ♕f6 with mate on f8 or h8.

38 ... ♗g6 *(54)*
39 ♗f3

This is hardly in keeping with the aim of pursuing the king, particularly since White can transpose to the

54
W

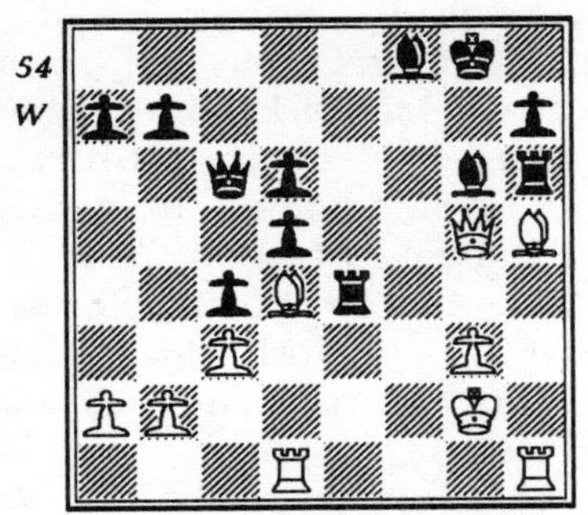

previous note with 39 ♖df1!, preparing 40 ♕f6. The immediate 39 ♕f6 just fails to clinch the game due to a spectacular combination: 39 ... ♖xd4! 40 ♗xg6 (40 cxd4 ♗e4+ 41 ♔g1 ♖xf6−+) 40 ... ♖d2+!! 41 ♖xd2 d4+ 42 ♔f2 ♖xg6 43 ♕f3 ♕xf3+ 44 ♔xf3 d3= Zagrebelni.

39	**...**	**♖xh1**
40	**♖xh1**	**♗e7**
41	**♕h6**	**♗f8**
42	**♕g5**	**♗e7**
43	**♕h6**	**♗f8**
	½–½	

Benschop – Maeckelbergh
Holland 1991

1	**e4**	**c5**
2	**♘c3**	**♘c6**
3	**g3**	**g6**
4	**♗g2**	**♗g7**
5	**d3**	**d6**
6	**f4**	**e6**
7	**♘f3**	**♘ge7**
8	**0-0**	**0-0**
9	**♗e3**	**♘d4**
10	**♕d2**	

The most straightforward response preparing for ♘d1 and c3 to oust the black knight from d4. Other options are the possibility of ♕f2-h4 for attacking purposes or the support of ♗h6 if f5 is achieved.

10 ... ♖b8

It is necessary to move the rook off the diagonal before advancing the b-pawn, otherwise White can seize the initiative: 10 ... b6?! 11 ♗xd4! cxd4 12 ♘b5 ♘c6 13 e5 dxe5 14 ♘xe5 ♘xe5 15 ♗xa8 ♗d7 16 ♗e4 ♗xb5 17 fxe5 ♗xe5 18 a4 ♗d7 with a definite advantage to White, Medina – Andersson, Las Palmas 1974. A more cautious approach is 10 ... ♘ec6 (10 ... d5 11 ♗f2!) 11 ♘d1 ♘xf3+ 12 ♗xf3 ♖b8 13 c3 b6 14 h4!? ♗b7 15 ♕g2 with equal chances, Arapovic – Cebalo, Medrisio 1988.

11 ♘h4 *(55)*

55
B

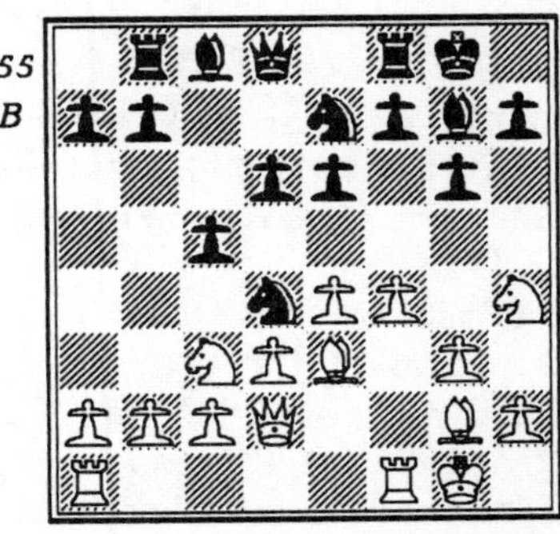

The idea of this move is to add support to the proposed f5 break and to prevent the exchange on f3 after the eventual c3-advance. There is a wide choice of alternatives available:

a) 11 ♖ab1 b6 12 ♘e2 ♘xe2+ 13 ♕xe2 ♗b7 14 g4 f5 15 ♗d2 ♕d7 16 h3 ♖be8 17 ♖fe1 ♘c6 18 c3 d5 19 gxf5 gxf5 20 e5 d4 21 c4= Dobrich - Gadia, Canada 1971.

b) 11 ♕f2 ♘ec6 12 g4 d5 12 ♘e1 ♘xc2, followed by d4∓, Medina - Balinas, Tel Aviv 1964.

c) 11 g4 f5 12 gxf5 and now:

c1) 12 ... exf5 13 ♖ae1 ♔h8 14 ♔h1 ♘xf3 15 ♖xf3 b6 16 ♗f2 ♗b7= Medina - Smyslov, Siegen Ol 1970.

c2) 12 ... gxf5 13 ♔h1 ♘g6 14 ♖g1 b5 15 ♖af1 b4 16 ♘d1 ♘xf3 17 ♖xf3 ♗b7= Wade - Matulovic, Skopje 1968.

d) 11 ♘d1 b6 12 ♘h4 and now:

d1) 12 ... d5 13 c3 ♘b5 14 a4 ♘d6 15 e5 ♘df5 16 ♘xf5 exf5 17 d4 c4 18 ♗f2 ♗e6 19 ♘e3 ♕c8 20 ♖fb1 ♖d8 21 b3 with the better game, Fuderer - Udovic, Yugoslav Ch 1953.

d2) 12 ... f5 13 ♗f2 (13 c3!?) 13 ... ♗a6 14 ♖e1 ♕d7 15 ♘e3 ♖bd8 16 c3 ♘dc6 17 ♖ad1 ♗b7 18 ♘c2= Biyiasas - Sigurjonsson, Lone Pine 1975.

11 ... ♗d7

12 ♘d1

White has managed to unsettle Black into making a slight error as ... ♗d7 is not advisable in lines featuring ♘d1, since it blocks the ... d5 advance. It would be better suited on b7 after 11 ... b6 or 11 ... b5, so White's switch in move order has had the desired effect.

12 ... b5

Whilst this is consistent with the strategy of expanding on the queenside, here it is a mistake because it fails to take account of White's intentions on the other flank. A better idea was 12 ... f5!, which blocks the immediate attack and would shift the game's focus to the centre, with equal chances.

13 c3 ♘dc6

14 f5! *(56)*

56

B

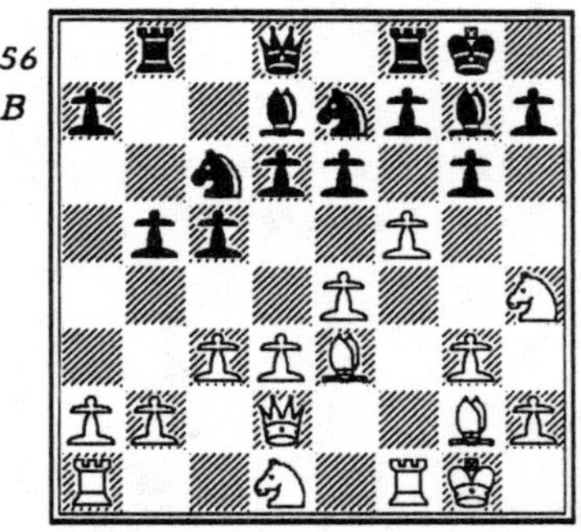

Now White's pieces are perfectly poised to exploit his space advantage and to launch an attack. A common feature of the Closed Sicilian is that White is often keen to trade dark-squared bishops, which is possible here now that h6 is ready for occupation. For Black, the most pressing problem is the threat of 15 f6 which, if blocked by 14 ... f6, leaves a dour struggle ahead with much more space for White. However, this was probably the best strategy.

14 ... exf5
15 exf5 ♗f6?

The appearance of an active defence is an illusion, 15 ... f6 was the best way to conduct the resistance. The text aims to force White to swap pawns on g6 rather than allow an exchange on h4, after which the f5-pawn can be taken.

16 ♗h6! *(57)*

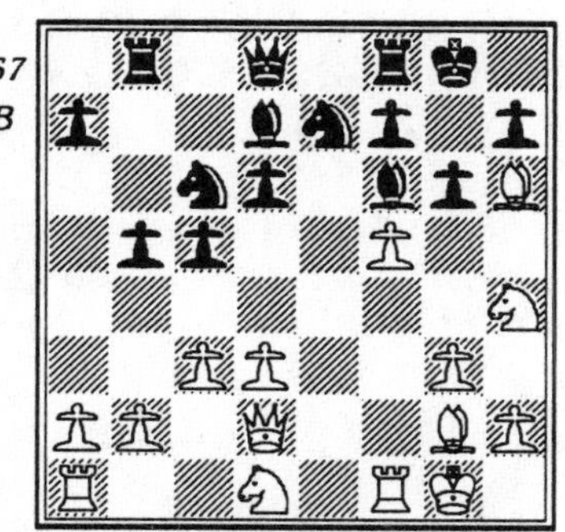

A satisfying solution to the problem, making no attempt to defend f5 but going on the offensive to exploit the gap left by the bishop. Now the meek 16 ... ♗g7 loses to 17 ♗xg7 ♔xg7 18 f6+, so the course of the game is now dictated.

16 ... ♖e8
17 fxg6 ♘xg6

Despite the exposed nature of the kingside pawns, this is forced due to the need to allow the queen to protect f6. The only hope is that the attack might falter, allowing Black time for recovery, since otherwise the pressure on the f-file will be too strong.

18 ♘f5 ♗e5
19 ♗d5

The threats to f7 are difficult to meet as 19 ... ♗e6 is out of the question due to the knight on c6 being unprotected.

19 ... ♖e6
20 ♗g5 f6
21 ♗e3 1-0

Kupreichik - Yakovich
Palma (GMA) 1989

1 e4 c5
2 ♘c3 ♘c6
3 g3 g6
4 ♗g2 ♗g7
5 d3 d6
6 f4 e6
7 ♘f3 ♘ge7
8 0-0 0-0
9 ♗e3

If one wishes to avoid the main body of theory, then the strange looking 9 ♕e1 might be worth considering. I have only been able to trace one game involving this idea: 9 ... b6 10 ♕f2 ♗b7 11 h4 ♕d7 12 h5 ♘d4 13 ♘xd4 ♗xd4 14 ♗e3 ♗g7 15 d4 ♘c6 16 dxc5 dxc5 17 hxg6 fxg6 18 ♖ad1 ♕e7 19 ♖d2 ♖ad8 20 ♖fd1 and the long-term weakness of e6 gives White a small plus, Abramovic - Paunovic, Yugoslav Ch 1989. A more common alternative is 9 ♗d2, which is discussed in the next illustrative game (Spassky - Beikert).

9 ... b6?!

A rather passive continuation, allowing White to achieve his d4-advance. Black is hoping to use White's occupation of the centre as a target and embark on a process of undermining it. After 9 ... ♖b8 10 d4 ♕b6 11 dxc5 ♕xb2 12 ♖b1 ♕xc3 13 ♖b3 ♕a5 14 cxd6 ♘d5 15 exd5 White has more activity, Sakarello - James, Skopje Ol 1972.

10 d4

The most exact reply. The whole system is geared towards playing d4, so it would be rather doubtful not to take advantage of the situation. Those players who decline the opportunity are usually anxious to transpose back into main lines:

a) 10 ♗f2 ♖b8 11 ♖e1 e5 12 fxe5 ♘xe5 13 ♘xe5 dxe5 14 ♗e3 ♗e6 15 ♕d2 ♕d6 16 ♖f1 ♖bd8 17 ♖f2 h5 18 ♖af1 f6 19 a4 ♔h7 20 b3 and White is slightly better, Abramovic - Lobron, New York Open 1987.

b) 10 ♕d2 d5 11 ♗f2 d4 12 ♘e2 f5 13 h3 ♗b7 14 g4 ♕d7 15 ♘g3= Benschop - Maric, Novi Sad Ol 1990.

c) 10 ♖b1 ♗b7 11 d4 and now:

c1) 11 ... h6 12 ♕d2 f5 13 ♖bd1 ♔h7 14 dxc5 dxc5 15 e5 ♗a6 16 ♖fe1 ♕xd2 17 ♖xd2 ♖ad8 18 ♖ed1 ♖xd2 19 ♖xd2 ♖d8 20 ♖xd8 ♘xd8 21 ♗f1= Hawthorne - Ward, London 1980.

c2) 11 ... ♕c7 12 dxc5 dxc5 13 ♕d2 ♖fd8 14 ♕f2 ♘a5 15 ♘d2 ♘ec6 16 e5 ♘d4 17 ♘de4 ♘c4 18 ♗c1 ♖d7 19 g4 ♕d8 20 b3 ♘a5 21 ♗e3 ♕e7 22 ♖bd1 ♖ad8 23 ♖d2 ♘dc6 24 ♔h1 ♖xd2 25 ♗xd2 ♘b4 26 ♗c1 ♘ac6 27 a3 ♘d5 28 ♘xd5 exd5 29 ♘d6 ♖xd6 30 exd6 ♕xd6 31 f5 ♘e5 32 ♕g3 f6 33 fxg6 hxg6 34 g5 ♗a6 35 ♖e1 1-0 Lane - Jean, Jersey 1982.

10 ... ♗a6

11 ♖e1 *(58)*

White decides to keep the rooks connected, which is the best policy. The alternative has also been tested: 11 ♖f2 ♕c7 12 a4 ♖ad8 13 ♘b5 ♗xb5 14 axb5 ♘xd4 15 ♘xd4 cxd4 16 ♗xd4 e5 17 ♗c3 d5 18 exd5 exf4 19 ♗xg7 fxg3! 20 hxg3 ♔xg7 21 ♕d4+ ♔g8 22 g4 ♘c8 23 c4, when the mass of pawns on the queenside provide compensation for the exposed kingside, Abramovic - Damljanovic, Yugoslavia 1989.

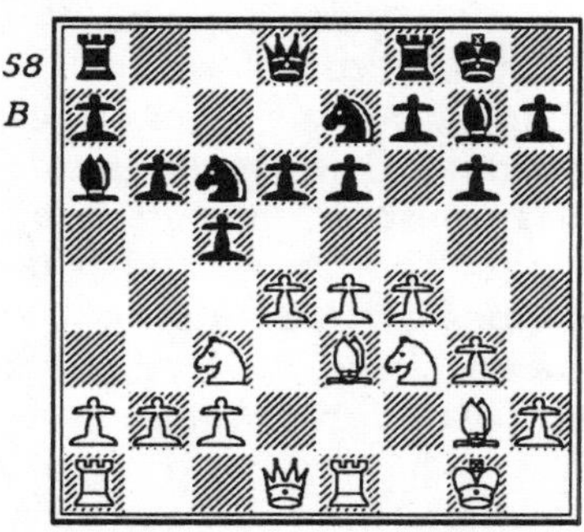

11 ... ♖c8

Evans - Lombardy, USA Ch 1973, continued 11 ... e5 12 fxe5 cxd4 13 ♘xd4 ♘xd4 14 ♕xd4 ♗xe5 15 ♕a4, when the active queen gives White the advantage.

12 a4 cxd4
13 ♘xd4 ♘a5
14 ♗f2

Now 14 ... ♘c4 can be defused by 15 b3, so Black adopts a more sedate approach.

14 ... ♕d7
15 ♕f3 ♗b7
16 ♖ad1

It is sensible to give the dormant rook a more central role. The prospect of 17 ♘db5 has to be seen as a real threat to the weak d-pawn.

16 ... a6
17 g4 *(59)*

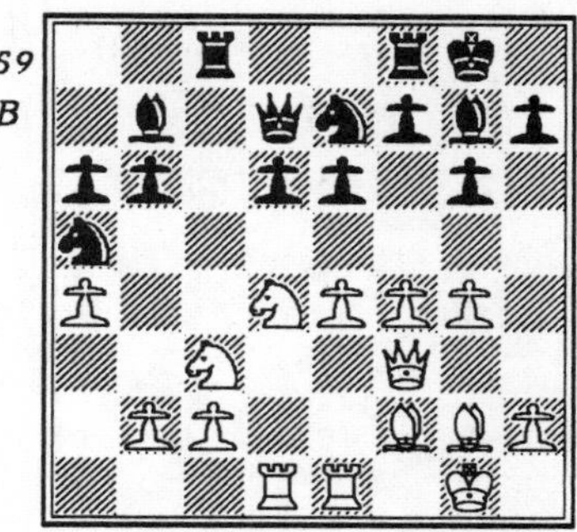

It is always good to be able to reserve f5 until all the preparatory measures have been taken. In the meantime, the text acts as a reminder that the game can change direction whenever White wishes to open up the kingside.

17 ... ♘ac6
18 ♘b3 ♘b4
19 ♗xb6 ♘xc2
20 ♖e2 ♘a3
21 ♗d4

The capture 21 bxa3 would be madness since Black would immediately regain the material by 21 ... ♖xc3, with a big initiative. Instead White offers to trade off bishops while renewing the threat to the knight.

21 ... ♘c4
22 ♗xg7 ♔xg7
23 f5

The thematic breakthrough is now possible since the key defensive bishop has just left the board, weakening the squares near the black king.

23 ... exf5
24 gxf5 gxf5 *(60)*

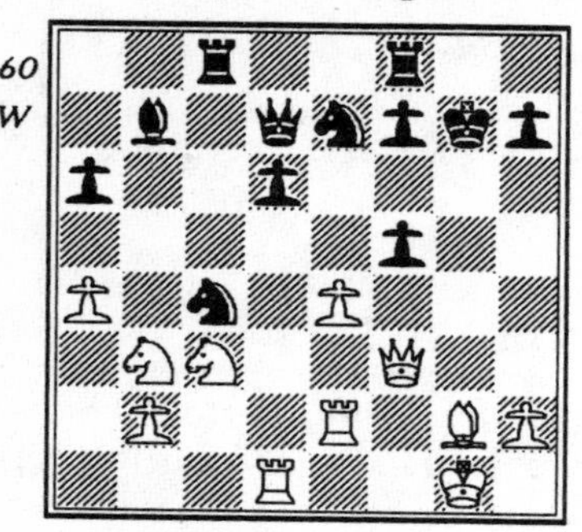

25 ♕f2!

Despite having sacrificed a pawn to expose the king. White conducts the attack in a subtle manner without resorting to a random check. The main intention is 26 ♕d4+, causing Black to make another concession by blocking with the f-pawn.

25 ... ♔h8
26 ♘c5 ♕c6

The knight fork is made possible by the pin. After 26 ... ♖xc5 27 ♕xc5 dxc5 28 ♖xd7, White wins the exchange and hits b7 and e7.

27 ♘xb7 ♕xb7
28 ♕d4+ f6

A poor reply is 28 ... ♔g8 29 ♖d3!, swinging the rook to the g-file with murderous consequences.

29 e5!

The discovered attack on the queen seals Black's fate. With the rook defending the bishop, there is no point in 29 ... ♖g8 as 30 exf6 forces a quick victory.

29 ... fxe5
30 ♗xb7 exd4
31 ♗xc8 dxc3
32 ♗xa6 ♘xb2
33 ♖xd6

The series of exchanges have made Kupreichik's advantage much clearer. Even though the rooks will be occupied with stopping the c-pawn there still remains the formidable passed a-pawn, which should divert the opposing forces sufficiently long enough to convert the extra material into a win.

33 ... ♘g6
34 ♗b5 ♘f4
35 ♖c2 ♖c8
36 a5 ♖c5

Black is certainly not in the mood to give up, and tries to tempt White into making a mistake.

37 ♖b6 ♘d1
38 a6 ♖c8
39 a7 ♖g8+
40 ♔f1

An absolute disaster results after 40 ♔h1 when Black is able, astonishingly, to force mate by 40 ... ♘h3 with the twin threats of 41 ... ♖g1+ and ♘f2+.

40 ... ♘e3+
41 ♔f2 ♘xc2

42 Rb8 1-0

Spassky - Beikert
French Cup Final 1991

1	e4	c5
2	Nc3	Nc6
3	g3	g6
4	Bg2	Bg7
5	d3	d6
6	f4	e6
7	Nf3	Nge7
8	0-0	0-0
9	Bd2	

Spassky has dabbled with this more cautious bishop move on a number of occasions. It is normally used to restrain the advance on the queenside by meeting it with a similar expansion policy.

9 ... b6 *(61)*

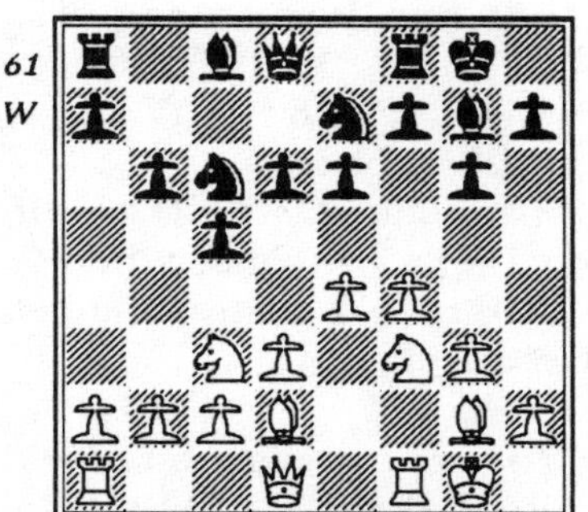

The main alternative is also quite playable, after 9 ... Rb8 10 Rb1 b5 11 a3 and now:

a) 11 ... f5 12 Be3 (12 b4 cxb4 13 axb4 a5 14 Na2 axb4 15 Nxb4 Nxb4 16 Bxb4 Nc6 gives White a slight edge, Karpov - Ribli, Budapest 1969) 12 ... Qc7 (12 ... Nd4 13 Ne2 Nxf3+ 14 Bxf3 Qc7 15 b4!± Marjanovic - Damjanovic, Yugoslavia 1978) 13 Bf2 Kh8 14 Re1 b4 15 axb4 cxb4 16 Ne2 fxe4 17 dxe4 e5 18 Qd2 Be6 19 Nc1! d5?! 20 Nxe5 Nxe5 21 fxe5 dxe4 22 Bxe4 Rbd8 23 Nd3 a5 24 Qe2 Bc4 25 Qe3 Nf5 (25 ... Bxe5 26 Nxe5 Qxe5 27 Qc5 Qxc5 28 Bxc5 Rfe8 29 Bb6+-) 26 Qc5 Qxc5 27 Bxc5 Rfe8 28 Bb6 Rb8 29 Bc7+- Spassky - Larsen, Malmo (7) 1968.

b) 11 ... b4 12 axb4 cxb4 13 Ne2 Qb6+ 14 Kh1 a5 15 b3 35 (Marjanovic - Matulovic, Sombor 1978) and now 16 h3!? gives White a small plus.

c) 11 ... a5 12 a4 b4 13 Nb5 d5 14 c4 bxc3 15 bxc3 c4 (15 ... Ba6 16 e5 d4 17 c4 Nb4 18 Qe2 Nc8 19 Rb2 Nb6 20 Ra1± Marjanovic - Damjanovic, Belgrade 1976) 16 Be3 cxd3 17 e5 Ba6 18 Qxd3± Spassky - Larsen, Malmo (3) 1968.

d) 11 ... c4 12 h3!? b4 13 axb4 cxd3 14 cxd3 Qb6+ 15 Kh2 Nxb4 16 Be1 Ba6 17 Bf2 Qc7 18 Ne1 Rfc8 19 Rc1 Qd7 20 Qd2= Marjanovic - Lputian, Erevan 1989.

10 Qe1!?

The beginning of an unusual plan to transfer the queen to the kingside for an attack, or to put pressure on e6 when the position is more open. The usual continuations are also worth investigating; after 10 ♖b1 ♗b7 and now:

a) 11 a3 ♕d7 12 ♘e2 ♘d4 13 ♘exd4 cxd4 14 ♕e2 ♖ac8 15 ♖bc1 a5 16 ♕f2 e5 is unclear, Balashov - Adorjan, Munich 1979.

b) 11 ♘e2 ♕d7 12 g4 f5 13 gxf5 exf5 14 c4 ♘d8 15 ♘c3 ♘e6 16 ♘g5 ♘xg5 17 fxg5 ♖f7 (Spassky - Portisch, Mexico (1) 1980) and now 18 ♕e2 results in an equal position.

10 ... ♗b7

11 g4

This is consistent with the aggressive stance of the queen, attempting to control more space and preparing the traditional f5-thrust.

11 ... f5?!

A reflex move which fully justifies White's opening novelty as it allows White to exploit the exceptional circumstances of the position. A possible improvement is 11 ... ♕d7, to cover the e6-square.

12 exf5 exf5

12 ♘g5 *(62)*

Now the knight heads for e6, to which the normal response is to parry with ... ♕d7, but with the white queen already on e1 everything is in White's favour. It is this twist in the opening that Black failed to perceive and he must now suffer accordingly.

62
B

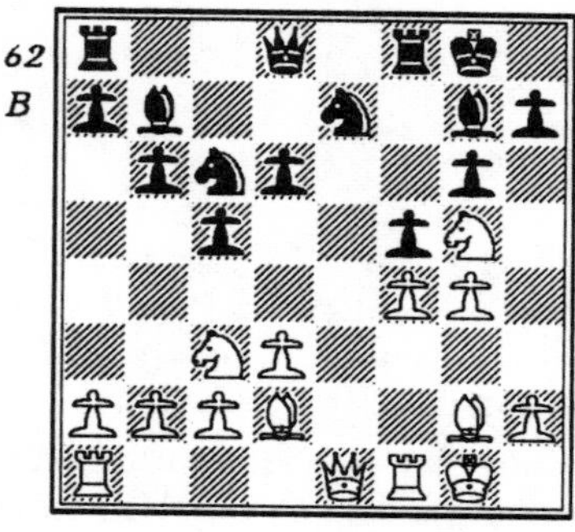

13 ... ♕d7

14 ♕e6+!

The ending gives White a huge advantage because he can pinpoint the weakness of the d6-pawn once the important dark-squared bishop has been traded off.

14 ... ♕xe6

15 ♘xe6 ♖f7

16 ♘b5

More accurate than 16 ♘xg7 ♔xg7 17 ♘b5, when 17 ... ♘c8 offers some chances of recovery.

16 ... ♘d8

Not very pleasant is 16 ... ♘c8 17 ♘ec7 ♖b8 18 ♗d5, winning.

17 ♘xg7

The start of a series of exchanges which appear on the surface to offer Black material equality, but Spassky has seen further than his opponent.

17	**...**	**♗xg2**
18	**♔xg2**	**♖xg7**
19	**♗c3**	**♘d5**

Otherwise 19 ... ♖f7 20 ♘xd6 ♖f8 gives Black a bleak future. The idea of the text is to threaten ... ♘e3+, which, if covered, allows ... fxg4 with an unbalanced game.

20	**♗xg7**	**♘e3+**
21	**♔g1**	**♘xf1**
22	**♗c3**	

This is probably what Black failed to appreciate at the beginning of the combination. By retreating the bishop, White really highlights the deficiency in the black king's position.

22 ... ♘e3 *(63)*

63
W

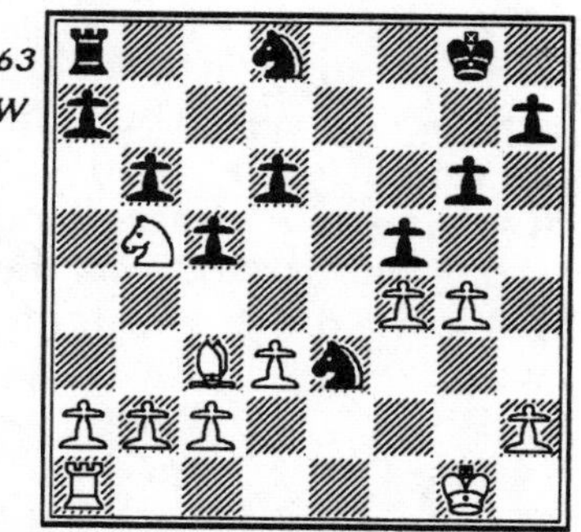

Black forks two white pawns, but the weakness of the back rank invites a nasty surprise.

23 ♖e1 1–0

Black resigned, in view of 23 ... ♘xg4 24 ♖e8+ ♔f7 25 ♘xd6 mate.

It is to be expected that there will be some players who are unwilling to contest the complex theoretical variations of the main line. Therefore, it is useful to have an idea of how to confront a small twist which deliberately avoids the accepted continuation. On balance, I suspect that White should be fine in these cases as long as the general considerations already discussed are followed. The following game is a good example of how to cope with a surprise weapon:

Spassky – Hort
West Germany 1981

1	**e4**	**c5**
2	**♘c3**	**♘c6**
3	**g3**	**g6**
4	**♗g2**	**♗g7**
5	**d3**	**d6**
6	**f4**	**e6**
7	**♘f3**	**♘ge7**
8	**0–0**	**♗d7!?**

Castling is delayed whilst Black seeks to rapidly complete his queenside development. Now the rook can come to c8, introducing the possibility of ... c4, probably with the queen on a5 to lend support. The problem facing White is whether he should continue his kingside attack with the black king still uncastled, or should he aim to restrict

Black's counterplay?

An independent line which contests the centre is 8 ... d5?!, but this is not really good enough after 9 ♘h4 f5 10 e5 a6 11 ♘e2 ♗d7 12 c3 0–0 13 ♗e3± Knezevic – Tot, Yugoslav Ch 1960. Clearly bad is 8 ... ♖b8? 9 e5! which transposes to the game Bronstein – Keres in Chapter six.

9 ♗e3 ♘d4

Before d4 can be played, the knight is entrenched on d4.

10 ♖b1

There is also a sharper alternative available: 10 e5 ♘ef5 11 ♗f2 h5!? 12 ♘e4 ♗c6 13 ♘fg5! dxe5 14 fxe5 ♗xe5 15 c3 ♘b5 16 ♗xc5 ♗d6 17 ♘xd6+ ♘bxd6 (17 ... ♘fxd6? 18 ♗xc6+ bxc6 19 ♕f3+-) 18 ♗xc6+ bxc6 (Donev – Balashov, Lenk 1991) and now 19 ♕a4! ♕c7 (19 ... 0–0 20 ♘e4!; 19 ... ♕xg5 20 ♕xc6+ ♔e7 21 ♗xd6+ ♘xd6 22 ♕c7+ wins) 20 ♘e4 0–0 21 ♘f6+ ♔g7 22 ♗d4 ♘xd4 23 ♕xd4 ♕b6 24 ♘e8++ ♔g8 25 ♕xb6 axb6 26 ♘xd6+-.

10 ... ♖c8

11 ♗f2 *(64)*

Even at this early stage there is clear evidence that Spassky is happy to rely on his considerable experience in the system and decides not to change his usual strategy at all. This is de-

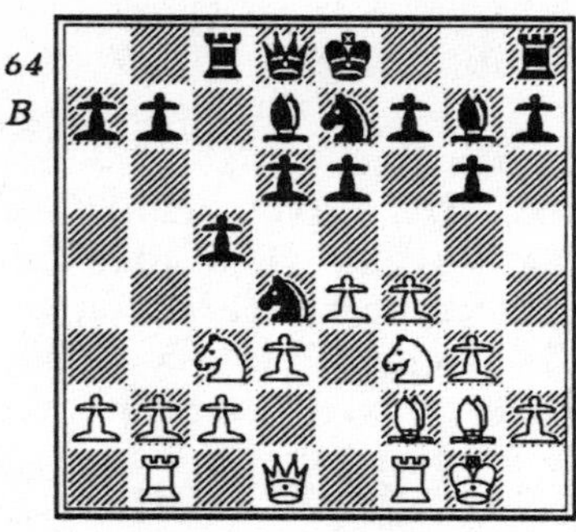

64

B

spite the unusual set-up employed by Hort aimed at provoking a reaction that will weaken the overall strength of White's position.

The fact that White can act with indifference is further proof of the value that such an opening has compared to the Open Sicilian. Of course, there are fewer tactics here, but the white positional plan of controlling the centre and starting an attack on the kingside is quite straightforward.

11 ... ♘ec6

12 ♘e2 ♕a5

The queen enters the scene to challenge a2. White cannot go passive with 13 ♖a1 due to 13 ... ♘xe2+ 14 ♕xe2 ♗xb2, so another approach is required.

13 ♘exd4 ♘xd4

14 c3!

Spassky is conducting the game logically. He has

managed to exchange a pair of knights in preparation for c3, shifting the remaining knight from its strong outpost. Although Black wins the pawn that he was counting on, he faces a dangerous attack.

14 ... ♘xf3+
15 ♕xf3 ♗c6
16 g4! *(65)*

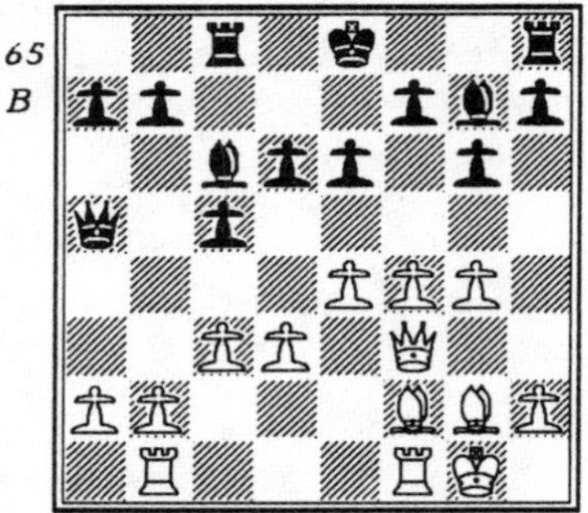

With the black queen out of the way there is an opportunity to furiously attack the king.

16 ... 0-0

Under the circumstances it is understandable that Black is keen to form some sort of defence. However, White has gathered considerable momentum and can create serious pressure on the black position.

17 f5 f6
18 fxe6 ♕xa2

At long last Black is unable to resist the temptation of the a2-pawn, now that he has developed his pieces and the queen can retreat by taking on e6.

19 b3 ♖fe8

Despite the fact that the queen has been locked out of taking on e6, the lone pawn still seems an easy target. Now the rook takes over the job of securing a material advantage,

20 ♕d1! *(66)*

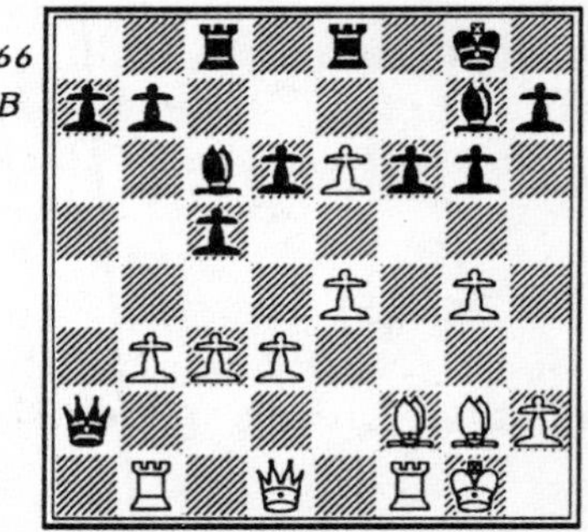

White turns his attention to the other possibility of trapping the queen. The sequence 20 ... ♖xe6 21 ♖a1 ♕b2 22 ♗e1, intending ♖f2, is fatal for Black.

20 ... ♕a5
21 b4 cxb4
22 cxb4 ♕a4

The full power of the e6-pawn becomes apparent after 22 ... ♕c7 23 b5, and the bishop has no square to escape the attentions of the white pawns.

23 b5!

White is keen to transpose into an ending in which his rook is able to invade the seventh rank, and the bothersome e-pawn suddenly becomes a serious problem. Not so convincing is 23 d4 ♕xd1 24 ♖fxd1 ♗b5, putting things on hold for a while, since Black has control of the open c-file.

23 ... ♗xb5
24 ♕xa4 ♗xa4
25 ♖xb7

The mini-combination has succeeded in getting the rook to its best position, where it can wreak havoc with the black pawns.

25 ... ♖xe6
26 g5! ♖e5

Black responds to the threat of ♗h3 by promptly moving out of the firing line. Tougher resistance could have been mustered after 26 ... ♖f8 adding further protection to f6. Now, however, White can set another tactical device in motion.

27 ♖xa7 ♗b5
28 gxf6 ♗xf6
29 ♗d4

At least the exchange must be lost due to the pin, allowing White an easy win.

29 ... ♗h4
30 ♗xe5 dxe5
31 ♗h3 ♖c6
32 ♖b1 ♖c5
33 ♖a5 1–0

5) 6 ♘h3 and 5 ... b6

In this chapter we discuss two variations which, although not very often seen, have a unique character of their own. The first involves an early ♘h3 by White; the second an immediate black queenside fianchetto.

Smyslov – Romanishin
USSR Ch 1976

1	**e4**	**c5**
2	**♘c3**	**♘c6**
3	**g3**	**g6**
4	**♗g2**	**♗g7**
5	**d3**	**d6**

The move-order is important because Black would now lose a move if he now prepared for ... d5. The ♘h3 plan is less effective against 5 ... e6, e.g: 6 ♘h3 ♘ge7 7 0–0 0–0 and now:

a) 8 ♗e3 b6 9 ♕d2 d5 (9 ... ♗b7 10 ♗h6 d6 11 ♖ae1 ♕d7 12 ♗xg7 ♔xg7 13 f4± transposes to the next illustrative game, Hort – Toran) 10 exd5 exd5 11 ♗f4 ♘d4 12 ♔h1 ♖e8 13 ♘g1 ♗b7 14 ♖ae1 ♕d7= Smyslov – Taimanov, USSR 1947.

b) 8 ♗d2 h6 9 a3 ♖b8 10 ♖b1 b5 11 b4 cxb4 12 axb4 d6 13 ♘f4 ♗d7 14 ♘ce2 e5 15 ♘d5 ♘xd5 16 exd5 ♘e7 17 ♕e1 ♕c7= Taimanov – Matulovic, USSR 1966.

6 ♘h3 *(67)*

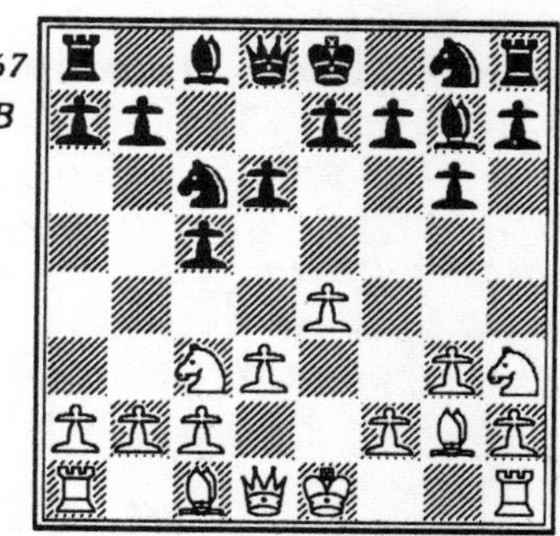

67
B

This early development of the knight has experienced fluctuating levels of popularity through the years. There is a school of thought that believes it to be too commital, and that clearing the f-file for the rook is not sufficient compensation for having a piece on the edge of the board. However, others believe that the position facilitates greater attacking opportunities because time is gained by not having to move the knight out of the way to play f4-f5. This system is a quite feasible alternative to the main lines and requires more of an understanding about the ideas in the system than precise theoretical knowledge.

A more obscure idea which needs more practical tests before a final judgement can be made is 6 ♗g5 ♘f6 (6 ... ♕d7 7 ♘f3 b6 8 0-0 ♗b7 9 ♕d2 e5 10 ♘h4 ♘d4 11 ♗e3 ♘e7 12 f4 f6 [Hazai - Csom, Pula 1975] 13 f5 g5 14 ♘f3 h6= Csom) 7 h3 0-0 8 ♕d2 ♘d4 9 ♘ge2 ♕a5 10 ♖c1 ♕b4 11 ♘xd4 cxd4 12 ♗xf6 ♗xf6 13 ♘d5 ♕xb2 14 0-0 ♗e6 with an unclear position, as in Romanishin - Ivanov, Moscow 1979.

6 ... h5

A rather optimistic assessment of the position which declares Black's contempt for White's whole idea. Naturally, 6 ... e5 transposes to chapter three after 7 f4 but Black has several alternatives:

a) 6 ... ♘f6 7 0-0 and now:

a1) 7 ... 0-0!? 8 f4 ♗g4 9 ♕d2 ♘d4 10 ♔h1 ♕c8 (10 ... ♕d7 11 ♘g1 ♗e6 [Medina - Benko, Malaga 1970] 12 ♘d5!±] 11 ♘g1 ♗d7 12 ♘d1 b5 13 c3 ♘c6 14 ♘f3 ♖b8 15 ♘e3 b4 16 c4 ♘g4 17 ♘xg4 ♗xg4 18 ♘h4 h6 19 f5± Ivanov - Faibisovic, USSR 1977.

a2) 7 ... ♗g4 8 f3 ♗xh3 9 ♗xh3 0-0 10 ♗e3 ♘e8 (10 ... ♘d4?! 11 ♗xd4 cxd4 12 ♘e2, intending c3, ± Geller) 11 ♕d2 ♘c7 12 ♖ae1 b6 13 ♘d1 d5 14 ♕e2 e6 15 f4= Spassky - Petrosian, World Ch (15) 1966.

b) 6 ... e6 7 0-0 ♘ge7 8 ♗e3 b6 (8 ... ♖b8 9 ♕d2 0-0 10 ♗h6 b6 11 ♗xg7 ♔xg7 12 f4± Ost Hansen - Hulak, Plovdiv 1983) 9 ♕d2 h6 10 ♘f4!? ♗b7 11 ♖ab1 ♕d7 12 ♘ce2 e5 13 ♘d5 ♘xd5 14 exd4 ♘e7 15 c4 g5?! (15 ... ♘f5!?) 16 f4! exf4 17 gxf4 g4 18 ♘g3 h5 19 f5 ♗e5 20 d4 cxd4 21 ♗xd4 ♗xd4+ 22 ♕xd4 0-0-0 23 f6 ♘g6 24 ♗e4 ♘h4 25 ♗f5 ♘xf5 26 ♘xf5 ♔b8 27 ♖be1 ♕a4 28 ♖e7 ♗c8 29 c5! ♕c2 30 c6 ♖dg8 31 ♘e3 ♕e2 32 ♘c4 ♕c2 33 ♖xa7 1-0 Augustin - Kavalek, Czechoslovakia 1968.

7 f4

White could also try 7 ♘d5 ♗g4 8 f3 ♗xh3 9 ♗xh3 e6 10 ♘e3 h4 11 f4 hxg3 12 hxg3 d5 13 exd5 exd5 (Hug - Kasparov, Simultaneous, Switzerland 1987) 14 ♔f2!? when White is slightly better.

7 ... ♗g4

8	**♕d2**	**♘d4**
9	**♘g1!**	

This is probably what Black had overlooked. The backward knight move puts a stop to ... ♘f3+ and allows White to meet 9 ... h4 with 10 h3! and 11 g4

9	**...**	**♕d7**

Smyslov suggests 9 ... ♕a5 as a possible improvement, so that the bishop can go to d7.

10	**h3**	**♗e6**
11	**♘ce2**	

Now White has the option of encouraging an exchange by c3.

11	**...**	**h4**
12	**g4**	**f5**
13	**exf5**	**gxf5**
14	**g5** *(68)*	

68
B

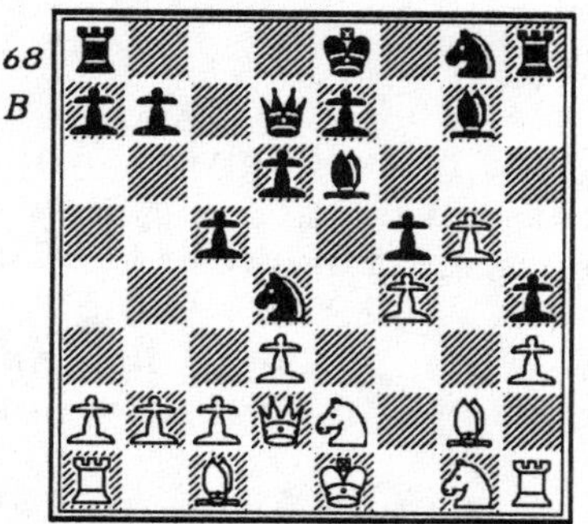

Black will now experience problems in developing the dormant and congested kingside. Now a cumbersome manoeuvre has to be undertaken to free the e7-square for the knight. In the meantime, White can proceed to create a grip on the position.

14	**...**	**0-0-0**
15	**♘xd4**	**cxd4**

White has no reason to fear the alternative after 15 ... ♗xd4 16 c3 ♗g7 17 ♘e2±.

16	**♘e2**	**♗f7**
17	**c3**	**dxc3**
18	**bxc3**	**♔b8**
19	**♖b1**	

Since the b-file has been opened, it is only natural that the rook should take up a threatening pose. Black has no counterplay and already he must take defensive measures to ward off the attack by blocking out the white-squared bishop.

19	**...**	**d5**
20	**0-0**	**e5**
21	**fxe5**	**♗xe5**
22	**d4**	**♗c7**
23	**c4!**	

The pawn is immune from capture as otherwise ♖xf7+ is fatal. Now it is easier for the white queen to join the attack and there is more room to get the forces directed towards the opposing king.

23	**...**	**♘e7**
24	**c5**	**♖dg8**

Black has to stage some sort of distraction in an effort to divert White from his mating ambitions.

25	**♕b4**	**♗d8**
26	**♖f3!** *(69)*	

69 B

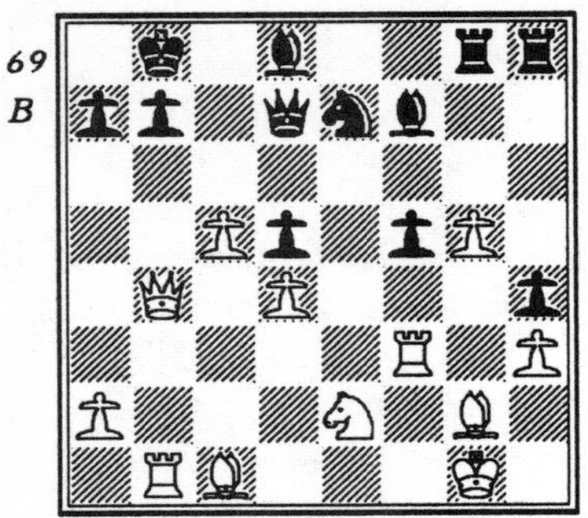

Correctly seeking to treble on the b-file because Black will have problems forming a reasonable defence.

26 ... ♘c6

In his analysis, Smyslov demonstrates that immediate attempts at counterplay lead to a ferocious attack: 26 ... ♗h5 27 ♖fb3 ♗xe2 28 ♕xb7+ ♕xb7 29 ♖xb7+ ♔c8 30 ♗f4 ♗c4 32 ♖xe7! ♗xe7 33 c6+-.

27 ♕b5 ♗h5
28 ♖fb3 ♖g7
29 ♘f4 ♗xg5

Black is neatly thwarted if he enters a series of exchanges hoping for complications: 29 ... ♘xd4 30 ♕xd7 ♖xd7 31 ♗b2 ♘xb3 32 ♗xh8 ♘d2 33 ♘xh5 ♘xb1 34 g6+-.

30 ♘xh5 ♖xh5
31 ♕e2! ♗xc1

There is no respite after 31 ... ♖h8 32 ♗xg5 ♖xg5 33 ♖xb7+ ♕xb7 34 ♖xb7+ ♔xb7 35 ♔h2 ♖d8 36 ♕e6 f4 37 ♕f7+ ♔c8 38 ♕f6+-.

32 ♖xb7+ ♕xb7
33 ♕e8+ ♔c7
34 ♖xb7+ ♔xb7
35 ♕xh5 ♘xd4
36 ♔f1 ♗e3
37 ♕h8 ♖d7
38 ♕e8 1-0

Hort – Toran
Palma de Mallorca 1969

1 e4 c5
2 ♘c3 ♘c6
3 d3 g6
4 g3 ♗g7
5 ♗e3

A strategy similar to the game can be adopted by Black after the more normal bishop move: 5 ♗g2 b6 and now:

a) 6 ♘h3 ♗b7 7 0-0 d6 8 f4 h6 9 f5 ♗xc3 10 bxc3 g5 11 ♘f2 ♕c7 12 ♘g4 ♘e5 13 ♘e3 ♘f6 14 ♕e2 ♖g8 15 ♘d5 ♗xd5 16 exd5, giving White the advantage, Smyslov – Portisch, Portoroz (4) 1971.

b) 6 ♘ge2 d6 7 0-0 ♗b7 8 f4 f5 9 ♗e3 ♘d4 10 ♗xd4 cxd4 11 ♘b5 e5 12 a4= Botvinnik.

c) 6 f4 ♗b7, with two alternatives:

c1) 7 ♘f3 d6 8 0-0 ♕d7 9 ♗e3 ♘h6 10 h3 f5 11 ♕d2 ♘f7 12 ♖ae1 0-0-0 13 exf5 gxf5 14 d4 e5 15 fxe5 cxd4 16 e6 ♕xe6 17 ♘xd4 ♘xd4 18 ♗xd4 ♗e5 19 ♕f2 ♘h6 20 ♘b5 ♗xg2 21 ♕xg2 ♔b8 22 ♕a8+ 1-0 Lane – Menadue,

West of England Ch 1981.

c2) 7 ♘ge2 d6 8 0–0 ♕d7 9 ♗e3 ♘d4 10 ♕d2 f5 11 ♘d1 e6 12 c3 ♘xe2+ 13 ♕xe2 ♘f6 14 ♘f2 0–0–0 15 b4 cxb4 16 cxb4 ♔b8 17 a4 ♘e8 18 ♖a3 d5 19 b5 d4 20 ♗d2 ♗f8 21 ♖b3 ♘c7 22 ♖fb1 ♖c8 23 ♗b4 ♗xb4 24 ♖xb4 ♖hd8 25 ♕a2 ♘a8 26 a5 bxa5 27 ♖a4 ♖c5 28 ♖xa5 ♖dc8 29 ♖b2 ♖c1+ 30 ♗f1 ♕c7 31 ♖xa7 ♕c3 32 b6 ♕e1 33 ♖xa8+ 1–0 Lane – Ashby, Torbay 1982.

5 ... **b6!?** *(70)*

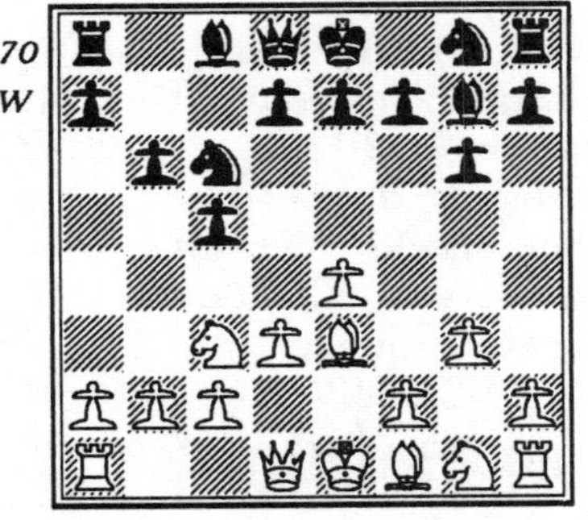

The plan of a queen's fianchetto is a rare guest against the Closed, mainly because it rules out the plan of counter-attacking with a pawn storm on the queenside. On the positive side, it can be helpful with an early ... d5 in an attempt to open the centre or just to challenge White's light-squared bishop.

6 **♕d2** **♗b7**
7 **♗g2** **d6**
8 **♘h3!**

Although White is following the usual plan of trying to trade dark-squared bishops, he takes full account of Black's unusual strategy. This explains why the text is favoured as now f4–f5 is a clear threat without the bishop on c8 to defend the f5-square. Also, if the knight goes to f3 then Black would be eager to exchange it by ... ♘d4 in order to widen the scope of his own queen's bishop.

8 ... **♕d7**
9 **0–0** **e6**
10 **♖ae1**

As there is no real prospect of active play on the queenside, the rook is moved to a more central role.

10 ... **♘ge7**
11 **♗h6** **0–0**
12 **♗xg7** **♔xg7**
13 **f4** *(71)*

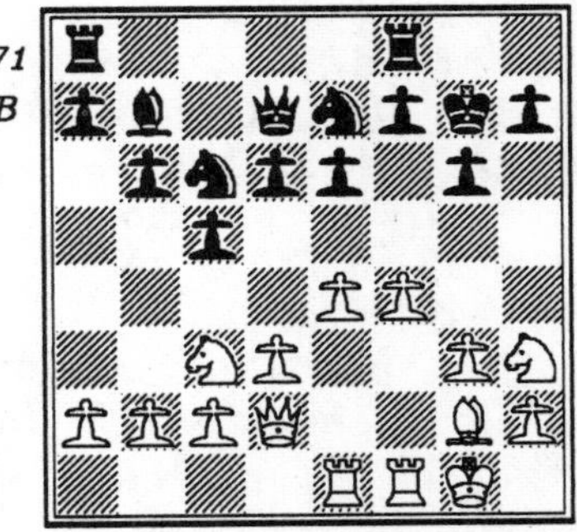

Now the first stage of the longer-term plan is completed (the exchange of dark-squared bishops), the second stage can be embarked upon. The f5-thrust is not yet an immediate threat as it is not clear that White could justify the sacrifice of a pawn. However, Black evidently did not want to leave White with this option, as the mere possibility of f5 prevents him from organising counterplay.

13 ... f5
14 ♘g5

The knight targets the weakness at e6 by threatening exf5 and ♘e6+.

14 ... ♖ae8
15 ♘e2 d5
16 exd5 ♘xd5
17 d4

White determines to exploit the backward e-pawn by firmly eliminating the proposed ... e5. Black is losing after 17 ... cxd4? 18 ♘xd4 ♘xd4 (18 ... ♘d8 19 c4 ♘f6 20 ♘dxe6+ ♘xe6 21 ♕xd7 ♘xd7 22 ♘xe6++-) 19 ♕xd4+ ♔g8 20 c4 ♘f6 21 ♕xd7 ♘xd7 22 ♗xb7+-.

17 ... h6
18 ♘f3 c4
19 ♘c3

The position becomes rather cramped for White after 19 c3 ♘f6!, so the knight is restored to its former post to prevent Black from putting a piece on e4, and clears the path of the rook on e1.

19 ... ♘f6
20 ♖f2 ♖d8
21 ♖fe2

Instead of passively defending the loose pawn, White goes on the offensive by doubling against e6. Not advisable here is 21 ... ♘xd4? 22 ♘xd4 ♗xg2 (23 ... ♕xd4 23 ♕xd4 ♖xd4 24 ♗xb7+-) 23 ♘xe6+ ♔g8 (23 ... ♕xe6 24 ♕xd8! ♕xe2 25 ♕xf8++-) 24 ♘xf8+-.

21 ... ♖fe8
22 h3 a6
23 ♕e3 b5

Both sides are trying to steadily improve their position; Black belatedly creates some play on the queenside whilst White transfers his queen to a better square.

24 a3 ♗a8
25 ♘e5 ♕c7
26 ♖d2

The strong knight on e5, together with a territorial advantage, gives White a good game. The problem posed by the vulnerable d-pawn has been solved by replacing the queen with the rook to act as a guard and now attention can be turned to the kingside.

26 ... ♘e7
27 g4! fxg4
28 hxg4 ♗xg2
29 ♖xg2 *(72)*

In the space of a few moves, White's attack has

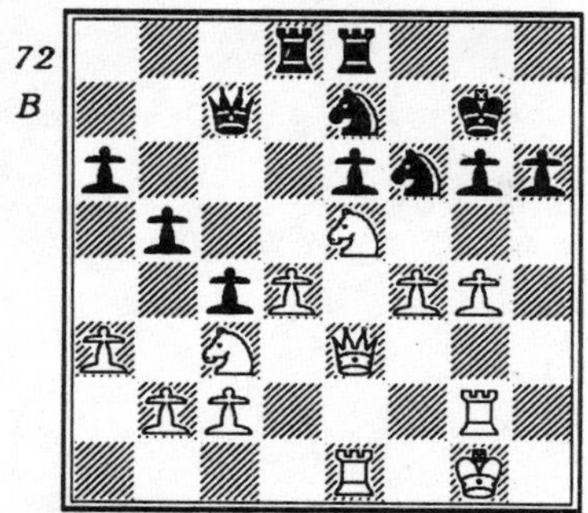

72
B

gathered considerable momentum. The white army is poised for a breakthrough and the black knights are purely defensive. Black's remaining pieces also lack significant influence.

29	...	♕b6
30	♘e2	♘c6
31	g5!	

Commencing a devastating plan; the lunge with the g-pawn is clear evidence that Black is in deep trouble, as the white queen and rook will now be able to infiltrate into the heart of the kingside bastion.

31	...	hxg5
32	♖xg5	♘xe5
33	fxe5	♘h7
34	♖g4	♔h8

A last try to salvage the position by removing the king behind the shelter of the knight. The main hope is for 35 ♖xg6? ♖g8! 36 ♖xg8+ ♖xg8+ 37 ♔h2 ♕b7, when the tables have turned and it is White's exposed king that is in imminent danger.

35	♖f1	♖f8
36	♘f4	

This seals Black's fate. The knight check on g6 is the key to a mating net as it will lure the king out into the open.

36	...	♖g8
37	♘xg6+	♖xg6
38	♖xg6	♖xd4
39	♖f8+!	1-0

6) Systems with ... ♖b8

In this chapter we look at variations in which Black seeks immediate counterplay with ... ♖b8, intending ... b5–b4. He tries to utilise the closed nature of the position to assume supremacy in the centre and on the queenside, reasoning that White is not well-placed to meet an early flank attack.

Bronstein – Keres
Zurich Ct 1953

1	e4	c5
2	♘c3	g6
3	g3	♗g7
4	d3	♘c6
5	♗g2	♖b8

In his comments on the game, upon which these notes are based, Bronstein regards the rook move as rather too rigid and one which severely reduces the number of options open to Black. He also doubts the benefits of the onrush of the b-pawn when the White king is safely on the other side of the board.

6 f4 *(73)*

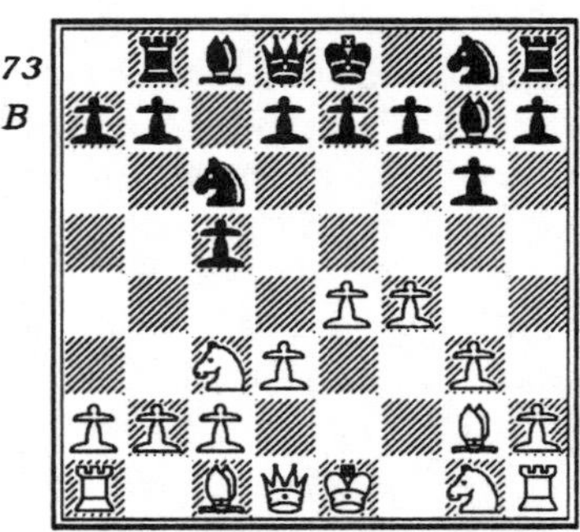

The most exact reply. The text is a reliable choice because it keeps to the basic developing plan that is similar to other lines, but there is an alternative choice for the more adventurous: Todorcevic – Ivanovic, Rakovica 1982, continued instead: 6 ♘h3 b5 7 f4 (7 0–0 e6 8 ♗g5 ♘ge7 9 ♕d2 b4 10 ♘d1 d5 11 exd5 exd5 12 ♗h6 0–0 13 ♗xg7 ♔xg7 14 ♘e3 ♗xh3 15 ♗xh3 ♘g8 16 a3 a5 17 axb4 axb4 18 ♖a6 ♘d4 19 ♗g2 ♘f6 20 c3 bxc3 21 bxc3 ♘e6± ½–½ Spassky – Ljubojevic, Bugojno 1981) 7 ... b4 8 ♘d5 e6 9 ♘e3 ♘ge7 10 f5 exf5 11 exf5 d5 12 fxg6 hxg6 13 ♘f4 ♕d6 14 ♘exd5

♘xd5 15 ♘xd5 ♗h3 16 ♕e2+ ♔f8 17 ♗f4 ♘e5 18 0-0-0 ♗xg2 19 ♕xg2 and White has the safer king and an extra pawn.

6 ... d6
7 ♘f3 e6
8 0-0

Simply getting on with the job of activating the pieces.

8 ... ♘ge7
9 e5! *(74)*

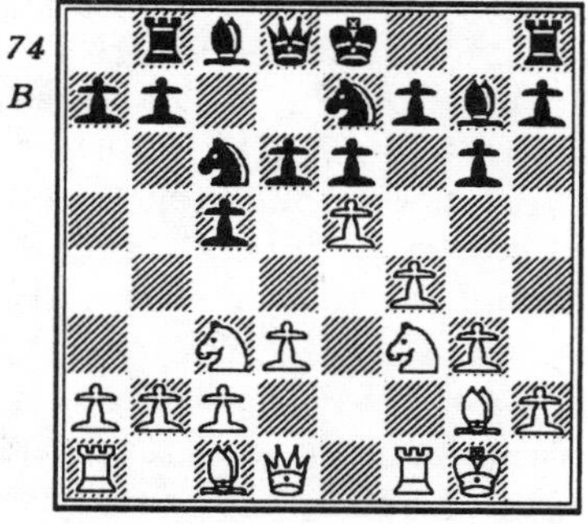

The position seemed destined to follow traditional paths, but White is not prepared to allow the extra rook move to pass without punishment. The idea behind the move is to open up the c1-h6 diagonal, and the e-file, as well as providing the ideal e4-square for the knight. All these factors combined are sufficient to promise White good chances.

9 ... dxe5

Black is not impressed by White's compensation and is satisfied that he can cope with the ensuing initiative. A more cautious approach suggests itself to defuse the situation; the best practical try was 9 ... d5 where the neglected development of Black's pieces is not so easily exposed.

10 fxe5 ♘xe5
11 ♗f4 ♘xf3+

An attractive way out of the immediate crisis, releasing the pin with check. Trying to remain firm on e5 spells trouble for the king:

a) 11 ... f6 12 ♗xe5 fxe5 13 ♘g5 and the threat of ♘f7 is strong.

b) 11 ... ♘7c6 12 ♘xe5 ♘xe5 13 ♕e2, when the pin continues to cause problems.

c) 11 ... 0-0 12 ♘xe5 ♕d4+ 13 ♔h1 ♗xe5 14 ♘b5 ♕xb2 15 ♖b1+-.

12 ♕xf3 ♖a8

Blocking the diagonal with 12 ... e5 is merely an encouragement for White to hack it off and come smashing down on f7. For example, 13 ♗xe5 ♗xe5 14 ♕xf7+ ♔d7 15 ♘d5 ♖e8 16 ♖ae1 ♗d4+ 17 ♔h1 and Black has a hopeless task.

13 ♗e3

The ploy to win a piece is an illusion 13 ♗e5 0-0!, when f7 and g7 are protected at one stroke. Whilst 13 ♗c7 ♕d4+ 14 ♔h1 0-0, when once again castling renders harmless any ambitions against f7.

13 ... 0–0

14 ♗xc5

Material equilibrium is restored.

14 ... ♗d4+

It is ironic that White usually strives to trade dark-squared bishops and here it is Black who forces the issue. The inherent weakness of f6 and g7 associated with such an action is ignored in the quest to lessen the number of pieces directed towards the king.

15 ♗xd4 ♕xd4+

16 ♔h1 ♖b8

Keres cannot be faulted for consistency. The rook returns to the square that triggered off all the original problems in order to enable the bishop to develop. Despite Black's positional problems, either ... ♘c6 or ... e5 should be preferred.

17 ♘e4 *(75)*

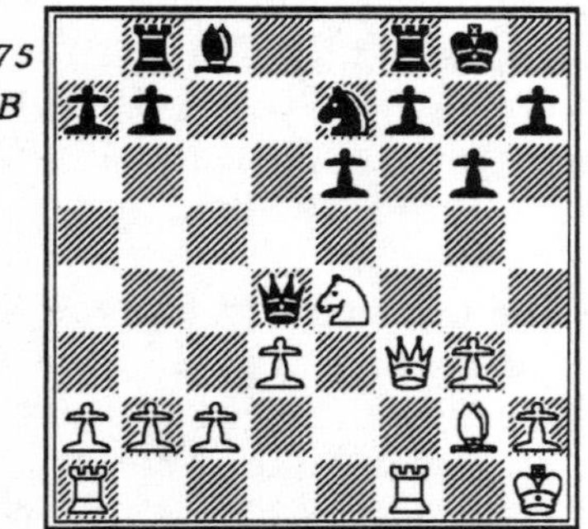

Leaping to the centre stage in readiness to take up residence on f6. This outpost would be extremely dangerous for Black so he cannot tolerate it.

17 ... f5

The pawn structure is foregone in order to meet White's direct threat. Now the backward e-pawn is a target.

18 ♕f4 ♗d7

Provided with the chance to get his last piece off its starting square, Black does not hesitate. Of course, moving the rook back to a8 looks like a foolish move, but in fact it was the only way to stay in the game. Although White will enjoy a considerable advantage in terms of space and targets, the long-term nature of these factors at least leaves some room for error.

19 c3!

A clever move that shows up the defects in the black position.

19 ... ♕b6

Taking on d3 is not advisable due to 20 ♘c5 ♕b5 21 ♕d6, winning a piece. Therefore, the queen retreats to cover c5 and d6, the squares on which the white knight and queen had real designs.

20 ♘f6+

The loose rook finally

proves to be Black's downfall as it allows White to trick his way into the enemy camp.

20 ... ♖xf6

The prospect of 20 ... ♔g7 21 ♘xd7, forking all three major pieces, cannot be contemplated.

21 ♕xb8+ ♗c8
22 d4 ♖f8

This is a time for stubborn defence rather than reckless stunts: 22 ... ♕xb2? 23 ♖ab1 ♕xa2 24 ♖xb7+-.

23 ♖f2 ♘c6
24 ♕f4 ♗d7
25 ♖e1

With the extra exchange to his credit for no apparent compensation, the win should just be a matter of time.

25 ... ♘d8
26 d5 ♘f7
27 dxe6 ♗xe6
28 b3 ♗d7
29 ♕d4 ♗c6
30 ♕xb6 axb6
31 ♗xc6 bxc6
32 ♖e6

The ending should be straightforward but Bronstein takes a rather long route to victory.

32 ... ♖c8 33 ♖fe2 ♔f8 34 h4 b5 35 a4 bxa4 36 bxa4 ♖a8 37 ♖xc6 ♖xa4 38 ♖c7 ♖a6 39 ♖b2 h6 40 c4 f4 41 c5 f3 42 ♔g1 ♖a8 43 ♖cb7 ♖a1+ 44 ♖b1 ♖a6 45 ♖d7 ♖a8 46 ♖e1 ♖a2 47 ♖e3 ♖a1+ 48 ♔f2 ♖a2+ 49 ♔xf3 ♖c2 50 ♖c7 h5 51 ♔e4 ♘h6 52 ♖a3 ♖e2+ 53 ♔f4 ♖e8 54 ♖h7 ♔g8 55 ♖xh6 ♔g7 56 c6 ♔xh6 57 ♖c3 g5+ 58 hxg5+ 1-0

Lane - Hutchings
Stroud 1980

1 e4 c5
2 ♘c3 ♘c6

Normally 2 ... g6 transposes to traditional lines but White has another possibility: 3 d4 cxd4 4 ♕xd4 ♘f6 5 ♗b5! a6 6 e5!±.

It is rare to find anybody willing to try out an early queen's fianchetto: 2 ... b6 3 g3 ♗b7 4 ♗g2 e6 5 ♘ge2 h5!? (5 ... d6 6 0-0 ♘d7 7 d4 cxd4 8 ♘xd4±; 5 ... ♘ge7 6 0-0 g6 7 d4! ♗g7?! 8 dxc5 bxc5 9 ♗e3 ♘a6 10 ♕d6 ♕b8 11 ♗xc5+- Lane - Perrett, Torbay 1981) 6 h4 f5?! 7 ♘f4 ♘f6 8 d3 fxe4 9 dxe4 ♘c6 10 e5! and due to the pin Black is in a terrible mess, Rosenthal - Anderssen, Vienna 1873.

3 g3

Quite bizarre is 3 g4?! e6 4 ♗g2 h5!? (quieter moves aimed at exploiting the weak squares f4 and h4 should be considered) 5 gxh5 ♘f6 6 d3 ♖xh5 7 ♘ge2 d5 8 ♘g3 ♖h8 9 ♗g5 with reasonable chances, Hort -

Kindermann, Bath 1983.

3 ... ♖b8 *(76)*

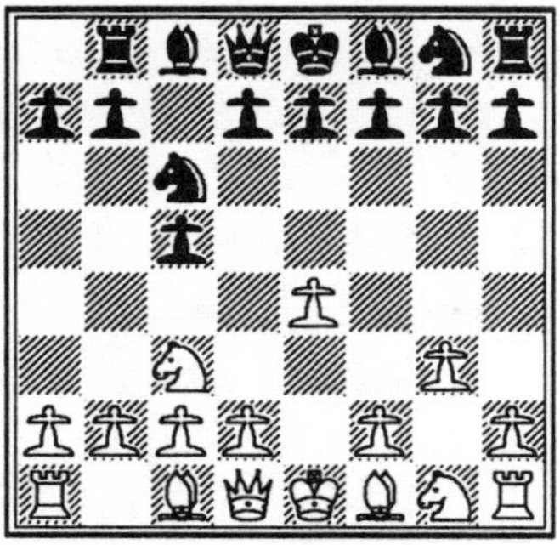

The rook supports the b-pawn in a rapid assault on the queenside. This move has the same drawback as in the illustrative game Bronstein - Keres, in that it lacks flexibility. At this juncture Black should be careful to adhere to the standard move order, otherwise he can face disaster:

a) 3 ... e5 4 ♗g2 g6 5 ♘h3 ♗g7 6 0-0 d6 7 f4 ♘ge7?! 8 f5! gxf5 9 ♕h5 ♘d4 10 ♘g5 ♘g6 11 exf5 ♗xf5 12 ♗d5 ♕d7 13 ♘xf7+- Taimanov - Minic, USSR 1965.

b) 3 ... ♘f6 4 ♗g2 d5?! 5 ♘xd5 (5 exd5 ♘b4 6 ♘ge2 ♘bxd5 7 0-0± Pachman) 5 ... ♘xd5 6 exd5 ♘b4 7 ♘e2 ♘xd5 8 d4 e6 9 0-0 ♗e7 10 dxc5 ♗xc5 11 c4± Bronstein - Lisitsyn, USSR 1947.

c) 3 ... d6 4 ♗g2 ♘f6 5 d3 g6 (5 ... ♗g4!? 6 ♘ge2 ♘d4 7 h3 ♗f3 8 ♗xf3 ♘xf3+ 9 ♔f1 e5 10 ♔g2 ♘d4 11 ♗g5±) 6 f4 ♗g4!? 7 ♘ge2 ♘d4 8 0-0 ♗g7 9 h3 ♘xe2+ 10 ♘xe2 ♗d7 11 ♗e3 ♗c6 12 ♕d2 0-0 13 g4 e6 14 f5 exf5 15 gxf5 ♘h5 16 c4 ♕h4? 17 ♗g5+- Lane - Schofield, Paignton 1982.

d) 3 ... h5 4 ♗g2 h4 5 g4 e5 6 h3 ♘ge7 7 d3 ♘g6 8 ♘ge2 ♗d6 9 ♘d5 ♘ce7 10 0-0 ♘xd5 11 exd5± Nun - Gurgenidze, USSR 1978/79.

4 ♗g2 g6

The immediate launch of a full-scale pawn rush is pointless without the backing of minor pieces: 4 ... b5 5 ♘ge2 (5 f4, keeping e2 vacant for the queen's knight, should also be considered) 5 ... b4 6 ♘d5 e6 7 ♘e3 ♗a6 8 d3 ♘ge7 9 0-0 ♘c8 10 f4 ♗e7 11 g4 ♘d4 12 ♘g3 ♘b6 13 g5 gives White a sizeable advantage due to the imminent attack on the black king, Meleghegyi - Horvath, Hungary 1979.

5 d3 ♗g7
6 f4 b5
7 ♘f3

White is content to reel out the usual moves which is perfectly acceptable because the system is so solid against inappropriately active play. An alternative plan is to encourage Black to open the a-file with 7 a3 a5 8 ♘f3 b4 9 axb4 axb4 10 ♘e2 (10 ♘d5!?) 10 ... d6 11 0-0 ♘h6 12 h3 f5 (Tarve - Tal, Parnu 1971) 13 exf5!±.

7 ... b4
8 ♘e2 ♕b6

Not 8 ... e6 9 a3 bax3 10 ♖xa3 ♗xb2 11 ♗xb2 ♖xb2 12 ♕a1+-.

9 0-0

There is no need to fear the discovered check as 9 ... c4+ can even be met with 10 d4.

9 ... d6

After 9 ... ♘h6 10 ♔h1 d6 11 h3 f5 12 exf5 gxf5 13 ♘g5 e6 14 g4 0-0 15 ♘g3 ♘e7 16 ♕e2, the white knights look dangerous and the e6-pawn is under pressure. Bonsch – Zinn, Potsdam 1974.

10 ♔h1 ♘f6
11 h3 *(77)*

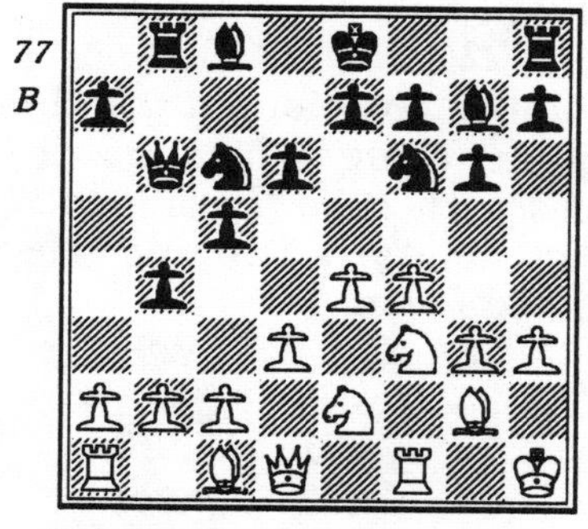

Primarily for the purpose of allowing 12 ♗e3 without fear of being molested by ... ♘g4 with a discovered attack on b2, this move has the benefit of preparing g4, gaining space, which is the typical way to treat ... ♘f6.

11 ... c4!?

In keeping with the game plan so far; Black perceives that the central pawns are the corner-stone of White's bastion of defence, without which Black has good prospects. He therefore makes a concerted effort to undermine them.

12 g4

The position is not looking promising on the other flank so White goes straight for the king. Very poor is 12 dxc4? ♘xe4, when Black is in control and the c4-pawn, faced with ... ♗a6, is decidedly weak.

12 ... cxd3
13 cxd3 0-0
14 f5

The thematic frontal assault on the king continues in earnest. Both players have a clear set of goals but Black must first stem the flow of the white attack. If he fails to take defensive measures now, it might be too late since his pieces are far from the kingside. Such a scenario is often repeated in the Closed where Black concentrates exclusively on the queenside whilst White burrows a direct route to the king.

14 ... ♗a6
15 ♘f4

This can only add weight to the mounting attack and at the same time acts as a deterrent to any vague ideas Black may have had about targeting the d3-pawn.

15 ... ♖fe8
16 g5 ♘d7
17 ♘d5 ♕a5

Hoping to activate the queen, but this is a lost cause with the powerful knight on d5. 17 ... ♕d8 should have been preferred.

18 ♘e1

It is now abundantly clear that White is angling for the f6-advance, with dire consequences for Black. The strategy employed by Hutchings has failed to produce any real counter-chances and he must now meekly retreat as a last resort.

18 ... ♕d8 *(78)*

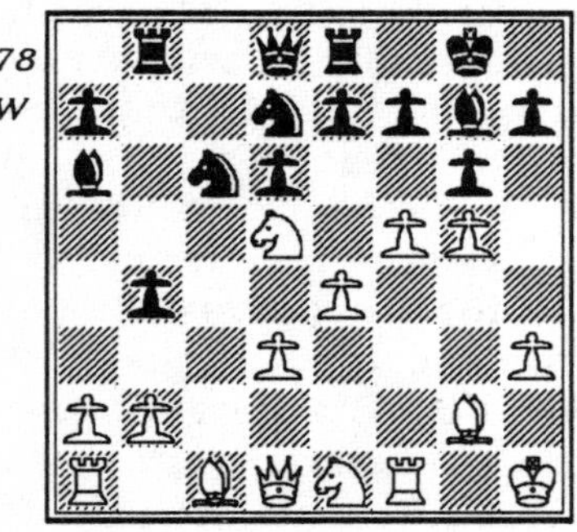

19 f6! exf6

Trying to save the game by hanging on to the extra pawn seems to be possible after the sequence 20 gxf6 ♘xf6 21 ♗g5 ♖e6 22 ♕f3 ♘e5 23 ♘xf6+ (23 ♕f2 ♘xe4; 23 ♕f4 ♘ed7 followed by ♗b7 and ♗xd5) 23 ... ♗xf6 24 ♗xf6 ♘xf3 25 ♗xd8 ♘xe1 26 ♗c7 ♖c8 27 ♖fxe1 ♖xc7 gives Black a superior ending because d3 is weak and the rook is poised to enter the second rank. However, there is a flaw in this logical analysis.

20 gxf6 ♘xf6
21 ♗g5 ♖e6
22 ♖c1!

A fine intermezzo that destroys any illusion that Black is still in the game. The significance of the rook sliding along to hit the knight is not immediately apparent, but soon all will become clear.

22 ... ♗b7

If the rook supports the knight then White continues with 22 ... ♖c8 23 ♖xc6 ♖xc6 24 ♕f3 winning the pinned piece.

23 ♕f3 ♘e5
24 ♘xf6+ ♗xf6
25 ♗xf6 ♘xf3
26 ♗xd8 ♘xe1
27 ♗c7

The point of 22 ♖c1 is revealed as the bishop is now protected here, and 27 ... ♖c8 28 ♖fxe1 wins a whole piece. Black must therefore lose material.

27 ... ♘xg2
28 ♗xb8 ♘e3
29 ♖f3 ♖xe4

A last ditch effort to

save the day.

30	**fxe4**	**♗xe4**
31	**♔g1**	**♗xf3**
32	**♔f2**	**1–0**

7) Systems with ♘ge2

The systems involving ♘ge2 are generally regarded as an effective way of achieving a solid position where White does not have to take any risks. White declares his intention to castle kingside, contest the d4 square, and retain the option of the f4 advance. The main drawback of this plan is that it is rather inflexible, although it can contain a sting in its tail if Black reacts carelessly.

Karpov – Schaufelberger
Groningen 1967

1	**e4**	c5
2	**♘c3**	♘c6
3	**g3**	g6
4	**♗g2**	♗g7
5	**d3**	d6
6	**♘ge2** *(79)*	
6	...	♕d7

This odd-looking move signals a bold attempt to refute White's plan and commits Black to an aggressive strategy involving a double fianchetto, castling queenside and the launch

79
B

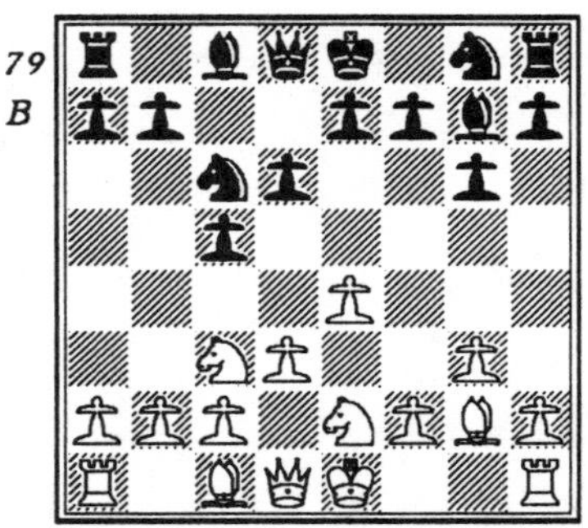

of an attack on the opposite wing. These ideas are sometimes a feature of the Open Sicilian, but here hold little fear for White because there are no weak targets in his solid structure.

7	**♗e3**	b6
8	**f4**	♗b7
9	**0–0**	

Karpov develops his pieces to their normal Closed Sicilian squares. This approach is strongly recommended when confronted with something unusual as there is no need to panic. The standard guidelines still apply here as in other variations. With the white forces converged on the centre and the pawns stifling any counter-attack, the White position is one that Black will have great difficulty in breaking down.

9 ... ♘d4
10 ♕d2 h5
11 h3 *(80)*

80
B

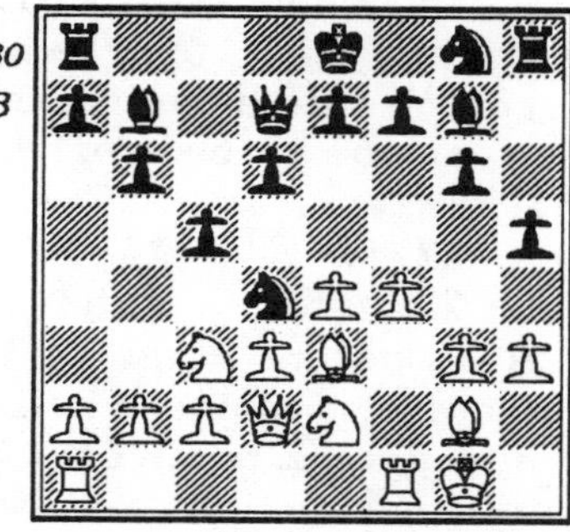

A key move to ensure that the h-file is not opened up to Black's benefit. The point is that after 11 ... h4 12 g4 the white kingside is a tough nut to crack, particularly since Black has only a few pieces out in the open.

11 ... f5
12 ♗f2 0-0-0
13 ♘xd4! ♗xd4

Schaufelberger feels obliged to swap the dark-squared bishops, a sure indication that things are not going right. Normally, it is jealously guarded as it tends to be the lynch-pin of the defensive strategy. In this case, the alternative is not particularly comforting: 13 ... cxd4 14 ♘e2 e5 15 c3 dxc3 16 ♘xc3 ♘e7 17 a4! and White gets his attack in first.

14 ♗xd4 cxd4
15 ♘e2 e5
16 c3! *(81)*

81
B

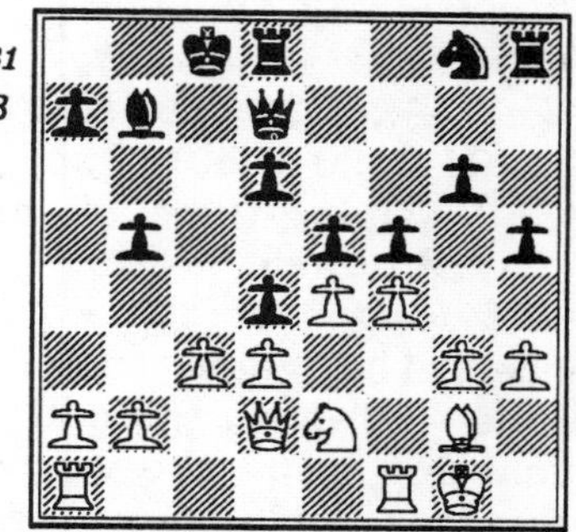

One must remember that when there is opposite-side castling, it is important not to blindly push the pawns without a certain amount of positional judgement and precise calculation. These qualities have been missing from Black's play and Karpov's straightforward move exposes this by opening up a direct line to the king.

16 ... h4

A gallant attempt at consistency but it is just not good enough. The drawback of launching pawns without the help of other pieces is evident from the analysis: 16 ... dxc3 (16 ... ♕g7 17 cxd4 exd4 18 ♕b4 and the d-pawn leaves the board) 17 ♕xc3+ ♕c7 18 ♖ac1 ♕xc3 19

♖xc3+ ♔b8 20 exf5 gxf5 21 fxe5 dxe5 22 ♖xf5, which gives White a winning advantage.

17 cxd4 hxg3

It is too late to change tactics by capturing on d4: 17 ... exd4 18 ♘xd4 hxg3 19 ♕c3+ ♔b8 (19 ... ♕c7 20 ♕xc7+ ♔xc7 21 ♘e6+ ♔d7 22 ♘xd8+-) 20 ♘c6+ ♗xc6 21 ♕xh8, gaining the exchange.

18 dxe5 ♘e7

At long last the knight enters the game to offer some defence against an incursion on the c-file. However, this move was needed earlier to lend support to d4 and is indicative of the faults in Black's policy of all or nothing. Hopeless is 18 ... dxe5 19 ♕c3+ ♕c7 20 ♖ac1 ♕xc3 21 ♖xc3+ ♔b8 22 exf5 exf5 23 fxe5, when the connected passed pawns will romp home to promotion.

19 ♕c3+ ♔b8

There is nothing constructive that can be done, e.g. 19 ... ♕c7 (19 ... ♘c6 20 d4!) 20 ♖ac1 ♕xc3 21 ♖xc3+ ♔b8 22 exd6 ♖xd6 23 ♘xg3, when White is a clear two pawns up.

20 ♘xg3

A minor miracle for Schaufelberger would arise after the foolish 20 exf5? ♘xf5 21 d4 ♗xg2 22 ♔xg2 ♘e3+! 23 ♕xe3 ♕xh3+ 24 ♔g1 ♕h2 mate. The text eliminates the prospect of any revival, as a protected pawn on g3 might be a real menace.

20 ... fxe4
21 dxe4 d5
22 ♖ad1

There is no need to give Black any chances: 22 exd5?! ♗xd5 22 ♖ad1 ♕e6 when Karpov would have to exercise caution to beat off the black attack.

22 ... d4
23 ♕d2 ♖xh3?

A desperate lunge to try and confuse matters before White gets a total grip on the game. Against accurate defence it should fail, if only because there is very limited support available from the black forces since the White pawn mass in the centre blocks direct involvement.

24 ♗xh3 ♕xh3
25 ♕g2 ♕h4
26 ♖f3!

Perhaps Black missed this idea, which puts paid to the threat of transferring the knight to f5, relying on the pin provided by the bishop.

26 ... ♖h8
27 ♖xd4 ♘f5
28 exf5 gxf5

The futility of the situation has become clear, e.g. 28 ... ♗xf3 29 ♕xf3 ♕h2+ 30

♔f1 and the attack has run out of steam after one check.

29 ♖dd3 ♖g8
30 ♕h2 1-0

Spassky - Kindermann
Dubai Ol 1986

1 e4 c5
2 ♘c3 d6
3 g3 ♘c6
4 ♗g2 g6
5 d3 ♗g7
6 ♘ge2 e6
7 0-0 ♘ge7
8 ♗g5!? *(82)*

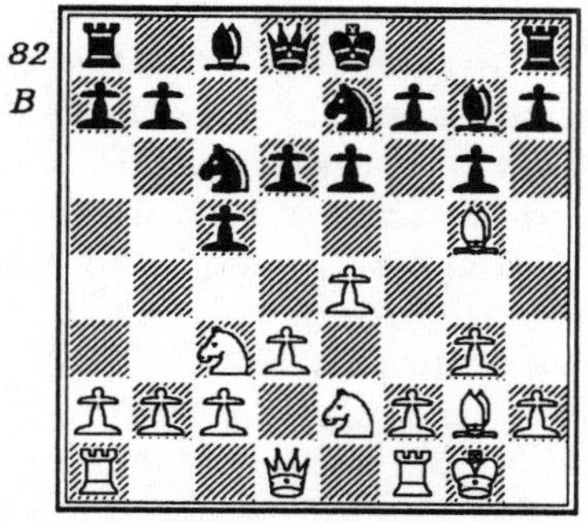

Spassky has done a great deal to popularise this move, which pins the knight and prepares ♕d2. It poses Black more problems than those normally associated with 6 ♘ge2, because a decision has to be made on whether to kick it away or continue with the normal plan of just getting the pieces out.

8 ... h6

Probably the best choice, although it is often avoided for fear of giving White a target. Black just has to delay castling to smooth matters out. There are two other possibilities.

a) 8 ... 0-0 9 ♕d2 ♕d7 (9 ... ♖e8 10 h4 ♖b8 11 h5 b5 12 ♔h2?! b4 13 ♘d1 ♘e5 14 f3 d5 and Black has equality, Preziuso - Komljanovic, Zurich 1989) 10 ♗h6 ♘d4 11 ♘xd4 cxd4 12 ♗xg7 ♔xg7 13 ♘e2 e5 14 f4, with the idea of undermining the pawn chain by c3!, is slightly better for White, Spassky - Arnason, Reykjavik 1985.

b) 8 ... b6 9 ♕d2 h6 10 ♗e3 ♗a6 11 ♖fe1 ♘d4 12 f4 ♖c8 13 ♖ab1 ♕d7 14 ♗f2 0-0 15 ♘xd4 cxd4 16 ♘e2 ♘c6 17 c3 dxc3 18 bxc3 d5 19 e5!, which gives White the better game because the strong closed centre allows a kingside pawn storm, Spassky - Panno, Lucerne 1985.

9 ♗e3 ♘d4
10 ♖b1

An interesting solution to the typical Black plan of planting a knight on d4. The early advance on the queenside with b4 presents some fresh problems for Black to handle, demonstrating just how versatile the Closed Sicilian can be. A reliable alternative is 10 ♕d2, to prevent castling, when the best retort is ... ♗d7, followed by ... ♗c6 and ... ♕d7 with roughly equal chances.

10 ... ♖b8
11 b4! b6
12 bxc5 dxc5
13 a4

This is a logical reflection of White's desire to act quickly before Black can cut off any active play.

13 ... 0–0

There is a flaw in the plan of surging forward with the queenside pawns: 13 ... a6 14 ♕d2 b5? 15 axb5 axb5 16 ♗xd4 cxd4 17 ♘xb5, giving White a material advantage.

14 ♘b5 *(83)*

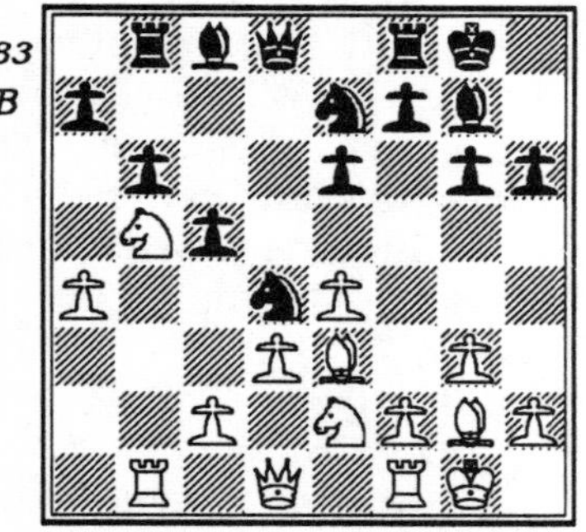

14 ... ♘xb5?!

Kindermann has a bewildering choice of alternatives, only one of which appears to offer him very much.

a) 14 ... a6 15 ♘bxd4 cxd4 16 ♗f4 e5 (16 ... ♖a8 17 ♕c1 ♔h7 18 ♕b2 when b6 is a target) 17 ♗d2 ♗e6 18 c4, which gives White a slight edge due to his strength on the b-file.

b) 14 ... ♘xe2+ 15 ♕xe2 ♘c6 16 e5 ♘xe5? 17 ♗f4 f6 18 ♘xa7 and Black is struggling.

c) 14 ... ♘ec6 15 ♗xd4 (15 ♗f4 e5 16 ♗d2 ♘xe2+ 17 ♕xe2 a6=) 15 ... cxd4 16 f4 a6 17 ♘a3 e5 18 f5, when White's pawn wave is compensated for by the weak dark squares now his bishop has been swapped off.

15 axb5 a6
16 bxa6 ♗xa6
17 ♕d2

White seems to have fair prospects. The weakness of b6 is one important factor, and another is the marooned bishop on a6, which is not destined to figure in the main conflict.

17 ... ♔h7
18 h4

Once again in the Closed a wing advance is used as a ploy to keep Black bottled up.

18 ... ♘c6

The attempt to ease the tension by using the queen's bishop backfires after 18 ... c4? 19 ♖fd1, when White will be eager to increase operations on the b-file now that the bishop is lined up against the weak pawn on b6.

19 f4 ♘d4

20 Nxd4

More exact is 20 e5 Nf5 21 Bf2 f6 22 exf6 Qxf6, when Black has similar problems to the game.

20 ... cxd4
21 Bf2 h5

Kindermann is understandably not prepared to allow a pawn-break with 22 f5, but according to Hickl this is precisely how he could have taken advantage of the slip on move 20. The correct prognosis is 21 ... e5! 22 f5 gxf5 23 exf5 Bb7, when the bishop returns to exchange on g2 with equality.

22 e5

A typical strategy to muster increased pressure against the d4-pawn. This threat is enough to force a weakening on the black pawn structure to allow the dark-squared bishop to resume its defensive role on the diagonal.

22 ... f6

The backward pawn on e6 is now vulnerable and g6 is also a worry. Here Black cannot afford to trade bishops: 22 ... Bb7 23 Bxb7 Rxb7 24 Rb4 Rd7 25 Rfb1 winning a pawn.

23 exf6 Qxf6

Not much good is 23 ... Bxf6?! 24 Ra1 Bb7 25 Ra7, when the pin along the seventh rank causes all sorts of problems.

24 Rfe1

The weak points of b6 and e6 are now under surveillance, severely limiting Black's options.

24 ... Qf5
25 Qe2 Qc5

Rather rash is 25 ... e5? 26 Be4 Qf7 27 Qxh5++-.

26 c4 Rfe8
27 Be4

No time is lost in pursuing the pawn on g6 which, after 22 ... f6, can no longer rely on its natural defender. We now see the culmination of Spassky's forceful play as all the weaknesses in Black's position will be revealed by direct action. The threat now is 28 g4.

27 ... Rf8

Keeping an eye on f4.

28 Rb2

Clearing the way for 29 Ra1 Bb7 30 Rb5 Qd6 31 Rxh5+, winning easily.

28 ... b5
29 Ra1 Bc8
30 Be1! *(84)*

84
B

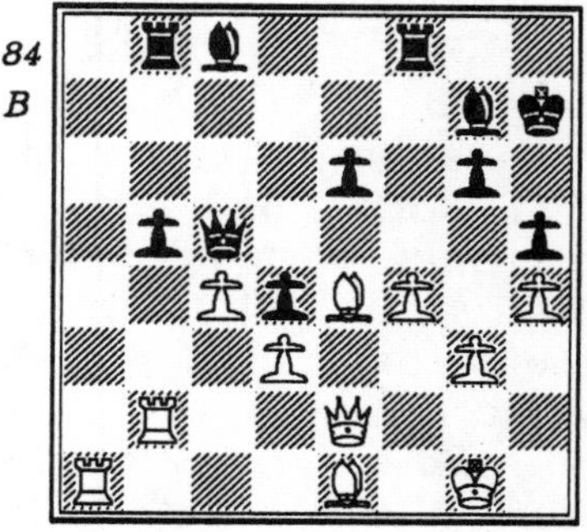

Black is completely lost. The dual threat posed by ♗b4, winning the exchange or knocking the queen away from the protection of h5, is extremely potent. It is worth noting that Spassky found this move by mobilising the only piece not already involved in the main skirmishes.

30	**...**	**♖f5**
31	**cxb5**	**♗b7**
32	**♗b4**	**♕c8**
33	**♗xf5**	**exf5**

Compensation for the exchange rests on the light-squared bishop that should provide Black with some attacking chances. Perhaps, more importantly, White has emerged from the mêlée with a powerful passed pawn.

34	**♗d6**	**♖a8**
35	**♖e1**	

There is no point in exchanging as after 35 ♖xa8 ♗xa8, the follow-up ... ♕b7 is tricky.

35	**...**	**♕c3**
36	**♖c2**	**♕b3**
37	**♖c7**	**♕d5**
38	**♖xb7!**	

It is better to be safe than sorry. Although the exchange is handed back, White can still count on the b-pawn to win the game.

38	**...**	**♕xb7**
39	**♖b1**	**♕d5**
40	**♕g2**	

Stamping out any resistance by virtue of a pin. Promotion can only be stopped at the cost of heavy material losses.

40	**...**	**♕g8**
41	**b6**	**♖a2**
42	**♖b2**	**1-0**

In the next game Karpov resorts to the standard 8 ♗e3 rather than Spassky's more intriguing 8 ♗g5!?, which only came into tournament practice quite recently, albeit in a position where Black has castled rather than played ... d6.

Karpov - Palatnik
USSR 1967

1	**e4**	**c5**
2	**♘c3**	**♘c6**
3	**g3**	**g6**
4	**♗g2**	**♗g7**
5	**♘ge2**	**e6**
6	**d3**	**♘ge7**
7	**0-0**	**0-0**
8	**♗e3**	**♘d4**
9	**♕d2**	**♕a5** *(85)*

Black has chosen a variety of ways to continue apart from the text:

a) 9 ... ♖b8 and now:

a1) 10 a4 (10 ♘d1!? intending c3 is also playable) 10 ... d6 11 f4 a6 12 g4 f5 13 gxf5 exf5 14 ♘g3 is roughly equal. Tochtermann - Bianco, Zurich 1988.

a2) 10 f4 d6 11 g4!? f5 12 gxf5 gxf5 13 ♘g3 ♕e8 14 ♘d1 b6 15 c3 ♘dc6 16 ♔h1= Mortazavi - Emms, Upminster 1990.

b) 9 ... ♘ec6 10 ♘d1 ♕a5 11 c3 ♘xe2+ (11 ... ♘b3? 12 axb3 ♕xa1 13 ♗xc5 ♖e8 14 ♗a3 the queen is trapped) 12 ♕xe2 d6± Rjumin - Kirilov , Moscow 1931.

c) 9 ... d5 10 exd5 exd5 10 ♘f4 with pressure on d5 giving White an edge, Alexander - Botvinnik, Nottingham 1936.

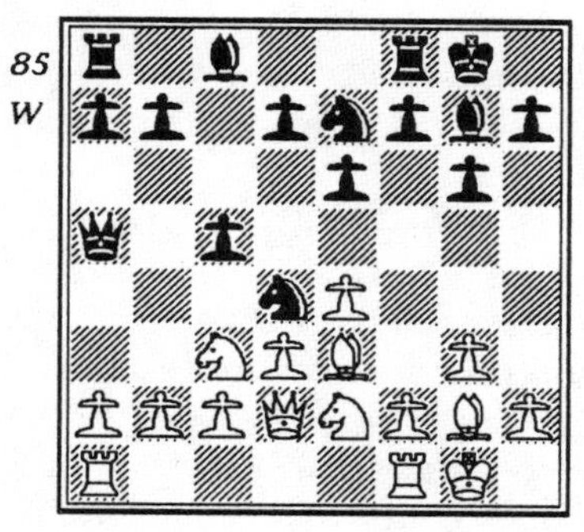
85
W

10 ♘f4 d6
11 ♖ab1

The queen presents itself as a natural target for White's intended expansion by a3 and b4.

11 ... ♘ec6
12 a3 a6
13 ♕d1!?

A curious decision but a change of plan was needed, otherwise Black could snap off on a3 after White's b4-advance. The text prepares to shift the black knight on d4 by ♘ce2 and c3.

13 ... b5
14 ♘ce2 ♗b7 *(86)*

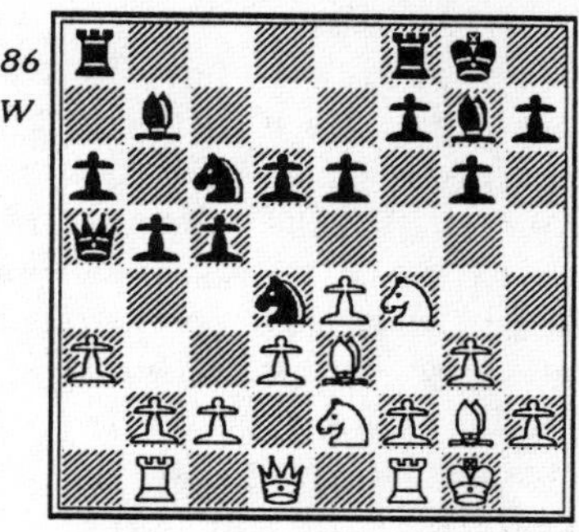
86
W

15 c3

It should be noted how Karpov handles the position very calmly, happy to lose time in order to achieve his objective. The inclusion of ♖b1 and a3 also has its points, since now the rook covers b2 and White is ready to exchange after ... b4. Having a queen rather than a pawn on a5 has the significant drawback that after Black's intended ... b4 he must recapture with the c-pawn on b4 as otherwise his pawns would lose co-ordination. However, this allows White to dominate with his extra pawn in the centre.

15 ... ♘xe2+
16 ♕xe2 ♖ac8
17 h4

A favourite tool in such closed systems to probe for weaknesses and perhaps provoke the pointless 17 ...

h5.

17 ... b4
18 axb4 cxb4
19 d4

A normal strategy in this opening is to aim for eventual control of the central squares. White has a sound set-up with few weaknesses and chances to consolidate his spatial advantage. Black now carelessly adopts a futile plan of exchanging pawns in the centre which only highlights his own weak pawns.

19 ... e5
20 ♖a1 ♕d8
21 dxe5 ♘xe5
22 ♗d4 ♖e8 *(87)*

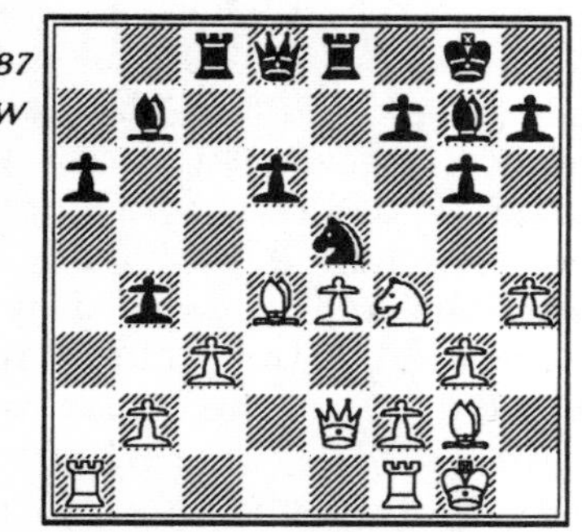

Although a lone pawn on d6 is weak, at least Palatnik has established the knight on a strong outpost. The black rooks are also posted in active positions but White's play can be based upon always having a draw in hand.

23 ♖fd1 f5
24 ♕c2

Not 24 exf5? ♘f3+ 25 ♗xf3 ♖xe2. The simple text move seems to refute the whole black concept of relying on the pin to undermine the position as White not only proposes to take on f5, but also to give check to start another combination.

24 ... fxe4
25 ♕b3+ ♘c4

Beset with difficulties but probably best in the circumstances is 25 ... ♔h8 26 ♕xb4 ♗c6 (26 ... ♕d7 27 ♗h3 ♘g4 28 ♗xg7+ ♔xg7 29 ♖xd6+-; 26 ... ♕e7!?) 27 ♖xa6 with a clear advantage.

26 ♗h3! ♗h6

It would be a pointless exercise to move the attacked rook because then 27 ♗e6+ forces the win of the exchange anyway. Therefore, Black accepts that he will have to shed material and seeks to confuse matters by shattering the white kingside pawn cover.

27 ♕xb4 ♗a8
28 ♖xa6 ♗xf4
29 ♗xc8

There might well be hope for Black if White had to immediately recapture on f4, but there is no reason for him not to take the black rook. The point is that after 29 ... ♕xc8 30 ♖xa8 (30 ♖a7!?) 30 ... ♕xa8

31 ♕xc4+ d5 32 ♕c5 ♗e5 33 ♗xe5 ♖xe5 34 ♕d6, White is winning.

29 ... ♗d5
30 ♗b7 ♗f7
31 ♖a8

With a material advantage, it is an ideal time to start swapping off material, especially as the opposing rook supports Black's last chance, ... e3.

31 ... ♕d7
32 ♖xe8+ ♕xe8
33 ♖a1 e3
34 ♖a8 1-0

Karpov - Tsamryuk
USSR 1967

1 e4 c5
2 ♘c3 ♘c6
3 g3 g6
4 ♗g2 ♗g7
5 ♘ge2

It really makes little difference whether this is played now or after 5 d3.

5 ... d6
6 0-0 ♘f6

The swift deployment of the knight to castle early has long been one of Black's favourite formations. The long-term plan is to weather the storm on the kingside, and then break through on the other wing, primarily by advancing the queenside pawns.

7 d3 0-0
8 h3 *(88)*

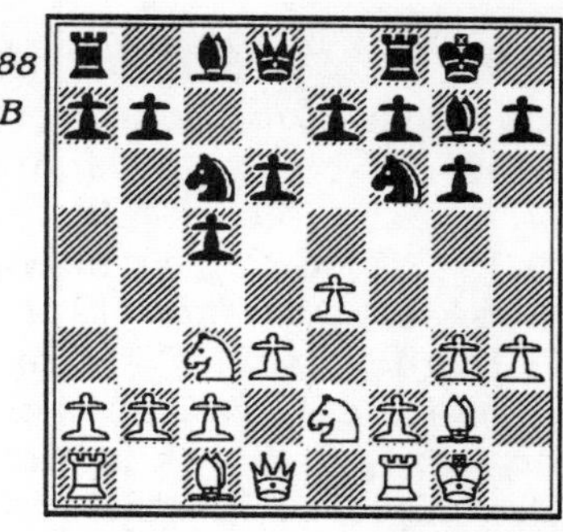

As the aim is to continue with ♗e3 and ♕d2, it makes sense to deter the annoying ... ♘g4. A more original approach is 8 ♘f4 ♗d7 9 a4 ♕c8 10 h4!? ♖e8 11 f3 ♘d4 12 ♗e3 ♗c6 13 g4 e5, when despite White's bold style the position offers equal chances. Kopilpov - Smyslov, USSR 1947.

8 ... ♗d7

A whole host of alternatives are possible:

a) 8 ... e5 9 ♗e3 (9 f4 exf4 10 ♘xf4 h5?! 11 ♗e3 ♘h7 12 ♕d2 h4 13 g4 ♗d7 14 ♘fd5 ♘e7 15 d4 Ignatiev - Osnos, Leningrad 1962) 9 ... ♗d7 10 ♔h2 ♘d4 11 f4 b5 12 ♕d2 b4 13 ♘d1 ♘h5 14 f5! gxf5 15 exf5 ♘xf5 16 ♖xf5 ♗xf5 17 g4 ♗xg4 18 hxg4 ♕h4+ 19 ♗h3 ♘f4 20 ♘xf4 exf4 21 ♗xf4 ♖ae8 22 ♘e3!, when the two pieces for a rook give White excellent attacking prospects, Keres - Darga, USSR 1954.

b) 8 ... ♘e8 9 ♗g5 ♘c7 10 ♕d2 ♖e8 11 ♖ae1 ♖b8 12 ♗h6

♗h8 13 f4 ♘d4 14 f5 b5 15 ♘f4 b4 16 ♘cd5 ♘xd5 17 ♘xd5 with good chances, Koslov - Shipov, Moscow 1964.

c) 8 ... ♖b8 9 ♗e3 b5 10 ♕d2 b4 11 ♘d1 ♕c7 12 f4 ♘d7 13 g4 ♘d4 14 ♘g3 ♗a6 and White can continue to build up on the kingside with high expectations, Wibe - Korchnoi, Havana 1966.

d) 8 ... ♘d4 9 f4 ♘d7 10 f5 b5 11 g4 ♗b7 12 ♘f4 ♗e5 13 ♔h1 e6 14 ♘ce2 ♕h4 15 ♘g1 exf5 16 gxf5 g5, when Black's immediate attacking threats do not look convincing because White has sufficient forces to fend him off, Lutikov - Romanishin, Tbilisi 1979.

9 ♗e3 ♖b8
10 ♕d2 b5
11 ♘d1

Refraining from 11 a3 and withdrawing the principal target from Black's queenside attack. White hopes to be able to play a quick d4 and take control of the centre.

11 ... ♕a5!?

More astute would be 11 ... b4 reaching exactly the same position as if Karpov had done something else on his 11th move. The psychological ploy of the keeping his options open causes Black to offer a transposition into a drawish endgame.

12 c3

The offer to exchange is rightly declined as White's prospects lie in the middlegame, where the stress is on finding the optimum posts for the pieces.

12 ... ♖fc8
13 ♗h6 ♗h8
14 g4

Black has managed to preserve his bishop, albeit on the temporarily restrictive square h8. Now Karpov can aim to open up the f-file for the rooks, which would make use of his control over f8 and it is actually quite difficult for Black to foil such a straightforward plan of action.

14 ... ♘e8
15 f4 b4
16 f5! *(89)*

89
B

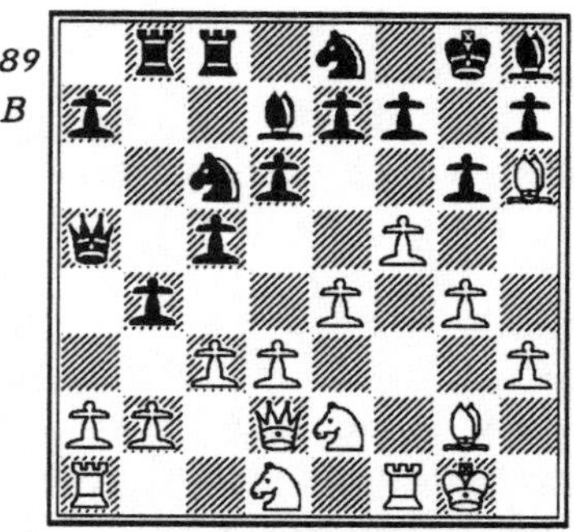

A position has been reached with a similar pawn structure to that in many other games where 6 ... ♘f6

is employed. The question is whether Black can use the e5-square as a pivot for his pieces or can make his queenside pressure more urgent, in answer to White's obvious but steady on-slaught against the black king's fortress. In practical terms Black has real problems over-the-board in trying to work out just how much the attack is illusory. On the other hand, White must strive to contain the counter-attack and turn his spatial advantage into something more tangible.

16 ... bxc3
17 bxc3 ♘e5
18 ♘f4 ♕d8

Reluctantly admitting that the contentious early sortie by the queen was rather rash, now that it is evident that White has almost a free hand in conducting operations on the kingside.

19 ♘e3 ♘c7
20 ♕f2 ♕e8
21 ♖ad1

It is remarkable how Karpov has systematically approached the business of transferring his forces to one side of the board, and achieved it with consummate ease. Black really lacks any way of creating counterplay to divert the white pieces from his own king.

21 ... ♖b6
22 h4 ♖cb8
23 ♖d2 ♖b1
24 d4

Dislodging the knight from its central role and cramping Black even more.

24 ... cxd4
25 cxd4 ♖xf1+
26 ♗xf1 ♘c6
27 ♘ed5 ♘xd5
28 ♘xd5 *(90)*

90
B

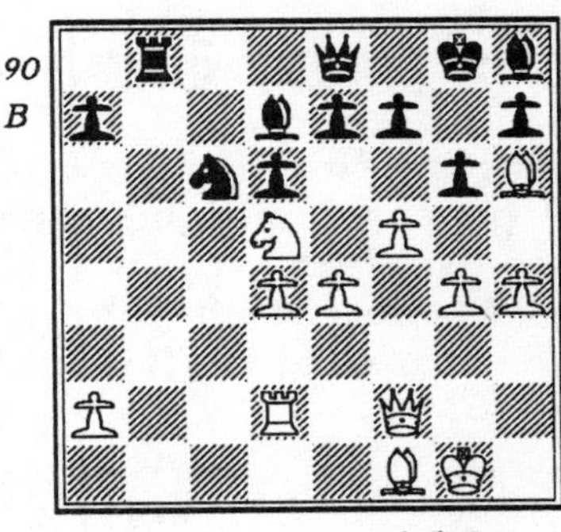

28 ... ♘b4

After the series of exchanges it is evident that Karpov has achieved a clear advantage. The remaining black pieces are rather passive and can only cause White mild irritation by probing the weak d4-pawn, whilst White can easily reorganise his pieces for maximum effect.

29 ♘f4 ♘c6
30 h5 ♖b4
31 ♘e2 a5
32 ♖d3

The struggle for d4 is a side-show as far as White

is concerned and now he prepares to swing the rook across to the real battleground.

32 ... ♖c4
33 hxg6 fxg6
34 fxg6 hxg6
35 ♖f3!

The bishop's control of f8 now assumes great importance and Black is forced into further concessions on the kingside.

35 ... ♗g7
36 ♗xg7 ♔xg7
37 g5

Angling to infiltrate with the queen on h6 and then mate by ♖f4-h4. Clearly 38 ♕h4 cannot be met by ... ♕h8 because of 39 ♖f7+.

37 ... ♗g4
38 ♖f4 ♗xe2
39 ♗xe2 ♖xd4
40 ♗b5 ♖d1+
41 ♔g2 ♖c1
42 ♕b2+

Sealing Black's fate.

42 ... e5
43 ♕xc1 exf4
44 ♕xc6 ♕e5
45 ♕d7+ ♔h8
46 ♕e8+ 1-0

Tompa – Sunye
Luanda 1981

1 e4 c5
2 ♘c3 d6
3 g3 ♘c6
4 ♗g2 g6
5 d3 ♗g7
6 ♘ge2 ♖b8

A game Thomas – Aitken, England 1946, saw Black play 6 ... ♗d7 but White won a fine game after 7 ♗e3 ♘d4 8 h3 ♕c8 9 ♕d2 b5 10 ♘d1 e5 11 c3 ♘xe2 12 ♕xe2 ♘e7 13 f4 0-0 14 ♘f2 ♗c6?! 15 0-0 ♕b7 16 fxe5 ♘f5 17 exf5! ♗xg2 18 f6! ♗xf1 19 ♖xf1 ♗h8 20 ♘e4 dxe5 21 ♗xc5 ♖fc8 22 ♕e3 ♕d5 23 ♗e7 ♖c7 24 ♕h6 ♖xe7 25 ♘g5! ♗xf6 26 ♖xf6 ♖d7 27 ♕xh7+ ♔f8 28 ♘e6+ ♔e8 29 ♕g8+ ♔e7 30 ♕xf7+ ♔d6 31 ♘f4+ ♔c5 32 b4 mate.

7 0-0

Lesser known alternatives are:

a) 7 a4 a6 8 0-0 b5 9 axb5 axb5 10 f4 ♗d7 11 f5 ♘f6 12 ♘f4 0-0 13 g4 b4 14 ♘cd5 (14 ♘ce2!) 14 ... ♘xd5 15 ♘xd5 e6 16 ♘e3 ♕h4 17 ♖f3 ♖a8 18 ♖b1 ♘d4 19 ♖h3 ♕e7 20 ♕f1, with a level position, Georgadze – Ruban, Tbilisi 1989.

b) 7 ♗g5 b5 8 ♕d2 b4 9 ♘d1 h6 10 ♗e3 ♘f6 11 h3 h5 12 f4 ♗d7 13 0-0 ♕c8 14 ♔h2 a5 15 a3 0-0 16 ♗g1!? ♔h7 17 ♘e3 ♘e8 18 c3, when White enjoys the standard spatial advantage and the h5-pawn is a weak point to attack by an eventual g4, Schorr – Valvo, New York 1987.

7 ... h5!? *(91)*

This deviates from the typical plan to ... b5 in favour of a hopeful punt to disturb the kingside set-up. Such measures are often taken by players who are keen to get their opponent out of the book. However, against the Closed such a strategy is quite inappropriate because the solid positional basis of White's opening is ideally suited to take advantage of such exuberance. More consistent is 7 ... b5 8 a3 Bd7 9 f4 (9 Be3 and 10 Qd2 is another plan) 9 ... f5 10 Kh1 Nf6 11 b4 cxb4 12 axb4 Qb6 13 Rb1 e6 14 Bd2 0-0 15 Qc1 Kh8 16 Be3 Qc7 18 Qd2 Rfc8 18 Rfc1 a5 19 bxa5 Nxa5 20 exf5 gxf5 21 Na2 Nc6 22 Bg1 e5 23 Nac3 b4 24 Nd1 Ne7 25 Rxb4 and Black has active play in compensation for the pawn, Fries-Nielsen - Groszpeter, Copenhagen Open 1989.

91
W

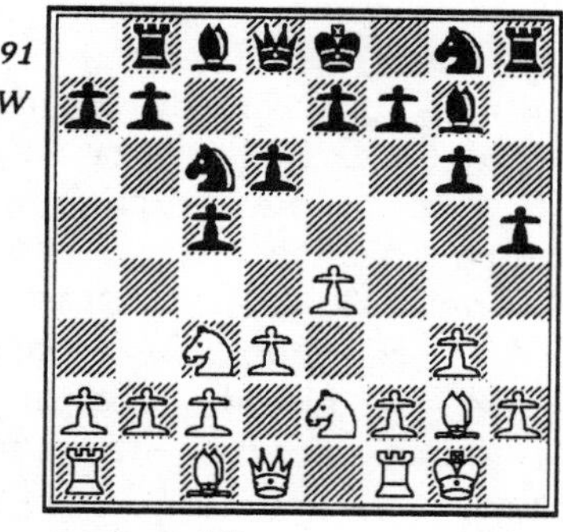

8 h3

Almost an impulse move to counter Black's clumsy advance. The text prepares to meet 8 ... h4 with 9 g4 and a subsequent f4 advance. This would leave h4 rather isolated and a real liability in any endgame.

8 ... Bd7
9 Nd5

Faced with such a limp opening, Tompa takes the initiative by re-routing the knight, nullifying any of Black's future queenside activity.

9 ... b5
10 c3 e6
11 Ne3 Qb6
12 b3 *(92)*

92
B

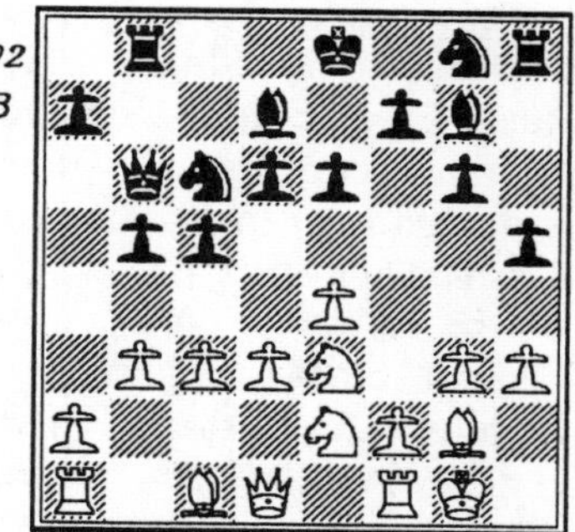

The double fianchetto is a novel way of coping with Sunye's ill-advised attempts at activity. This idea might be desirable in other lines, although White only only has the time for it here because Black has dallied with ... h5 and ... Bd7.

12 ... Nge7
13 Bb2 0-0
14 Kh2

There is no rush to occupy the centre, so Tompa gives added protection to the h-pawn in order to release the bishop from its duties. If 14 d4!? cxd4 15 cxd4 d5! 16 exd5 ♘xd5 (16 ... exd5 17 ♘f4±) 17 ♘xd5 exd5 18 ♘f4 ♘e7 takes advantage of the loose h-pawn if the bishop moves to give an equal position.

14 ... b4?!

Black fails to sense the danger and is too concerned with the worthy objective of preventing d4. In fact, already the black structure presents various positional problems because 14 ... e5 is ruled out by 15 f4, intending f5, putting additional pressure on the soft target at h5.

15 ♘c4 ♕c7
16 cxb4! ♗xb2?

Sunye considers that after 17 ♘xb2 ♖xb4 White cannot force an immediate d4, thereby reducing the tension in the situation. However, he makes a miscalculation. In fact, the right way to handle things was 16 ... ♖xb4 17 ♗xg7 ♔xg7 18 d4, and Black can continue the struggle.

17 bxc5! *(93)*

A neat idea which gives White a big advantage. This kind of twist, neglecting what appears to be a forced recapture, is often very difficult to spot in complicated positions.

93
B

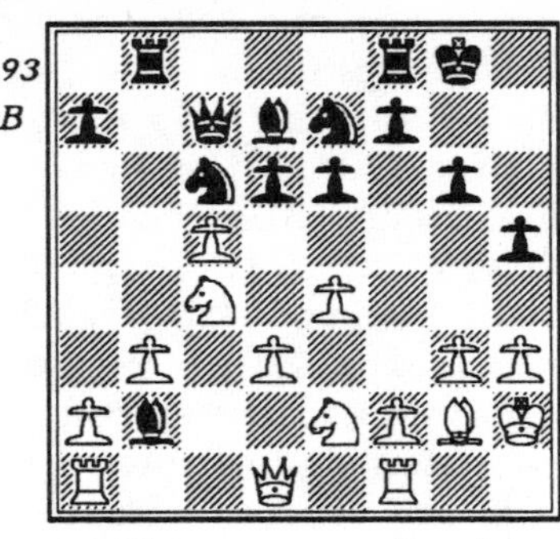

17 ... ♗xa1

This move, trying to hang on to the exchange, is probably the best bet in the circumstances. Not very enticing is 17 ... ♗e5 18 d4 ♘xd4 (18 ... dxc5 19 dxe5+-; 18 ... d5 19 ♘xe5, with eventually at least an extra pawn) 19 cxd6 ♗xd6 20 ♕xd4 and the material advantage should be enough to win.

18 cxd6 ♕d8
19 dxe7 ♕xe7
20 ♕xa1

White has ample compensation for the sacrifice with two pawns for the exchange. White can either try for a kingside attack, after reorganising his pieces, or simply advance his extra pawns up the board.

20 ... e5
21 f4 f6
22 d4

At last, the thematic

thrust is employed to break down the potential strong-point at e5.

22 ... ♘xd4
23 ♘xd4 exd4
24 ♕xd4

Having accomplished the centralisation of his queen, it only remains for the knight to take a more active role.

24 ... ♗b5
25 ♖d1 ♖fd8?!

It would be more prudent to exchange minor pieces on c4, as then the black rooks could try to stir up trouble on the open files. As played, the knight is useful in cutting down on entry squares or even blocking files, although White also maintains a lasting edge after 25 ... ♗xc4 26 ♕xc4+ ♔h7 (16 ... ♕f7 27 ♖d5 ♖bd8 28 e5!) 27 ♖d5 ♖fd8 28 ♖c5 - Tompa.

26 ♘d6! ♔h7
27 e5 ♖b6
28 ♖c1

With the knight firmly entrenched on d6, Tompa has established a clear advantage by severely reducing the capabilities of the opposing rooks. The black king is protected by a fragile shelter of pawns and it only remains for the white bishop to join the attack on e4.

28 ... h4
29 gxh4 ♗e2
30 ♖c5!?

Missing a clear chance to punish Black for trying to mix it with his speculative pawn sacrifice. Much better was 30 ♕f2! (31 ♘c8) 30 ... ♖bb8 (30 ... ♖a6 31 a4) 31 ♘e4 (31 ♕xe2 ♖xd6), and the dual threat of ♘xf6+ and ♕xe2 wins.

30 ... fxe5
31 fxe5 ♗h5
32 ♕c3?

The quality of the game now deteriorates in a period of mutual time trouble. The right course of action to crown a well-played game way 32 ♕f4 ♖f8 33 ♕g3, keeping an eye on d6 with no worries.

32 ... ♖bxd6!
33 exd6 ♕xd6+
34 ♕e5

Understandably White is so shocked at the sudden collapse of the position that he instinctively resorts to an ending to exploit the extra pawn on the queenside. With more time it is evident that the calm choice of 34 ♔g1 ♖d7 (34 ... ♕b6 35 b4!) 35 ♗d5 would have been the best winning try.

34 ... ♕xe5
35 ♖xe5 ♖d2

Now 36 ... ♗f3 is in the air and the game heads for a draw.

36 ♔g3 ♖xa2
37 ♖e7+ ♔h6
1–0

Black lost on time! Perhaps justice was done after Tompa's generally good handling of the game. The finish would have been 38 ♗d5 ♖d2! 39 ♗g8 ♖d3+ 40 ♔f4 ♖d4+ 41 ♔e5 ♖xh4 42 ♖xa7 ♖xh3=.

Karpov – Augustin
USSR 1966

1 e4 c5
2 ♘c3 ♘c6
3 g3 g6
4 ♗g2 ♗g7
5 ♘ge2 ♖b8
6 0–0

The plan of delaying d3 is interesting because it always makes Black hesitate in case something special has been prepared. More routine is 6 d3 d6, transposing to the previous game (Tompa – Sunye).

6 ... e6
7 f4 d6
8 g4!? *(94)*

A provocative sortie which is usually postponed until White is fully developed. White lets Black know of his intention to play f5 and invites Black to counter, hoping that in the process that he will overreach himself.

8 ... h5

94
B

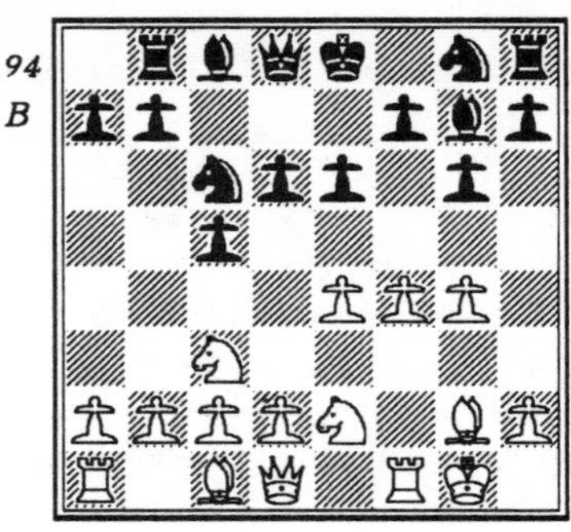

9 g5 ♘ge7
10 d3

Karpov has managed to steal more space than is usual in the opening. The challenge of 8 ... h5 has left Black with a long-term weakness that can be undermined by f5 at a critical point (since after a series of exchanges h5 will be hanging). Black has some vague ideas of combating White's early pawn-thrusts but, with the centre closed, a counter-attack is not easy to organise.

10 ... b5
11 ♕e1 ♘b4
12 ♕d2

If the queen retreats to d1, this would only justify the black knight hitting c2. Now the odd placing of the queen is compensated by the fact that the traditional queenside rush of black pawns has been delayed.

12 ... ♘bc6
13 ♔h1

A standard precautionary

measure – to wait and see what Black's intentions are, whilst, at the same time, avoiding potentially irritating checks on the g1–a7 diagonal.

13 ... d5

Opening up the centre is a creditable ploy, but when both knights are not in good defensive positions, it has severe drawbacks.

14 f5! exf5
15 ♘xd5 ♘xd5
16 exd5 ♘e5

A quick glance at the position might give the false impression that Augustin has managed to get out of the tangle with the better chances. His aim is to blockade the d-pawn and finally take it, keeping the central knight on its excellent outpost. In fact, White had calculated one move further, changing the whole picture.

17 ♕c3! *(95)*

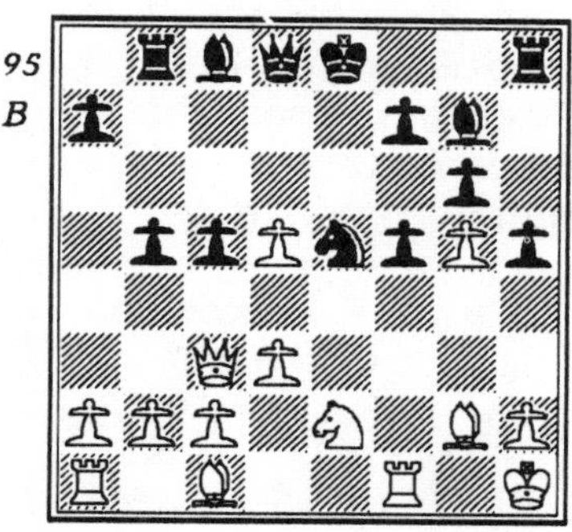

This exposes the supposed stronghold on e5 as the source of many problems, due to the nasty pin on the bishop. Now Karpov has the dual threats of simply taking on c5 or further increasing the pressure on e5. It is worth noting that the quiet 13 ♔h1 has made all this possible because there are no possibilities of a knight check, revealing a hidden attack on the queen.

17 ... ♕d6
18 ♗f4 b4
19 ♕b3 0–0

One would normally expect Black to have castled long ago but it is a tribute to Karpov's tricky opening move order that only now is the king whisked to safety. Clearly, with hindsight, this move should have been played long ago.

20 d4 cxd4
21 ♘xd4 ♗b7
22 ♘c6 *(96)*

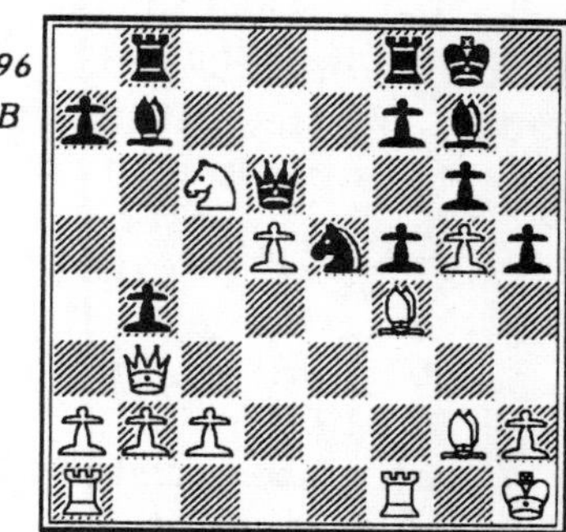

White is happy to allow the exchange of pieces because then the passed d-pawn is one step nearer its ultimate destination. It also acts as a potent weapon to split Black's forces, preventing them from establishing any harmony.

22 ... ♗xc6

Not 22 ... ♖e8, when White has the pleasant 23 ♘xb4, winning a pawn before returning to c6.

23 dxc6 ♕c5
24 ♖ad1 ♖bd8

Removing the last pin, which at least gives the knight some freedom of movement.

25 ♗e3 ♕b5
26 a4

The change of emphasis to harassing the queen, aided by the scope of the pair of bishops, is very difficult for Black to deal with. The main cause for concern for Augustin must be the lack of any real counterplay. Now that Black has moved his pieces to the kingside and the centre, White totally dominates on the queenside.

26 ... ♕c4
27 ♗xa7 ♕xb3
28 cxb3 ♖xd1
29 ♖xd1 ♖c8
30 ♖c1

A calculated risk, with the odds always heavily stacked in White's favour. The passed pawn, supported by the rest of the White pieces, must prove decisive despite the loss of a little irrelevant material in the process.

30 ... ♘d3
31 ♖c4 ♗e5
32 ♗b6 ♘xb2
33 ♖xb4

The three passed connected pawns ensure success despite Black's resourceful play.

33 ... ♗c3
34 ♖b5 ♘d3
35 c7 ♖e8

It is commendable that Augustin manages to extract anything from his dire situation, making his opponent proceed only after accurate analysis.

36 ♗a5 ♖e1+
37 ♗f1 ♖xf1+
38 ♔g2 ♖f2+
39 ♔g1 ♗d4
40 c8(♕)+ ♔h7
41 ♖d5 ♖c2+
42 ♖xd4 1-0

In the final game of this chapter we look at various ♘ge2 systems in which Black counters early in the centre with ... e5.

Karpov – Tsikhelashvili
USSR 1966

1 e4 c5
2 ♘c3 ♘c6
3 g3 g6
4 ♗g2 ♗g7

5 ♘ge2

More usual is 5 d3 which will normally transpose into standard lines unless Black tries for an early ... e5, for example, 5 ... d6 6 ♘ge2 e5 (6 ... ♘d4?! 7 ♘xd4 cxd4 8 ♘e2 e6 9 c3 dxc3 10 ♘xc3 ♘e7 11 ♗e3 0–0 12 0–0 b6 13 ♕d2± Smyslov – Cistjakov, USSR 1974) 7 ♘d5 and now:

a) 7 ... ♘ge7 8 c4 0–0 9 0–0 ♗g4 10 f3 ♗e6 11 ♗g5 h6 12 ♗e3 ♘d4 ½–½ Andonov – Gheorghiu, Warsaw 1987.

b) 7 ... ♗e6 8 h4 h5 9 ♗e3 ♘h6 10 ♘ec3 ♘d4 11 a4 ♕d7 12 f3!? f6 13 ♕d2 ♘f7 14 0–0 0–0 with equal chances, Steiner – Wittman, Yugoslavia 1981.

5 ... d6
6 0–0 e5
7 f4 *(97)*

97
B

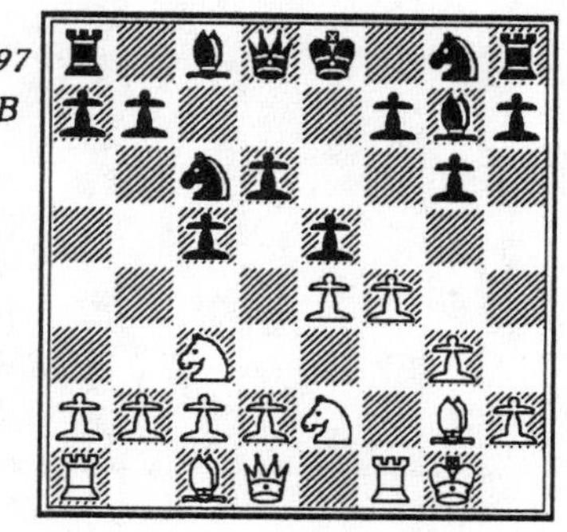

There is still time to pursue a more steady course of action: 7 d3 ♘ge7 8 ♗e3 h5 (8 ... 0–0 9 ♕d2 ♘d4 10 f4 ♗e6 11 ♖ae1 ♕d7 12 ♘c1 ♖ad8! 13 ♘d1 b6 14 c3 ♘dc6 15 c4 exf4 16 ♗xf4 ♘d4= Holmov – Tal, USSR 1964) 9 h3 ♗e6 10 ♘d5 ♕d7 11 h4 ♗xd5 12 exd5 ♘d4 13 c3 ♘df5 14 ♗g5 0–0 15 a4 ♕c7 16 a5 b5 17 axb6 axb6 18 ♕b3 b5 19 ♖xa8 ♖xa8 20 ♕xb5 ♖b8 21 ♕a4 ♖xb2 22 ♕e8+ ♗f8 23 ♖a1 ♕c8 24 ♕xc8 ♘xc8 25 ♔f1 ♘b6 26 c4 ♗e7 27 ♗e4 ♗xg5 ½–½ Kharitonov – Psakhis, Moscow 1989.

7 ... ♘ge7
8 d3 ♗e6
9 ♗e3

In some ways the position is similar to games such as Spassky – Gufeld (chapter two), in which White has a knight on f3, Black a pawn on e6, and a similar strategy is often followed. However, these small changes make a significant difference in practical play. With the pawn on e5 the black dark-squared bishop is impeded, although this might only be for a short while as Black can exchange on f4. However White has little hope of forcing through d4 and must concentrate on achieving activity on either wing. Unfortunately, the ruse of retreating the c3-knight to e2 and playing c3, which is common to other lines, is ruled out here, so White makes room for the knight on d1.

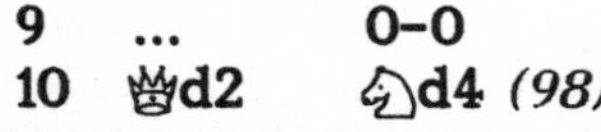

9 ... 0–0
10 ♕d2 ♘d4 *(98)*

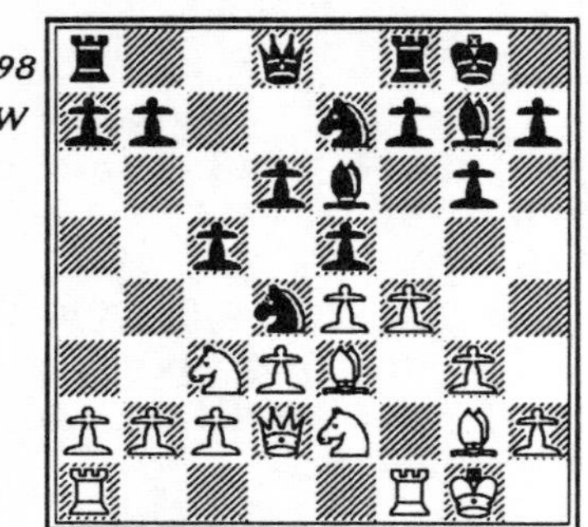

11 ♘d1

This sort of manoeuvre should soon be second nature to an experienced devotee to the opening. The queen's knight makes way for a pawn to shoo the offending piece away. The sooner this manoeuvre is carried out, the better, since it is not clear how White wants to place his pieces after either the capture on e2, or the knight retreat.

11 ... ♕d7
12 c3 ♘xe2+
13 ♕xe2 ♖ac8

Black brings the rook into play, preparing 14 ... d5 as now the loose c-pawn will be defended. Not possible is 13 ... b6? 14 f5 gxf5 15 gxf5 ♗d5 16 f6+-.

14 ♘f2 d5
15 ♗d2 d4

This is an error of judgement because it is in White's interests to close the centre so that his flank operations can proceed. Black should have maintained the tension here rather than try to force matters.

16 c4 b5
17 b3 bxc4
18 bxc4 ♖b8
19 ♖fb1 ♘c6
20 ♕d1!

Karpov realises that flexibility in such positions is the key to a successful strategy. He therefore prepares to transfer his major pieces to the queenside. One ploy is to transfer the queen to a4 followed by doubling rooks, starting with ♖b5.

20 ... a5
21 a3 ♕a7 *(99)*

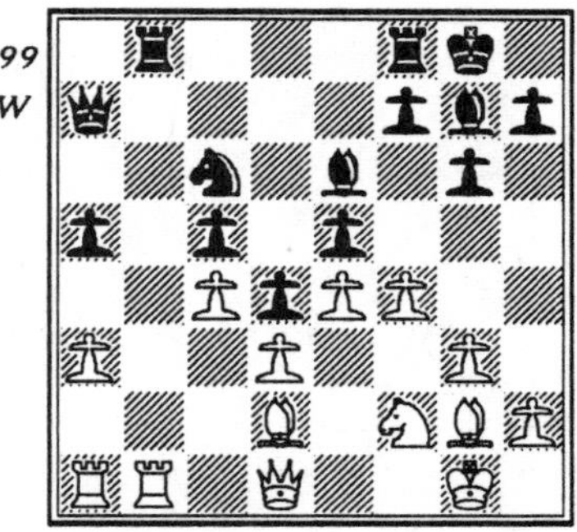

22 f5

A bolt from the blue! All the time during the game, Black has been careful to prevent such an advance, but now White seizes upon a tactical chance to force the pawn to the fifth rank. The cramping effect that is now exerted on the kingside leaves Black under pressure to counter-attack before he is swamped by the white pieces massing behind his powerful pawn shield.

22 ... Bd7

Useless is 22 ... gxf5 23 exf5 Bd7 (23 ... Bxf5?? 24 Bxc6) 24 g4, intending Ne4 with a clear advantage.

23 g4 Ne7
24 h4 a4
25 Qf3

The game flows for Karpov, who is content to transfer his major pieces to the other side of the board, whilst continuing to advance the pawns in search of a possible breakthrough.

25 ... f6
26 Bh3 Rb3
27 Rf1 Qb7

Tsikhelashvili makes a valiant attempt to get back into the game but, faced with overwhelming problems on the kingside, it is really only a matter of time before something cracks.

28 Kh1 h6
29 fxg6 f5

A surprising twist, made possible by the pin exerted on the diagonal by the queen. It is a desperate measure to open up the game and bring his pieces into play, but few players have strong enough nerves for a successful wait and see strategy.

30 gxf5 Bxf5
31 Bxf5 Rxf5
32 Qg2 Rh5

An understandable reaction to the prospect of 33 h5, which must surely win as Ng4 will place the h6-pawn in grave danger.

33 Qg4

It is clear that Black has no good moves as now the rook has run out of squares.

33 ... Nf5

33 ... Rf5 keeps the game going for a little longer, but the result would not be in doubt.

34 Kg1 Rb2
35 exf5 Rxd2
36 Qxh5 e4
37 dxe4 Qc7
38 Qf3 d3
39 Rad1 1-0

8) Systems with ♘f3

An early ♘f3, without the preliminary f4-advance, is generally frowned upon by most experts in the Closed Sicilian. It is not as aggressive as 6 f4, 6 ♗e3 or 6 ♘h3, and lacks the flexibility of 6 ♘ge2. However, if White is careful with his move order he may be able to persuade Black away from adopting his normal kingside fianchetto strategy, in which case ♘f3, which helps White to control d4, does have some advantages.

First we look at a game in which White followed a stereotyped move order allowing Black to adopt a standard set-up, before looking at examples where White tries to force Black's hand early on, and only then switches to the Closed Sicilian.

Smyslov – Kotov
Moscow 1943

1	**e4**	**c5**
2	**♘c3**	**♘c6**
3	**g3**	**g6**
4	**♗g2**	**♗g7**
5	**d3**	**d6**
6	**♘f3**	

A signal that White has no real opening intentions other than the simple, straightforward development of his pieces.

6 ... e6 *(100)*

100
W

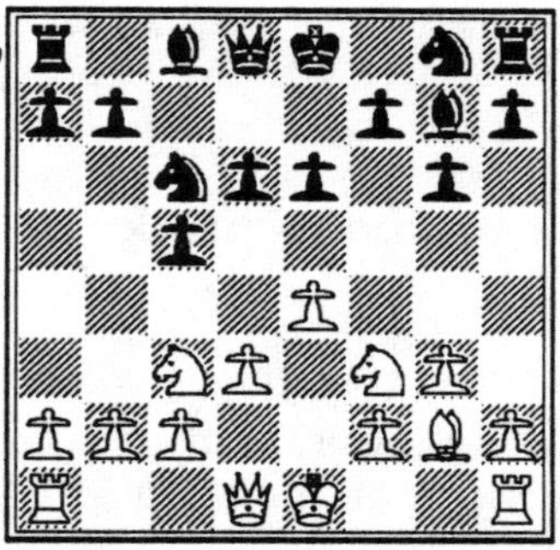

The usual assortment of alternatives are possible:

a) 6 ... e5 7 0–0 ♘ge7 8 ♘h4 (8 a3 h6 9 b4 0–0 10 bxc5 dxc5 11 ♖b1 ♖b8 12 ♗e3 b6 13 ♘d5 ♘xd5 14 exd5 ♘d4 15 c3 ♘xf3+ 16 ♗xf3± Westerinen – Olafsson, Geneva 1977) 8 ... 0–0 9 f4 exf4 10 ♗xf4 ♗e6 11 ♕d2 d5 12 ♗h6 d4 13 ♘e2 ♘e5 14 h3 f6 15 ♗xg7 ♔xg7 16 ♖f2 ♕d6 17

♖af1, Hodgson - Eingorn, Sochi 1986.

b) 6 ... ♘f6 7 0-0 0-0 8 h3 ♖b8 9 a4 a6 10 ♗e3 e5 (10 ... b5 11 axb5 axb5 12 ♕d2 b4 13 ♘e2 ♘d7 14 ♖b1 ♗a6 15 ♗h6 c4 16 ♗xg7 ♔xg7 17 d4 c3 18 bxc3 bxc3 19 ♕e3± Braga - Henley, Mexico 1980) 11 ♕d2 ♘d4 12 ♘e1 b5 13 axb5 axb5 14 ♗g5 ♘e6 15 ♗h4 h6 16 ♗xf6 ♗xf6 17 ♘d5 ♗g7 18 ♕a5 ♗b7 19 ♕xd8 ♖fxd8 20 c3 ♖a8 ½-½ Wahls - De Firmian, Novi Sad Ol 1990.

c) 6 ... ♖b8 (6 ... ♘d4?! 7 ♘xd4!) 7 0-0 b5 8 ♘h4 b4 9 ♘d5 e6 10 ♘e3 ♘ge7 11 a3 a5 12 axb4 axb4 13 f4 f5 14 g4 0-0= Hernandez - Miles, Las Palmas, 1980.

d) 6 ... ♗d7?! 7 0-0 ♕c8 8 a4?! (8 ♘d5!?) 8 ... ♗h3 9 ♗xh3 ♕xh3 10 ♘g5 ♕d7 11 f4 h5 12 f5 ♗d4+ 13 ♔g2 h4 14 ♘d5?! (14 fxg6 fxg6 15 ♘d5 hxg3 16 hxg3±) 14 ... hxg3 15 hxg3 gxf5 16 ♖xf5 ♘h6 17 ♕h5 0-0-0 18 ♖f4 ♗e5 19 ♖xf7 ♘xf7 20 ♕xf7 ♖dg8 21 ♗e3 ♖xg5 22 ♗xg5 ♕h3+ 0-1 Harris - Aston, Hastings 1991.

7 ♗g5!?

Consistent with White's opening strategy. The knight is used in conjunction with the bishop to irritate Black. White then follows the usual ploy of the queen supporting the trading off of the bishops via h6. Despite the fact this largely forgotten game was played decades ago, it is an exemplary example of how to make the most of such positions.

7 ... ♘ge7
8 ♕d2 h6

Kotov has no desire to let White have everything his own way so he pushes back the intruding piece and scuttles any ideas of occupying h6. Black can also try 8 ... ♘d4 9 h4!? h6 10 ♗e3 e5 11 ♘h2 ♗e6 12 f4 h5 13 0-0 exf4 14 ♗xf4 0-0 15 ♘d1 d5 16 c3 ♘dc6 17 ♘f2± Norwood - Hulak, Marseille 1990.

9 ♗e3 e5

Clamping down on any plans for the d4-advance.

10 0-0 ♗e6 *(101)*

101
W

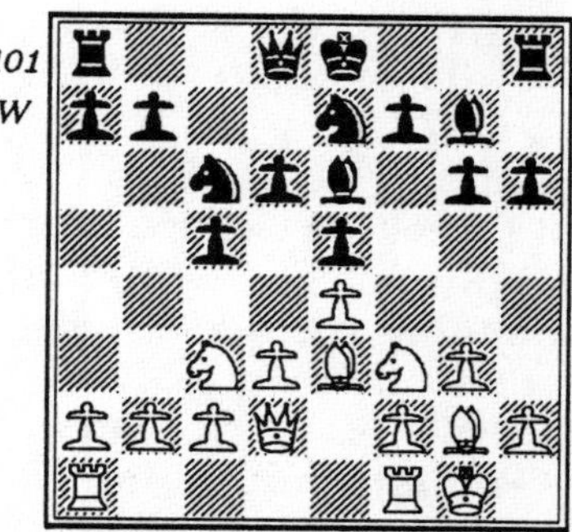

11 ♘e1

At some stage f4 is necessary to unlock the black pawn barrier. Whether this indicates that the early ♘f3 is a waste of a move is not clear, as it has caused

Kotov to compromise his position.

11 ... ♕d7
12 a3

A quiet move that is useful if Black advances on the queenside and discourages Black from castling long as 13 b4 would be a powerful riposte.

12 ... ♗h3
13 f4 ♘d4

Once again in this system the knight takes up its natural central post.

14 ♖b1

This has the merit of adding the plan of b4, opening up the file for the rook, to White's possible options. It also defends b2 from tactics when the black queen's knight moves.

14 ... exf4
15 ♗xf4 ♗xg2
16 ♕xg2 0-0
17 g4

Putting a stop to ... f5 and making space for a knight on g3, whilst also shielding the queen when it attacks h6 from h3.

17 ... ♖ad8

Foolish would be 17 ... f5? 18 gxf5 gxf5 19 ♗xh6, winning.

18 ♔h1 ♘e6
19 ♗d2

The bishop is vital in order to contest the mighty opposing dark-squared bishop, which has a double purpose as a key defensive piece and of exerting control on the important central zone.

19 ... d5
20 ♘f3 d4

The tension is released, which makes it easier for White to concentrate on his kingside activities.

21 ♘e2 ♘c6
22 ♕h3 ♔h7
23 ♘g3

The position has become highly complex, with White seeking to exploit his mounting kingside presence before Black can effectively shut up shop by blocking every avenue that leads to the king.

23 ... f6 *(102)*

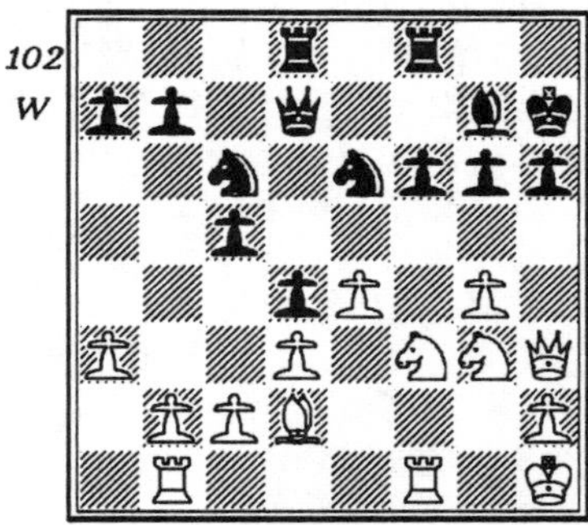

24 ♘f5!

An extraordinary sacrifice which blows a hole in Black's meticulous defence; this move comes from a mixture of calculation and inspiration. The weak point at h6 forces Black to accept the offering, as otherwise his important defensive bishop would be removed.

24 ... gxf5

25 gxf5 ♘c7

A quick breakthrough is achieved after 25 ... ♘g5 26 ♗xg5 fxg5 27 ♘xg5+, intending ♘e6, when the open g-file is occupied by the rook with devastating consequences.

26 ♖g1 ♘e8

Grimly holding on. The tactics flow after 26 ... ♖h8 27 ♗xh6 ♗xh6 (27 ... ♔g8 28 ♖xg7+ ♕xg7 29 ♖g1!+-) 28 ♖g6 ♕g7 29 ♖xg7+ ♔xg7 30 ♕g3+ ♔f7 31 ♕xc7++-.

27 ♖g6 ♖f7

28 ♖bg1

Bringing the other rook into the action, a reflex move in such situations.

28 ... ♔g8

29 ♖xh6 ♔f8

The king embarks upon a desperate trek, seeking sanctuary away from White's mass of forces.

30 ♖h7 ♔e7

31 ♕h5! *(103)*

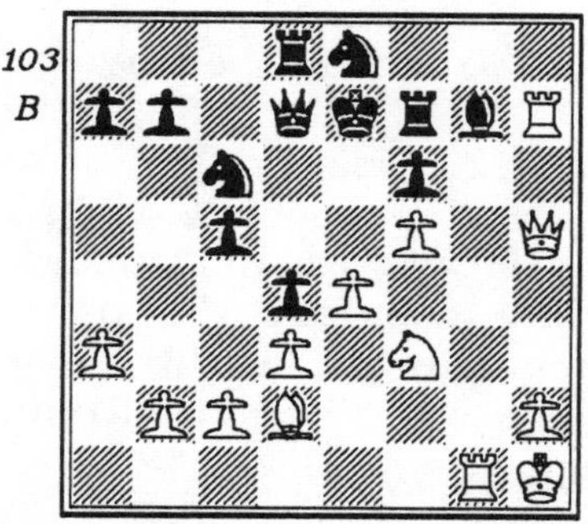

Smyslov displays commendable energy in prosecuting his attack.

31 ... ♔d6

The strength of the rampant attack can be judged from Smyslov's analysis: 31 ... ♖c8 32 ♘g5 fxg5 33 ♗xg5+ ♘f6 34 ♖xg7 ♖xg7 35 ♗xf6+ ♔xf6 36 ♕h6+ ♔e5 37 ♖xg7 ♕e8 38 ♖g6+-; or 33 ... ♔d6 34 ♗f4+ ♔e7 (34 ... ♘e5 35 f6!) 35 f6+ ♘xf6 36 ♖gxg7 ♘xh5 37 ♖xf7+ ♔e6 38 ♖xd7 ♘xf4 39 ♖xb7+-.

32 ♗f4+ ♘e5

33 ♗xe5+ fxe5

34 f6!

The relentless pursuit of the king continues in earnest. Now e5 must fall as the support of the bishop is cut off due to 34 ... ♗xf6 35 ♖xf7.

34 ... ♘xf6

35 ♕xe5+ ♔c6

36 ♖hxg7!

White is enjoying himself! Now it is a matter of time before Black must succumb to the inevitable.

36 ... ♔b5

Hopeless is 36 ... ♖xg7 37 ♕xf6+ ♔b5 38 ♖xg7, winning a piece.

37 ♘xd4+ ♔b6

There is no respite due to 37 ... ♕xd4 38 ♕xd4 cxd4 39 ♖xf7+-.

38 b4 ♖c8

The knight can still not

be removed: 38 ... cxd4 39 ♕c5+ ♔a6 40 ♕a5 mate.

39	♖xf7	♕xf7
40	♕d6+	♖c6
41	♘xc6	♘xe4
42	bxc5+	1-0

Timman - Polugaevesky
Amsterdam 1981

1	e4	c5
2	♘c3	♘c6
3	♘f3	e6
4	g3	♘f6
5	♗g2	d6
6	0-0	♗e7

Black passes up the chance of a kingside fianchetto since White's clever move order allows him to meet 6 ... g6 with 7 d4, exposing the weakness of the d6-pawn.

7 d3

The Scheveningen system of the Open Sicilian is reached after 7 d4 cxd4 8 ♘xd4.

7 ... 0-0
8 ♗f4 *(104)*

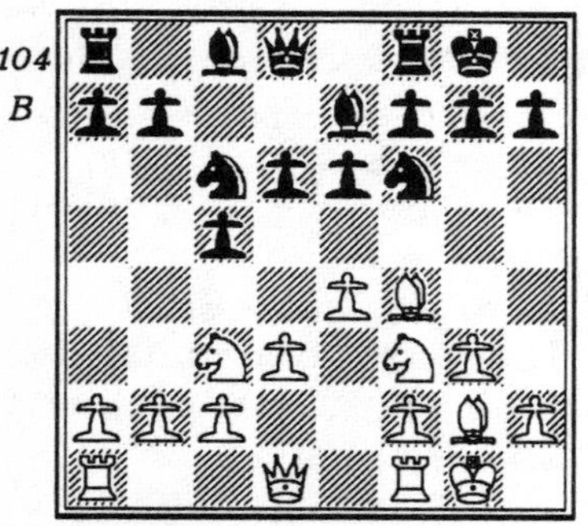

With the bishop on e7, White must choose an alternative scheme from the normal method of approach, which involves the exchange of Black's dark-squared bishop. For the time being he simply uses his territorial advantage to develop his pieces on active squares.

8 ... ♗d7

There is nothing to be gained from 8 ... e5, which merely encourages the usual thrust on the f-file after 9 ♗d2 ♘d4 10 ♘e1 ♖c8 11 f4.

9 h3

For the moment it would be rather pointless to force matters with 9 e5 dxe5 10 ♘xe5 ♖c8, which only leads to an equal position.

9 ... ♘d4
10 ♘xd4

As soon as Black seeks any kind of activity it is pounced upon. Although the doubled d-pawns are not a serious weakness, they lack the usual support of a bishop on g7.

10	...	cxd4
11	♘e2	e5
12	♗d2	♖c8

Krnic suggests 12 ... ♗a4 13 b3 ♗c6, when although White has lost the pawn support of c3, he still has a small but distinct advantage.

13 c3 dxc3

14 ♗xc3 *(105)*

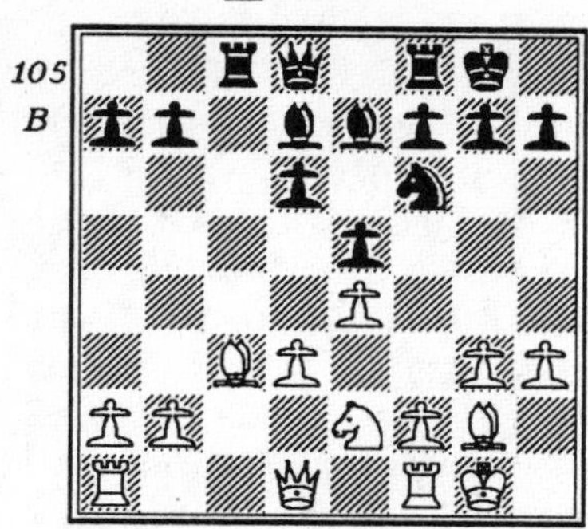

The bishop has received a new lease of life by operating on another diagonal, with the idea of undermining e5 with f4. Timman knows that once he gets going on the kingside the cramped nature of the black pieces will become more relevant.

14 ... ♗c6
15 f4 ♕b6+

There is no improvement over the text after 15 ... exf4 (15 ... ♘d7 16 d4!?; 16 ♕d2) 16 gxf4, when the bishop on c3 is even stronger now that the diagonal has been opened and White plans to place a rook on the g-file.

16 ♔h2 ♘d7
17 ♕d2 ♗f6
18 g4!

The strongpoint at e5 needs to be undermined if White is to make rapid progress. Black lacks any real counterplay in this position.

18 ... ♘c5
19 g5 ♗e7

More prudent is 19 ... ♗d8, but Polugaevsky was banking on White continuing with 20 f5 when he could mount a blockade with ... f6 or ... g6.

20 ♘g3 ♕d8
21 h4 exf4 *(106)*

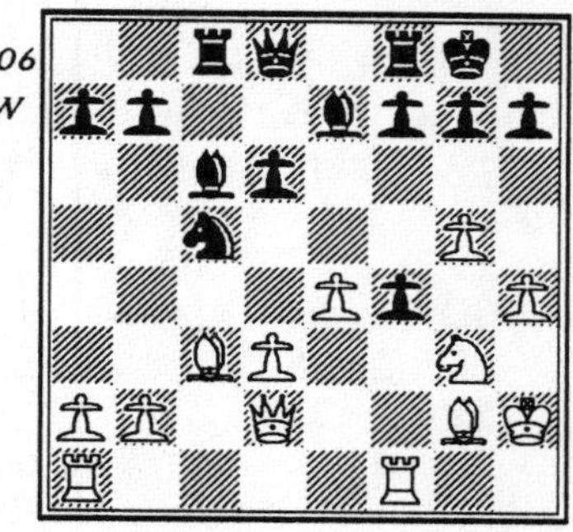

22 ♘f5!

Spurning the natural capture to strike deep into the black position with a direct attack on g7, this is the culmination of White's play.

22 ... f6

Matters are not helped by 22 ... ♘e6 23 d4!, when the threat of d5 forces resignation.

23 ♘xe7+ ♕xe7
24 gxf6 ♖xf6

The decision to mix things with this exchange sacrifice is forced as 24 ... gxf6 25 ♕xf4 is horrendous for Black.

25 ♗xf6 ♕xf6
26 ♖xf4 ♕d4

27 ♖d1

A necessary precaution to safeguard the d3-pawn.

27 ... ♘e6
28 ♖f5 g6
29 ♖f2

White keeps open the possibility of doubling the rooks. However, Black's crisis would be untenable if Timman had found 29 ♖ff1!, when the idea is 30 ♕f2, forcing an ending and effectively wrapping up the game.

29 ... d5
30 exd5 ♗xd5
31 ♗xd5 ♕xd5
32 ♕e3 ♘g7
33 d4 ♘f5

Black is tenaciously holding on in a vain battle to save the game. With so many open lines the pair of rooks are free to roam, although they are curtailed to a certain extent by the need to protect the isolated pawns on d4 and h4.

34 ♕e5 ♕d7
35 ♕f4 ♖e8
36 ♖c1 ♖e7
37 ♖c5 ♖f7
38 ♕e5

The squeeze is beginning to take effect. Even so, Polugaevsky demonstrates commendable fighting spirit by carrying on for so long: 38 ... ♕d8 39 ♖f4 b6 40 ♖c6 ♖d7 41 ♕e6+ ♔g7 42 ♕e5+ ♔g8 43 ♖g4 ♘g7 (43 ... ♖xd4 44 ♕xf5 ♖d2+ 45 ♔g3 ♖d3+ 46 ♔f2 ♖d2+ 47 ♔e3; 43 ... ♘xd4 44 ♖cxg6+ hxg6 45 ♖xg6+ ♔f8 46 ♕h8+ – Krnic) 44 ♖e4 ♘f5 45 ♖e6 ♔f7 46 ♖f6+ ♕xf6 47 ♕e8+ ♔g7 48 ♕xd7+ ♔h6 49 ♕e6 ♕d8 (49 ... ♕xe6 50 ♖xe6 ♘xd4 51 ♖e7 wins) 50 d5 ♕c7+ 51 ♕e5 ♕c2+ 52 ♖e2 ♕c4 53 ♕e4 ♕c7+ 54 ♔g1 ♕c1+ (54 ... ♕g3+ 55 ♕g2 ♕c7 [55 ... ♕d6 56 h5] 56 ♕g5+ ♔g7 57 h5) 55 ♔g2 ♕d1 56 ♖f2 ♔g7 57 ♕e5+ ♔g8 58 ♔h2 ♕d3 59 d6 1–0

Tal – Vogt
Riga 1981

1 e4 c5
2 ♘f3 e6
3 ♘c3 d6
4 g3 ♘c6
5 ♗g2 ♘f6
6 0–0 ♗d7
7 d3 ♗e7
8 ♗f4 0–0
9 h3 ♖c8

Up to this point the game has followed Timman – Polugaevsky (by transposition), but now Vogt introduces his prepared movement to stonewall White. Black is prepared to soak up the pressure and then break out of the restraints to take advantage of the overstretched white pawns.

10 g4

Tal is not ruffled by his opponent's passive attitude and gets on with the business of seizing more space.

10 ... ♕c7

With the idea of installing a knight on e5.

11 ♘d2 *(107)*

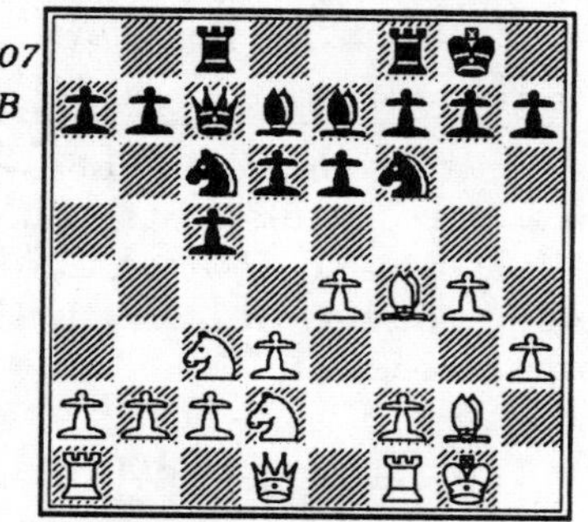

107 B

White embarks on an elaborate plan of forcing through f4 by moving the obstructing pieces. He happily flouts the principle of not moving the same piece twice in the opening because Black has posted his pieces in such a tame fashion that the loss of time is not significant.

11 ... ♘d4
12 ♗e3 e5

There is no way Vogt will allow White to have it all his own way. The text makes sure that the proposed wave of pawns can be broken up by ... exf4, when the e5-square would become available for occupation by Black.

13 g5

A change of tack is required, so the knight is pushed back to allow a fork on d5. Nothing can be gained from 13 f4 exf4 14 ♗xf4 ♗e6∓.

13 ... ♘e8
14 ♘d5

More precise than 14 f4 exf4 15 ♘d5 fxe3! 16 ♘xc7 e2 17 ♕e1 exf1(♕)+ 18 ♕xf1 ♘xc7, when the conclusion must be that it is Black who is on top.

14 ... ♕d8
15 f4

The time is now right for the long-prepared advance.

15 ... exf4
16 ♘xe7+ ♕xe7
17 ♗xf4 *(108)*

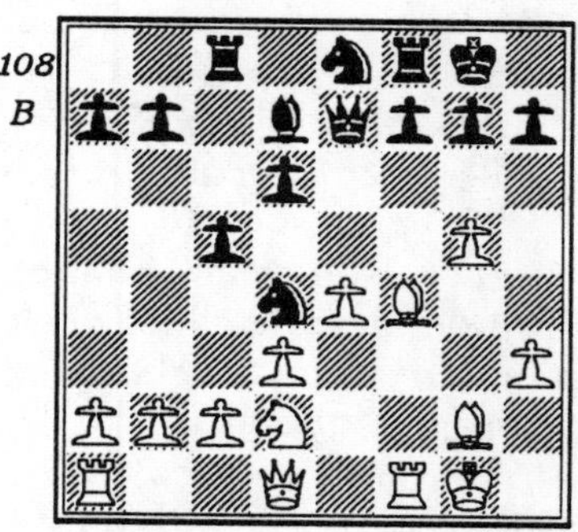

108 B

The position is roughly equal. White has managed to prise open the f-file and has the greater freedom of movement. Against this must be set the relatively weak pawn on g5 which will need to be looked after. If it is supported by the h4-advance, then ... f6 is flicked in, wrecking White's pawn structure.

17 ... ♘e6

Equality is reached after 17 ... f6 18 ♕h5 fxg5 19 ♗xg5 ♘f6.

18 ♕h5!? b5

Starting operations on the other flank, confident that f7 is well protected.

19 ♗e3 c4
20 dxc4

Less accurate is 20 d4 c3!, which is awkward to deal with.

20 ... bxc4
21 c3 ♗c6
22 ♖f2

Acceptance of the pawn offer would leave White in a mess: 22 ♘xc4 g6! 23 ♕g4 ♗b5∓.

22 ... ♕b7
23 b3 cxb3
24 axb3 a6
25 b4 g6

Vogt misses his chance to compensate for his weak a-pawn by 24 ... ♕b5, activating the queen

26 ♕e2

Once Tal is given a chance there is no respite. Now the vulnerable part of Black's position comes under fire and there is no reasonable resource available.

26 ... ♕b5
27 ♕xb5 axb5
28 ♖a7 *(109)*

A rook on the seventh is

109
B

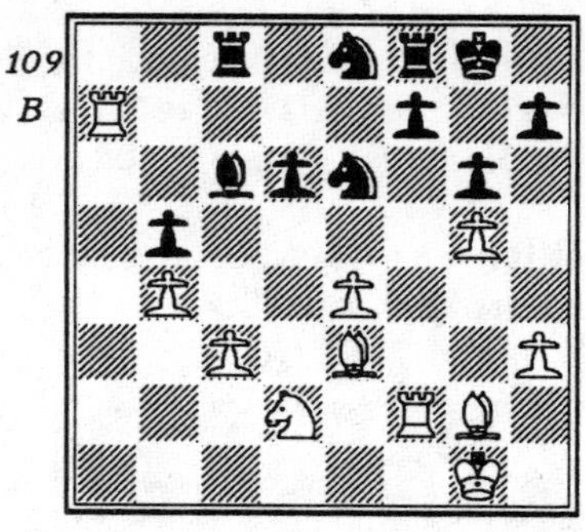

always an ominous presence as it disrupts co-ordination and, if it can get behind the pawns, they will soon be lost.

28 ... ♖c7
29 ♖xc7 ♘8xc7
30 ♘b3 ♖e8?!

Countering against e4 is the wrong approach since the fate of the d6-pawn will cause Black too many problems. More resolute is 30 ... d5 31 e5 d4! 32 ♘xd4 ♘xd4 33 ♗xd4 ♗xg2, intending ♘d5± (Tal).

31 ♖d2! ♘g7
32 ♗b6

This is the move that Black had missed. Now his assessment must be revised in line with the changing situation. It is now apparent that the real worry is the black queen's knight's complete lack of mobility. White only had a small advantage after the hasty 32 ♖xd6 ♗xe4 33 ♗xe4 ♖xe4 34 ♗d4.

32 ... ♘a8

33 ♖xd6 ♗xe4
34 ♗xe4 ♖xe4
35 ♗d8!

The knight is firmly stuck in the corner, effectively making White a piece up.

35 ... ♘e6
36 ♘c5

White is happy to exchange his other pieces so that the significance of the errant knight becomes more apparent.

36 ... ♖e3
37 ♘xe6 ♖xe6

Hopeless is 37 ... fxe6 38 ♗f6 ♖e1+ 39 ♔f2 ♖a1 40 ♖d7 threatening a murderous check on g7.

38 ♖xe6 fxe6
39 ♔f2 ♔f7
40 ♔e3

The ending is an easy win for White, since the king cannot be stopped from forcing a passed pawn on the queenside, which can then be used to divert the opposing king and gain entry on the other wing.

40 ... ♔e8
41 ♗a5 ♔d7
42 ♔d4 ♔d6
1–0

Kupreichik – Suba
Medina del Campo 1980

1 e4 c5
2 ♘f3 d6
3 ♘c3 e6
4 g3 ♘f6
5 ♗g2 ♗e7
6 0–0 0–0
7 h3 ♘c6
8 d3 a6?! *(110)*

110
W

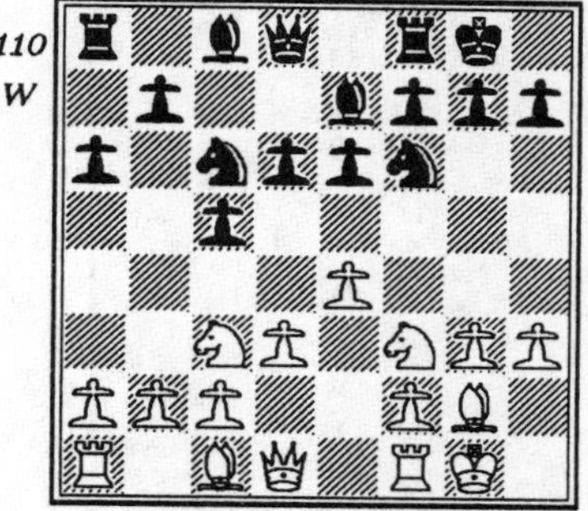

A common mistake. Since White has no intention of playing 9 a4 this is just a waste of time. Much more precise is 8 ... ♖b8, removing the rook from the h1–a8 diagonal and supporting the b-pawn.

9 ♘h2

Paving the way for the normal f4-advance, gaining space. This is the first instalment in White's overall attacking plan.

9 ... ♗d7

A necessary precaution in view of 9 ... b5 10 e5!, when the discovered attack wins material.

10 f4 b5
11 g4

In conjunction with f4 this is a familiar theme, particularly when Black has developed the knight at f6, as the blockade with ...

f5 costs Black too much time.

11 ... b4
12 ♘e2 e5
13 ♘f3 *(111)*

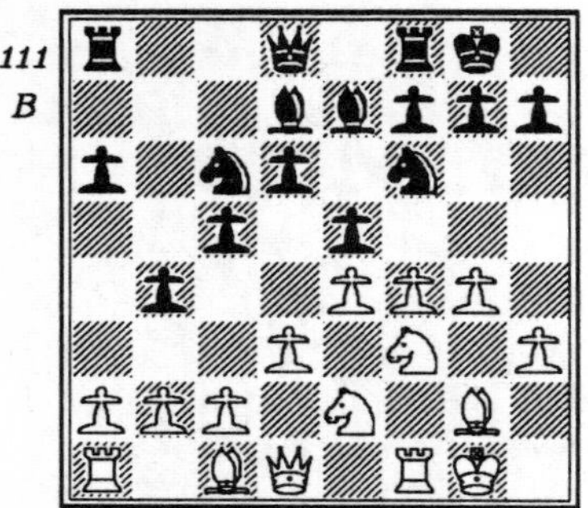

White is content to centralise his pieces before embarking on any ambitious pawn storms. This quiet approach has real merits because in the meantime Black is struggling to find something active to do, and will inevitably be drawn into moving more pieces over to the queenside. After 13 f5 White has a distinct edge, but the question is whether there is time for a knockout against the blockade based upon 13 ... h6, ... ♘h7 and ... f6.

13 ... exf4
14 ♗xf4 ♘e8
15 c3!

White seeks to control the centre and especially the vital d4-square where the black knight is heading, once support from the bishop on f6 is guaranteed. White has now achieved two major objectives, the opening up of the kingside and a clear control of the central zone.

15 ... bxc3
16 bxc3 ♖c8

This deters 17 d4, since 17 ... cxd4 18 cxd4 ♘b4! is irritating.

17 ♔h1 ♗e6

At the moment Black feels no need for caution and persists in trying to get his pieces onto more active squares. The right way to proceed is 17 ... ♗f6, intending to fianchetto.

18 ♗h2 ♕a5
19 ♕d2

Now the knight is released from the duty of defending c3. The queen now not only acts as a guard but it can also swing towards the kingside. This move also co-ordinates the rooks.

19 ... ♘c7
20 ♘g3

A classic confrontation has developed with White shifting the majority to his forces to the kingside while Black concentrates on the other wing. However, White has few weaknesses for his opponent to attack, whilst Black has barely sufficient pieces to fend off an attack against the king.

20 ... ♗f6

21 e5!

The breakthrough. Now Kurpreichik can mobilise with alarming speed, curtailing any faint hopes Black may have of regrouping.

21 ... dxe5

The root of the problem is the danger of allowing the king's pawn barrier to be broken open: 21 ... ♘xe5 22 ♘h5 ♘xf3 (22 ... ♗e7 23 ♘xe5 dxe5 24 ♗xe5 transposes to the text) 23 ♘xf6+ gxf6 24 ♖xf3 with a fine game; or 21 ... ♗xe5 22 ♘xe5 ♘xe5 23 ♘e4 ♖fd8 24 ♘xd6 ♖xd6 25 ♗xe5, followed by ♕g5, when ... f6 can be taken due to the pin.

22 ♘h5 ♗e7

23 ♘xe5 ♘xe5

24 ♗xe5 f6 *(112)*

112
W

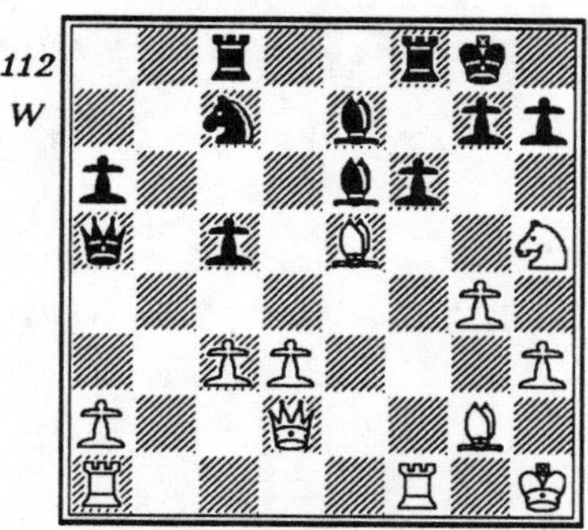

25 ♘xg7

Now the g-pawn bites the dust and suddenly Black is in all sorts of trouble. Snatching the bishop fails after 25 ... fxe5 26 ♘xe6 ♘xe6 27 ♗d5 ♕b6 28 ♕h6, regaining the piece with interest.

25 ... ♔xg7

26 ♕g5+

This is what White had forseen back as far as 21 e5; the pin allows the queen to join the fray with devastating results.

26 ... ♔h8

27 ♖xf6 ♗xf6

28 ♗xf6+ ♖xf6

29 ♕xf6+

Now that all Black's pawn cover has been obliterated it is just a question of involving the other pieces in the attack.

29 ... ♔g8

30 ♕g5+ ♔h8

31 ♕e5+ ♔g8

32 ♖f1

The rook prepares to infiltrate.

32 ... ♕b5

Having spent most of the game acting as a spectator, the queen emerges to try to tackle the onslaught by defending via d7 or even by taking on d3 and moving back to g6.

33 ♕g5+ ♔h8

34 ♕f6+ ♔g8

35 ♖e1

The change in direction of the rook brings the game to its natural conclusion. The point is that now c7 is undefended in critical lines so White can hope to pick off the knight.

35 ... ♗f7

No joy is to be gained from 35 ... ♕d7 36 ♖e5 ♕f7 37 ♖g5+ ♔f8 38 ♕h6+ ♔e8 39 ♖g7+-.

36 ♖e7 ♖f8
37 ♖xc7

The knight leaves the board and the two pawns now assume extra value.

37 ... ♕xd3
38 ♕g5+ ♕g6
39 ♖xc5 ♗xa2
40 ♕xg6+ hxg6
41 ♖c6

Hitting both the a- and g-pawn and ensuring that the ending is an easy win. Now it is just a matter of time.

41 ... ♗f7
42 ♖xa6 ♖d8
43 ♖a8 ♖xa8
44 ♗xa8 g5
45 ♔g2 ♔g7
46 h4 1-0

9) 2 ... e6

In this chapter we discuss a system, similar to the French Defence, in which Black avoids the main lines by an early ... e6 and ... d5. He thereby forgoes his usual kingside fianchetto but reckons on challenging White immediately in the centre. White, however, is happy to continue with his fianchetto, since from g2 the bishop exerts pressure against the d5-pawn.

The immediate 2 ... e6 and 3 ... d5 can be met either by 4 exd5 exd5 5 ♗g2 (Spassky – Kasparov) or by 4 exd5 exd5 5 d4 (Lane – Nunn) with very diferent types of position. Blatny – McCann is a good example of a delayed ... e6 and ... d5.

Spassky – Kasparov
Bugojno 1982

1	**e4**	**c5**
2	**♘c3**	**e6**
3	**g3**	**d5**
4	**exd5**	**exd5**
5	**♗g2**	**♘f6**

The tempting prospect of 5 ... d4 6 ♘ge2 d3 is easily side-stepped by the zwischenzug 6 ♕e2+, when the knight can leap to a central square at e4 or d5.

6 ♘ge2 *(113)*

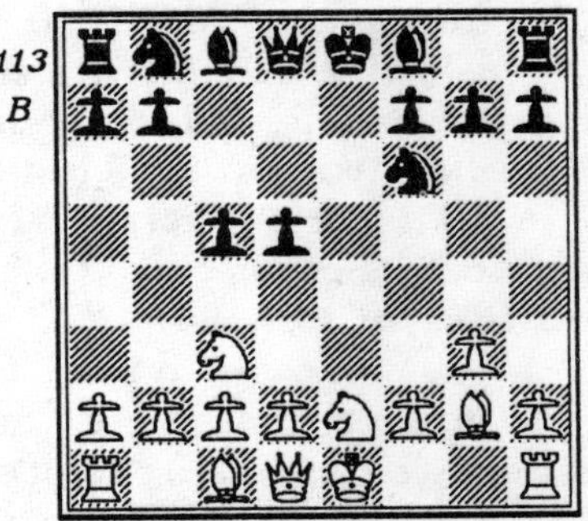

113
B

This is probably the most accurate move, although it can lead to quite drawish positions. There are a couple of alternatives for the more adventurous player:

a) 6 d4?! cxd4 7 ♕xd4 ♘c6 8 ♕d1 d4 9 ♘ce2 ♗c5 10 ♘f3 ♗f5 11 0-0 0-0 12 ♘f4, Suttles – Tal, Hastings 1973/4, and after 12 ... h6 Black may even be slightly better.

b) 6 d3 and now:

b1) 6 ... ♗e7 7 ♘ge2 d4 8

♘e4 0-0 9 0-0 ♘c6 10 ♘f4 ♘e5 11 ♘xf6+ ♗xf6 12 ♘d5 ♗g4 13 f3 ♗e6 14 ♘xf6+ ♕xf6 15 f4 ♘c6 16 ♕h5 ♗f5 17 g4 g6 18 ♕h3 ♗d7 19 f5!, starting an attack and clearing the way for the pair of bishops to dominate the game, Chigorin - Tarrasch, Ostend 1907.

b2) 6 ... d4 7 ♘e4 ♘xe4 8 ♗xe4 ♗d6 9 ♕h5 ♘d7 10 ♗g5 ♗e7 11 ♘f3 h6 12 h4 ♖g8! 13 ♗f4 ♘f6 14 ♕e5 ♘g4 15 ♕d5 ♕xd5 16 ♗xd5 ♘f6 17 ♗c4 ♗e6 18 ♗xe6 fxe6 19 0-0, when White can install the knight on e5 and consider doubling rooks on the e-file with the slightly better chances, Smyslov - Trifunovic, Moscow 1947.

6 ... d4

A modern strategy, designed to cancel out White's hopes of gradually building up pressure against an isolated queen's pawn. This is often the point at which players unfamilar with the special features of the position tend to blindly continue development, often with drastic consequences after 6 ... ♘c6 7 d4 and now:

a) 7 ... ♗g4 8 h3 ♗e6 9 0-0 ♕d7 10 ♗g5 0-0-0 11 ♔h2 h5 12 ♘f4 h4 13 ♗xf6 hxg3+ 14 fxg3 gxf6 15 ♘cxd5 f5 16 c3 ♗d6 17 ♕f3 ♖h6 18 ♖ad1 ♖g8 19 dxc5 ♘e5 20 ♕e2 ♘g4+ 21 ♔h1 ♗xc5 22 ♕c4 ♕c6 23 ♘xe6 fxe6 24 ♘e7+ ♗xe7 25 ♗xc6 ♖xh3+ 26 ♔g1 ♘e5 27 ♕xe6+ 1-0 Giddins - Coleman, British Ch 1989.

b) 7 ... cxd4 8 ♘xd4 ♗b4 9 0-0 ♗xc3 10 bxc3 0-0 11 ♖e1 ♗g4 12 ♕d3 ♕d7 13 ♗g5 ♘e4 14 ♗f4 ♘c5 15 ♕b5 ♘xd4 16 ♕xd7 ♗xd7 17 cxd4 ♘e6 18 ♗xd5 ♘xd4 19 ♖e7 ♗c6 20 ♗xc6 bxc6 21 c3 ♘e6 22 ♗e3 a6 23 ♖b1, with a superior ending due to the active rooks, Spassky - Gobet, Switzerland 1987.

c) 7 ... ♗e6 8 0-0 cxd4 9 ♘xd4 ♕b6 10 ♘xe6 fxe6 11 ♖e1 0-0-0 (11 ... ♔f7 12 ♘xd5! ♘xd5 13 ♗xd5 exd5 14 ♕xd5+ winning) 12 ♖xe6 ♗c5 13 ♗f4! ♗xf2+ 14 ♔h1 d4 15 ♖xf6!, and the prospect of ♗h3+ forces a win, Znosko-Borovsky - Bronstein.

7 ♘e4 ♘xe4
8 ♗xe4 ♘d7

The knight is heading for f6, where it can simultaneously control the important square d5 and safeguard the h7-pawn from attack.

9 0-0 ♘f6
10 ♗g2 ♗d6
11 c3! *(114)*

When playing somebody as brilliant as Kasparov it pays to take every chance to put him under pressure, particularly since his opening preparation is extremely deep. It is quite likely that Kasparov was ready to play an innovation if the game had developed along normal lines: 11 d3 0–0 12 ♗f4 ♗g4 13 ♗xd6 ♕xd6 14 h3 ♗d7 15 ♘f4 ♖fe8 16 ♕d2 ♗c6 17 ♖ae1 ♘d7= Spassky – Korchnoi, USSR 1968. Now the tables have been turned and it is Black who must solve an opening problem.

114
B

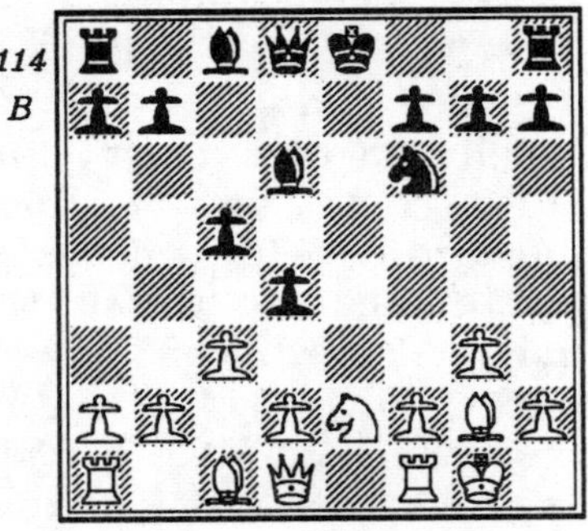

11 ... d3

The tame 11 ... 0–0 12 cxd4 cxd4 13 d3 gives White a small but lasting edge due to the influential white-squared bishop.

12 ♘f4 0–0

Black resists the temptation to capture the knight, which fails to wreck the opposing pawn structure after 12 ... ♗xf4 13 ♕a4+ ♗d7 14 ♖e1+! ♔f8 15 ♕xf4.

13 ♘xd3 ♗xg3
14 fxg3

Sensibly opening the f-file for rook. Obviously bad is 14 ♘xc5? ♗xh2+ 15 ♔xh2 ♘g4+ 15 ♔h1 ♕h4, with a certain win.

14 ... ♕xd3
15 ♕f3 ♕xf3

Black is keen to stop the two bishops from achieving an active presence on the board. This strategy rests on his ability to fix the d-pawn to its original square, not allowing the dark-squared bishop into the game. Thus 15 ... ♖d8 16 ♕xd3 ♖xd3 17 ♖e1 followed by ♗f1, when White can play d3.

16 ♗xf3 ♗h3
17 ♗xb7!

Much more energetic than 17 ♗g2 ♗xg2 18 ♔xg2 ♖ad8, when Black has the better chances.

17 ... ♖ae8

Kasparov is well advised to play for an inititiative, since 17 ... ♗xf1?! 18 ♗xa8 ♗d3 19 ♗f3 ♖e8 20 b3! is good for White.

18 ♗g2

Forced in view of 18 ♖d1 ♗g4 19 ♖f1 ♗e2 20 ♖e1 ♗d3, with no prospects of activating the queenside.

18 ... ♗xg2
19 ♔xg2 ♖e2+
20 ♖f2 ♖fe8
21 b3! *(115)*

Even though Spassky is temporarily a pawn up his dormant pieces give some cause for concern. This makes the text move so important, because it is essential to bring the pieces into play before Black's active forces take complete control of the position. The idea is to develop the queenside at the expense of the other wing. Not so good is 21 d4 cxd4 22 cxd4 ♖e1, with a stranglehold on the position.

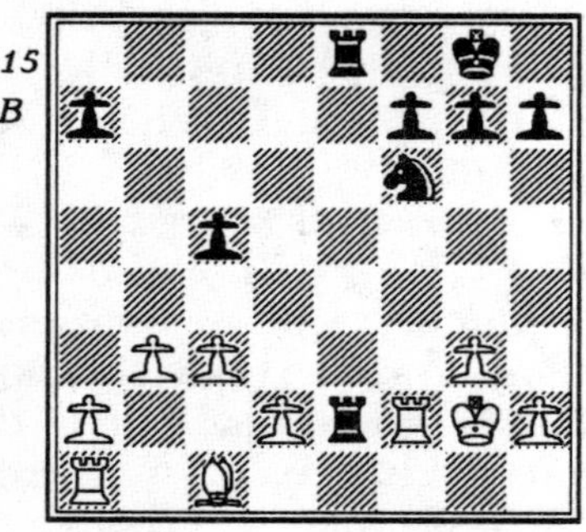
115
B

21 ... ♖xf2+

According to Kasparov, the imagination of White's idea can be measured from the way it handles the direct approach: 21 ... h5 22 ♗a3 ♖xf2+ (22 ... ♘g4 23 ♖xe2 ♖xe2+ 24 ♔f3, intending ♗xc5 and ♗xa7, with an advantage) 23 ♔xf2 ♘e4+ 24 ♔g2 ♘xd2 25 ♗xc5 ♖e2+ 26 ♗f2 ♘e4 27 ♔f3 ♖xf2+ 28 ♔xe4 ♖xh2, and the white king is ideally placed to support the promotion of the pawns.

22 ♔xf2 ♘g4+
23 ♔g2 f5!

More precise than 23 ... ♖e1 24 ♗b2 ♖e2+ 25 ♔f3 ♖xd2 26 ♗a3 ♘xh2+ 27 ♔e4, when suddenly the white pieces are very active and his queenside pawns will prove faster in the race for promotion.

24 h3 ♘e5
25 d4

This is essential since otherwise the knight will take up residence on d3 and severely restrict the mobility of the white bishop.

25 ... cxd4
26 cxd4

Relieved to extract himself from his confined quarters, White misses a subtle idea to utilise the bishop: 26 ♗d2 ♘d3 (26 ... dxc3 27 ♗xc3±) 27 ♔f1! dxc3 28 ♗xc3 ♖e3 29 ♗d4 ♖xg3 30 ♗xa7 ♖xh3, with a complex position in favour of White, from an analysis by Kasparov.

26 ... ♘d3
27 ♗g5

Even at this late stage care must be taken to avoid a trap such as 28 ♗a3 ♘e1+ 29 ♔f2 ♘c2.

27 ... h6
28 ♖d1 hxg5
29 ♖xd3 ♖e2+
30 ♔f3 ♖xa2
31 d5 ♔f7
32 d6 ♔e8
½–½

A clear draw arises after 33 ♖e3+ ♔d7 34 ♖e7+ ♔xd6

35 Rxg7 Rb2 36 Rxg5 Ke6.

Lane - Nunn
Stroud 1980

1	**e4**	**c5**
2	**Nc3**	**e6**
3	**g3**	**d5**
4	**exd5**	

It is possible to deviate at an early stage:

a) 4 d3 and now:

a1) 4 ... Nc6 5 exd5 (5 Bg2!?) 5 ... exd5 6 Bg2 d4 7 Ne4 Nf6 8 Ne2 Nxe4 9 Bxe4 Bd6 10 0–0 Bg4 11 Bg2 Qd7= Hug - Korchnoi, Biel 1986.

a2) 4 ... d4?! 5 Nce2 Nf6 6 Bg2 Nc6 7 f4 e5 8 Nf3 Bd6 and White has a pleasant choice of continuing with 9 c4, curtailing Black's prospects of queenside pressure, or immediately starting a promising attack with 9 f5, N. Lane - Nixon, Paignton 1976.

b) 4 Bg2 Nf6 5 d3 Be7 6 Nge2 dxe4 7 Nxe4 Nxe4 8 Bxe4 0–0 8 0–0 Nd7 10 Bg2 Nf6 11 d4 Qb6 12 c3 cxd4 13 Nxd4 Rd8= Marjanovic - Masic, Subotica 1978.

4	**...**	**exd5**
5	**d4** *(116)*	

This direct method of trying to take advantage of Black's early advance in the centre is quite sound, despite its rare appearances in tournament play. The Closed Sicilian is generally thought of as an opening which postpones the real battle until the middlegame, but it can surely do no harm to have the option of an occasional surprise in the opening. The challenge for the centre puts the opponent under immediate pressure and he must carefully avoid little wrinkles on the way to claiming equality. In short, this line is direct, unusual and tricky.

116
B

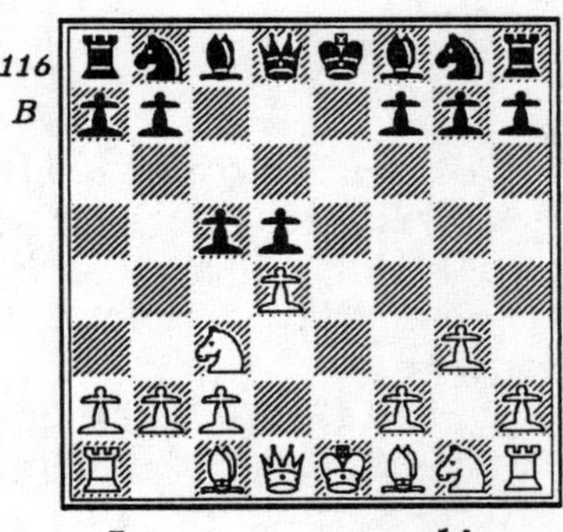

5	**...**	**cxd4**

The text lures the queen out in an effort to gain time by attacking it. The alternatives are less committal but in practice have tended to favour White.

a) 5 ... Be6 6 Nge2 and now:

a1) 6 ... Nc6 7 Bg2 Nf6 8 0–0 Be7 (8 ... Qd7 9 Re1 Be7 10 dxc5 Bxc5 11 Nf4 is close to winning Blackburne - Janowski, Vienna 1898) 9 Bg5 cxd4 10 Nxd4 Nxd4 11

♕xd4 0-0 12 ♖ad1 ♕a5 13 ♕d2 ♖fd8 14 ♗xf6 ♗xf6 15 ♘e4! ♕xa2 16 ♘xf6+ gxf6 17 ♕d4 and White has plenty of play against the shattered kingside, Lane - Franzoni, Lugano 1982.

a2) 6 ... ♘f6 7 ♗g2 c4 8 0-0 ♘c6 (8 ... ♗d6? 9 ♗g5 ♗e7 10 ♗xf6 ♗xf6 11 ♘f4 ♘c6 12 ♘cxd5 ♗xd4 13 ♕e2!, gives White the advantage due to the pressure on e6) 9 ♗g5 ♗e7, and White can continue to undermine d5 with the better chances, according to Schwarz.

b) 5 ... ♘c6 (5 ... ♘f6?! 6 ♗g5 ♗e7 7 dxc5±) 6 dxc5 d4 7 ♘e4 ♗xc5 8 ♘xc5 ♕a5+ 9 ♗d2 ♕xc5 10 ♗g2, and the two bishops are sufficient to give White a slight advantage.

6 ♕xd4 ♘f6

The isolated d-pawn is often a liability in the middlegame: 6 ... ♗e6 7 ♗g2 ♘c6 8 ♕a4 ♗b4 9 ♘ge2 a6 10 0-0 ♘ge7 11 ♘f4 0-0 12 ♘ce2 ♗c5 13 c3 b5 14 ♕d1 ♗b6 15 a4 b4 16 cxb4 ♘xb4 17 b3! ♖c8 18 ♗b2 ♗f5 19 ♘d4 ♗e4 20 ♕g4 ♘g6 21 ♗xe4 dxe4 22 ♘f5 ♖c5 23 ♘h5 f6 24 ♘hxg7 ♕d5 25 ♘e7+! ♘xe7 26 ♘f5+ ♔f7 27 ♕g7+ ♔e6 28 ♕xe7+ ♔xf5 29 ♕xf8+- Lane - Bologan, Cappelle la Grande 1992.

7 ♗g5 ♗e7
8 ♗b5+

The normal continuation is 8 ♗g2 ♘c6 9 ♕a4 with play directed against d5, Spielmann - Mieses, Austria 1910. Following that game, the accepted opinion was that Black could gain time by chasing the white queen around the board. The text move is somewhat surprising since White played g3 to prepare a fianchetto and now changes tack. However, sometimes general rules have to be broken.

8 ... ♘c6
9 ♗xf6 ♗xf6
10 ♕c5! *(117)*

117
B

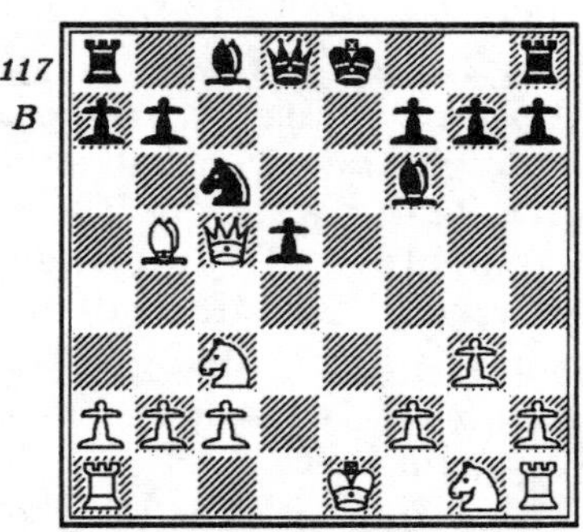

The last few moves have been forced since White has been probing for an opportunity to capture on d5. Now the queen takes up an unusual position, preventing castling, attacking c6, and threatening ♖d1. In fact, Nunn was hoping that I was not aware of the chosen move but I knew very well that we were merely following a line from the ancient Reversed Goring Gambit Declined! I suspect that the vast majority of Sicilian players would hardly welcome such a prospect, yet alone know that the opening existed. It normally arises after the move order: 1 e4 e5 2 Nf3 Nc6 3 d4 exd4 4 c3 d5 5 exd5 Qxd5 6 cxd4 Bg4 7 Be2 Bb4+ 8 Nc3 Bxf3 9 Bxf3 Qc4!, reaching an almost identical position to the one on the board. The only difference is that White has added g3, which probably weakens the kingside slightly but not enough to alter the assessment of the position being roughly equal. Even so, Black still has to overcome a few minor problems before reaching equality.

10 ... Bxc3+

The best practical chance is probably 10 ... Qb6 11 Qxb6 axb6 12 Nge2 0-0 13 a3 Ra5, keeping the pieces on although the doubled b-pawns are a serious long-term problem for Black. A risky venture is 10 ... Be6 11 Bxc6+ bxc6 12 Qxc6+ Kf8 13 Qc5+ Kg8 14 Nge2 Rc8 15 Qxa7 Ra8 16 Qc5 Rc8 17 Qb4 (17 Qa7=) when White should be able to cope with the pressure by giving back one of the pawns and then directing action against d5.

11 bxc3

The weakness of g3 is apparent after 11 Qxc3 0-0 12 Ne2 d4 13 Qd2 Qb6 14 Bxc6 bxc6 and Black's bishop should be able to utilise the a8-h1 diagonal.

11 ... Qe7+

The only move.

12 Qxe7+ Kxe7
13 0-0-0

The plan for White is fairly obvious, involving bringing the rooks to the centre and organising pressure against d5. It is almost certain that in the average game Black will have wasted precious minutes coming to terms with the opening, and would be ill-prepared for the quick transformation into a tricky endgame.

13 ... Be6
14 Ne2 Kd6!?

As the game rapidly heads for a draw, Black decides to steer the play to a more unclear situation where he hopes to take advantage of the resulting confusion. In fact, with so few pieces left on the board, this strategy is flawed; Black should prefer 14 ... Rac8 or 14 ... Rhd8.

15 Rhe1 Kc5

The plan of activating the king is a technique often used in endings, but is hardly likely to be effective when the opposing rooks are lying in wait.

16 c4!

This timely move reveals the pointlessness of the king manoeuvre and pushes the game towards a critical state for Black.

16 ... dxc4
17 Bxc6 bxc6

The last chance to opt out with a draw is forsaken in the quest for the full point. Much more sensible is 17 ... Kxc6 18 Nd4+ Kc7! 19 Nxe6 fxe6 20 Rxe6 Rhe8, which is completely level.

18 Nf4 Bg4
19 Re5+ Kb4

After 19 ... Kb6 20 Rd4, White regains the pawn with active play and threatens Rg5. The text is based on a misguided tactical idea of setting up mating threats by ... c3 or even ... Kc3, hoping that the black rooks will be able to deliver a decisive check.

20 Rd4

Black finds himself in big trouble now, the white rooks prepare to weave a mating net around the wandering king.

20 ... Be6

Nothing can save Black now:

a) 20 ... h5 21 a3+ Kc3 (21 ... Kxa3 22 Rxc4 a5 23 Re3+ Ka2 24 Ra4+ mate) 22 Ree4 Be6 23 Ne2 mate.

b) 20 ... Rad8 21 Nd3+ Kc3 22 Rxg4 cxd3 23 Rc5 mate.

21 a3+! *(118)*

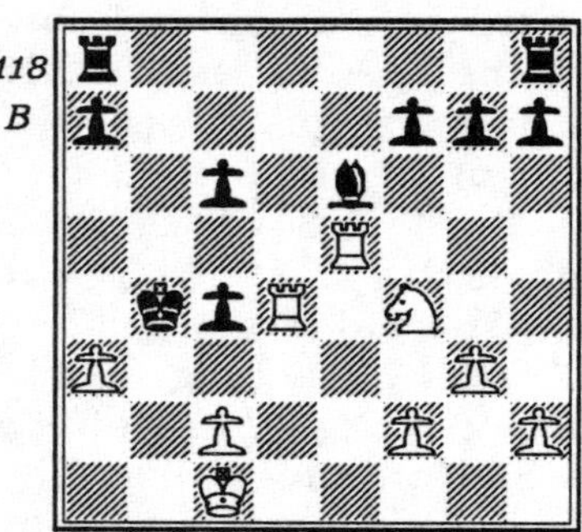

The final piece in the puzzle, forcing mate in every variation.

21 ... Kxa3

No better is 21 ... Kc3 22 Ree4 (intending 23 Ne2+) 22 ... Bg4 24 Rxc4 mate.

22 Nxe6 Kb4

Of course 22 ... fxe6 23 Rxc4 a5 24 Re3+ Ka2 25 Ra4 mate.

23 Rc5 1–0

Blatny – McCann
Adelaide 1988

1 e4 c5
2 Nc3 e6
3 g3 Nc6

This leads to a position when the 'French' formation is deferred in order to facilitate steady development before breaking out with ... d5.

4 Bg2 Nf6

A little-known idea is 4 ... Nge7, whose reputation was seriously tarnished by a typical pawn-storm upon its appearance on the international scene: 5 f4 d5 6 d3 d4 7 Nce2 e5 8 f5 f6 9 g4 Qd6 10 Ng3 Bd7 11 g5 0-0-0 12 gxf6 gxf6 13 Bf3 Kb8 14 Bh5 c4 15 Nf3 cxd3 16 cxd3 Nb4 17 0-0 Rc8 18 Ne1 a5 19 Bf7 and White can start queenside action by gradually pushing the pawns forward, while on the other wing Black has few prospects of a counter-attack, Zagorovsky - Eidlin, USSR 1969.

5 d3 Be7
6 f4 *(119)*

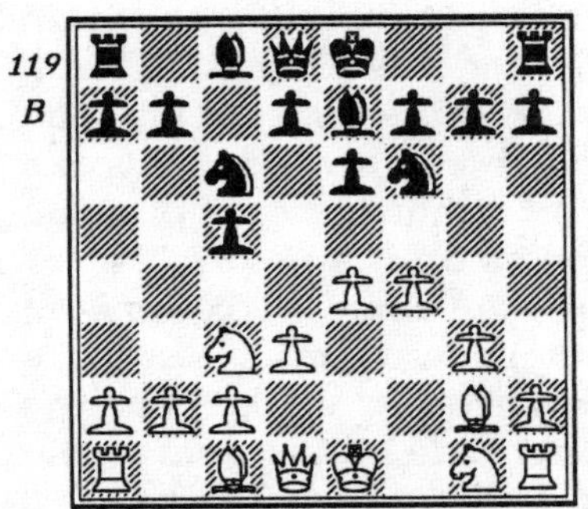

Although other moves have been played, in my view this is the best because it uses a straightforward strategy White should by now be acquainted with. The plan is the usual kingside attack, mobilising the pawns as a battering ram to invade the enemy territory. The main alternative is suitable for those who prefer to be more subtle in their intentions, ie: 6 Nge2 0-0 7 0-0 and now:

a) 7 ... a6?! 8 f4 d5 9 exd5 exd5 10 f5! d4 11 Ne4 Nxe4 12 Bxe4 Bf6 13 Nf4 Be5 14 Qh5 f6 15 Bd5+ Kh8 16 Ng6 mate, Hawthorne - Schofield, Paignton 1980.

b) 7 ... d5 8 h3 (8 exd5 exd5 9 Bg5! d4 10 Bxf6 Bxf6 11 Ne4 Be7 12 Nf4 Bf5 13 Nd5± Schwarz) 8 ... d4 9 Nb1 e5 10 f4 exf4 11 gxf4 Nd7 12 Nd2 f5 13 e5 Nb6 14 Nf3 Be6 15 Kh2 Qd7 16 Rg1 with equal chances, Kasparian - Simagin, 1952.

6 ... d5

Less consistent is the timid 6 ... d6?!, when Black has to suffer a cramped position and can only watch as White builds up momentum: 7 Nf3 0-0 8 0-0 Rb8 9 h3 b5 10 g4 b4 11 Ne2 d5 12 e5 Nd7 13 g5 Re8 14 Ng3 Bf8 15 h4 Ne7 16 h5 gives White a tremendous initiative, Zaitsev - Cebaneko, USSR 1976.

7 Nge2

White only makes Black's task easier if the position is simplified: 7 exd5 exd5 8 Nf3 0-0 9 0-0 Rb8 10 h3 b6= Lane - A. Wade, Paignton 1976.

7 ... d4

The decision to close down the centre is a ploy often used by Sicilian players, who are used to frantic play on either wing. The difference here is that the black king will be the first to come under attack, whilst as a last resort White can happily give up material on the queenside in order to gain time for a mating sequence. Certainly Black has to be careful with his defence.

8 ♘b1 e5
9 0-0 0-0
10 f5

The stage is now set for Blatny to pursue a typical simple and strong attack that Closed Sicilian devotees relish. Now White's advanced pawns guarantee him a spatial advantage and he is without structural weaknesses. His operation will be concentrated on the kingside with the major pieces huddled behind the pawn shield. In contrast, McCann must strive to create enough problems on the queenside to district White's forces and blunt his flank initiative.

10 ... b5?!

More normal is 10 ... ♖b8 followed by ... b5 and ... a5, and then only when the a-file is open will the rook return to a8. The text tries to gain a tempo on this line by inserting ... ♗b7 so that tha a-file can be challenged as soon as possible.

11 a4! *(120)*

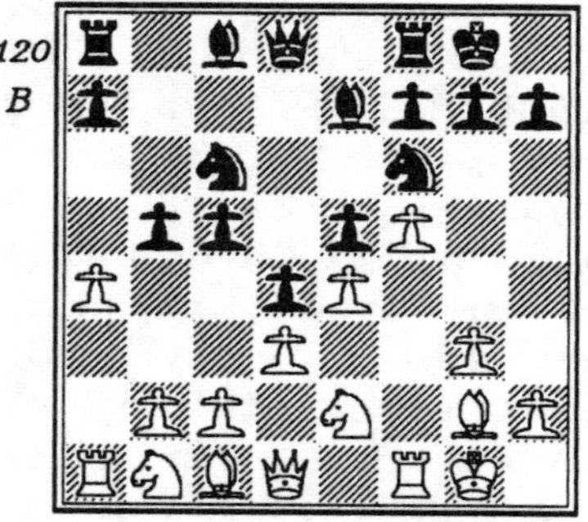

The problem with Black's short-cut now becomes clear. Ideally, Black would like to support the b5-pawn but after 12 ... a6 the white pawn simply takes on b5, and the hanging rook on a8 makes recapture impossible. In one stroke White manages to put the brakes on Black's ambitions for queenside expansion, and gains time to start a steamroller effect on the other side of the board.

11 .... bxa4

Not much better is 11 ... b4 12 b3!, which gives all the winning chances to White.

12 ♖xa4 ♘d7
13 h4

A precautionary measure to avoid the exchange of bishops on g5 and the bizarre possibility of 13 g4 g5!?, with hopes of establishing a blockade on the kingside.

13 ... ♘b6
14 ♖a1 c4
15 ♘d2

White can steadily get on with the job of shifting the pieces to their optimum squares in the full knowledge that his opponent can do little to stop him.

15 ... cxd3
16 cxd3 a5
17 ♘f3 ♘d7

It really is a matter of wait and see as far Black is concerned.

18 g4 h5

At least this gives Blatny something to think about although it weakens the king's protective pawn barrier. Catastrophic would be 18 .. ♗xh4 19 g5, winning the bishop. If White captured on h5 now then Black could take on h4, although even then White would remain the favourite to win.

19 g5 g6
20 ♘g3 *(121)*

This game provides us with a model example of how to handle kingside attacks when the centre is closed. White first ensures that the knights are in their desired place before taking any further action. Now there is also a real chance of the queen entering the fray with a knight sacrifice on h5 in some lines, making defensive organisation even more difficult for Black.

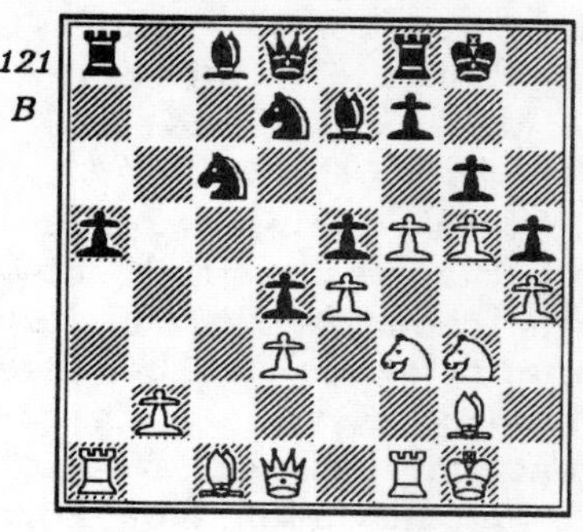

121
B

20 ... ♘b4
21 ♘e1 ♔g7
22 ♗f3!

A less experienced player might be tempted by the chance to pick up a piece: 22 f6+ ♘xf6 23 gxf6 ♗xf6, followed by ♗xh4, gives Black three pawns for a piece. True, White would have a technical win as the pawns would only come into their own in the ending but, more importantly, his attack would be halted. This, in itself, would be a psychological relief for Black, who can hardly make any constructive move at the moment. The text move is much better, continuing to turn the screw with no relief in sight.

22 ... ♖a6
23 ♗d2 ♖h8
24 ♕b3

With the kingside effectively paralysed by White's forces, the time is right to calmly exploit the weaknesses on the other wing. The threat is 25 fxg6 fxg6 26 ♗xh5! gxh5 27 ♕f7 mate.

24 ... a4
25 f6+!

White's timing is perfect and Black's position now falls apart. The bishop cannot take on f6 because b4 is loose, and a king retreat only allows 26 fxe7 hitting the queen. Not more than a second glance is needed to dismiss 25 ♖xa4? ♘c5!.

25 ... ♘xf6
26 gxf6+ ♖xf6
27 ♖xa4

Blatny is now a piece up and the game is effectivly over. It only remains for him to keep a grip on the game to force a prompt resignation.

27 ... ♘a6
28 ♕c4 ♘c5
29 ♖a7 ♖c6
30 ♕d5 ♖e6
31 ♗g2 ♗b7?
32 ♖xb7 ♘xb7
33 ♕xb7 ♖b6
34 ♕a7 ♖xb2
35 ♘f3 1-0

10) 2 g3

White can also play the Closed Sicilian without 2 ♘c3 although this allows Black to steer the game away from the traditional paths. On the positive side it disguises White's true intentions, making it more difficult for the opposition to decide which formation to adopt since it is not clear which direction White will eventually take. In general, 2 g3 is for those players who like to introduce an element of bluff to their opening repertoire and are happy to allow Black to counter with 2 ... d5.

Short - Hjartarson
Solingen - Reykjavik 1990

1	**e4**	**c5**
2	**g3**	**d5**

Recommended by Euwe and the logical choice to contest the centre. A more cautious approach might be 2 ... g6 3 ♗g2 ♗g7 4 f4 ♘c6 5 ♘f3 d6 6 d3 e6 and at any time ♘c3 can be played to transpose back into familiar territory. At this point, Black will be acutely aware of the possibility of White entering into a King's Indian Attack-type position, which is outside the scope of this book. A sample line indicates the sort of position to be expected: 7 c3 ♘ge7 8 0-0 d5 9 e5! b6 10 ♘a3 a6 11 ♗e3± Chandler - Celabo, Vrsac 1981.

3 exd5

Not so good is 3 ♗g2 dxe4 4 ♘c3 (4 ♗xe4 ♘f6 5 ♗g2 ♗g4 6 ♘e2 ♘c6∓) 4 ... f5 5 f3 exf3 6 ♘xf3 ♘c6 7 0-0 e5 8 d3 ♗e7 9 ♕e2 (Spielmann - Bogoljubov, Silac 1932), and now 9 ... ♗f6 leaves White with precious little compensation for the pawn.

3	**...**	**♕xd5**
4	**♘f3**	**♗g4**
5	**♗g2** *(122)*	

It is rather foolish to abandon the fianchetto plan: 5 ♗e2?! ♘c6 6 h3 ♗d7 7 ♘c3 ♕e6 8 d3 ♘d4 9 ♘xd4 cxd4∓ Novopasin - Saharov, USSR 1968.

122
B

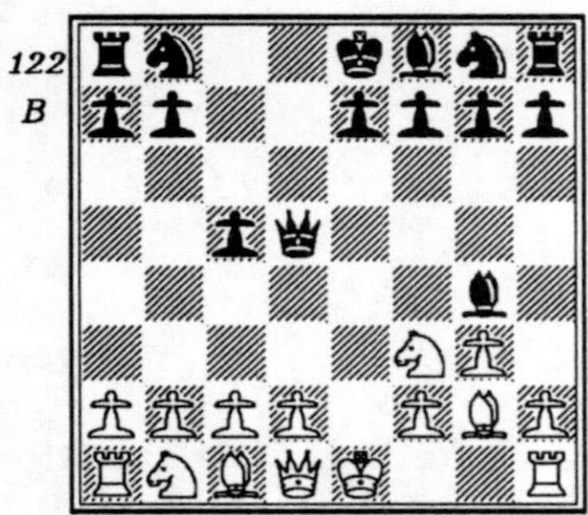

5 ... ♕e6+

The best place to register the check to avoid later harassment. A less forcing continuation allows White to consolidate: 5 ... ♘c6 (5 ... ♕e4+ 6 ♔f1 ♘c6 7 ♘c3±) 6 h3 ♗h5 (6 ... ♗f5 7 0–0 ♕d7 8 ♔h2 0–0–0 9 d3 e5 10 ♘c3 f6 11 ♗e3 ♘d4 12 a3! ♔b8 13 ♘d2±) 7 0–0 ♕d7 8 d3 e6 9 ♘bd2 0–0–0 10 a3 f6 11 b4, swiftly opening lines against the king to White's advantage, Taimanov – Korchnoi, USSR Ch 1965.

6 ♔f1 ♘c6

The natural move to bring another piece into play. It is also possible to exchange bishops by 6 ... ♗h3, but White might gain an initiative by rapid development, when the queen on e6 just gets in the way:

a) 7 d4 cxd4 8 ♘xd4 ♕d7 9 ♘c3 ♘c6 10 ♘xc6 ♕xc6 11 ♕d5 ♕xd5 12 ♘xd5 ♗xg2+ 13 ♔xg2 0–0–0 ½–½ Lane – Dunnington, Dudelange 1991.

b) 7 ♘c3!? ♘c6 8 d3 ♘f6?! 9 ♗e3 b6! 10 ♘g5 ♗xg2+ 11 ♔xg2 ♕d7 12 ♕f3 e6 13 d4! taking advantage of the pin on the diagonal and giving White the edge, Trifunovic – Bolbochan, Mar del Plata 1952.

c) 7 b4!? cxb4 8 a3 b3 9 ♘c3 ♘f6 10 ♖b1 g6 11 ♖xb3± Korolev – Rusakov, corr 1978.

7 h3

Also possible is the less forcing 7 d3 ♕d7 8 h3 ♗f5 9 ♘c3 e5!? 10 ♗e3 ♖d8 11 g4 ♗g6 12 ♘h4 b6 13 ♕e2 ♗d6 14 ♘xg6 hxg6 15 h4 ♘ge7= Trifunovic – Petrosian, Belgrade 1956.

7 ... ♗h5
8 ♘c3

A better try for the advantage than the harmless series of exchanges which featured in the game Suetin – Sveshnikov, Dulna 1979, which went: 8 d3 ♕d7 9 g4 ♗g6 10 ♘h4 e6 11 ♘xg6 hxg6 12 ♘c3 ♘f6 13 ♗e3 ♗e7 14 ♘e4 b6 15 ♘xf6+ ♗xf6 with equality.

8 ... ♘f6
9 d3

In the game Gurgenidze – Bykov, USSR 1960, White managed to extract an edge from a knight manoeuvre with 9 ♘e2 ♕d7 10 ♘f4 ♗g6 11 d3 e5?! (11 ... e6=) 12 ♕e2 ♗d6 13 ♘xg6 hxg6 14 c4 0–0–0 15 ♘g5±.

9 ... ♕d7
10 a4 *(123)*

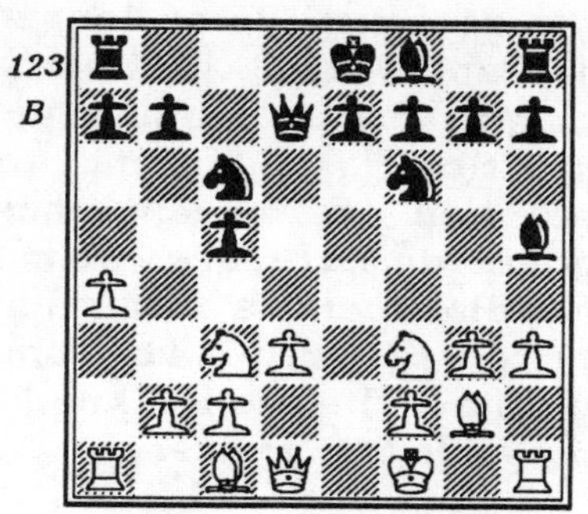

Short is not prepared to see what improvement Black has prepared on the standard game in this line, and takes the opportunity to deviate. Previous play had continued 10 g4 ♗g6 11 ♗f4 e6 12 g5! ♘g8 13 ♕e1 ♘ge7 14 h4 ♗h5 15 ♘e5 ♘xe5 16 ♗xe5 ♘c6 17 a4, and White had the better chances, Speelman - Sunye, Graz 1981.

10 ... e6
11 a5 ♖c8

An interesting alternative is 11 ... ♖d8 intending ... c4 to use the pin, but it is easily rebuffed by 12 ♗e3, when the queen is protected (12 ... c4 12 dxc4).

12 g4 ♗g6
13 ♘h4 ♗e7

A novel idea, suggested by Hjartarson, is 13 ...♗d6!? to activate the bishop via e5, although White would still maintain a slight plus.

14 ♘xg6 hxg6
15 h4 0-0

Whilst the king is on f1 Black can see no reason to fear the advance of the pawns, bravely believing that it will be difficult for White to muster sufficient forces to create serious threats. Less ambitious is 15 ... ♘d5 16 ♘xd5 exd5 17 g5 ♘d4 18 c3 ♘e6, when Black will have difficulty in organising counterplay as his pieces are cramped.

16 h5 *(124)*

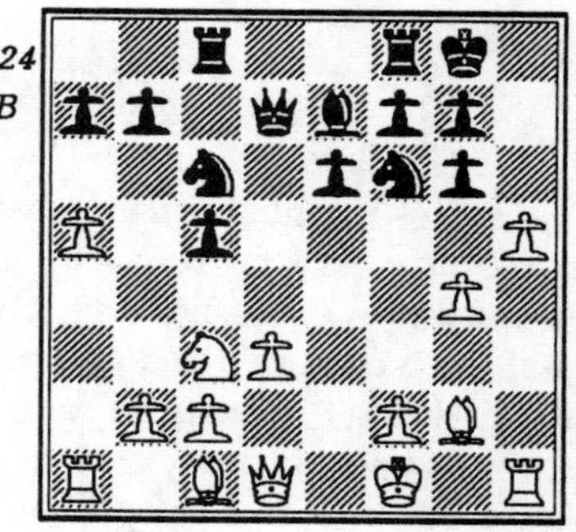

16 ... gxh5?!

In expectation of the automatic reply 17 gxh5, when a reasonable defence can be erected, but this is a clear error. Hjartarson goes astray at the critical moment and his notes confirm that he could have found a way to have a more comfortable position: 16 ... ♘d4! 17 hxg6 (17 ♗e3? gxh5 18 g5 ♘g4 19 ♖xh5 ♘xe3+ 20 fxe3 ♘f5 with a strong initiative; 17 ♘e4 ♘xe4 18 ♗xe4 g5! is unclear) 17 ...

fxg6 18 ♘e4 (18 g5 ♘h5 19 ♖xh5? gxh6 20 ♕xh5 ♘f5!∓) 18 ... ♘d5, when the open f-file gives Black good chances relative to the game.

17 g5!

This move changes the direction of the game. Short manages to achieve the primary goal of opening the h-file by ignoring the immediate recapture in order to force the knight to move away from the protection of h5.

17 ... ♘g4
18 ♖xh5 f5
19 gxf6!

The knight must take back the pawn, leaving the e6-pawn weak and the king rather vulnerable, as now only the g7-pawn offers it any cover.

19 ... ♘xf6
20 ♖h3 ♘d4

The knight is heading for the kingside in an effort to fend off the attack.

21 ♘e4 ♘f5
22 ♘g5 g6
23 c3!

Now the queen is free to probe for weaknesses as the d4-square is no longer available for the black knight. Even a cursory inspection is sufficient to see that the opening has gone disastrously wrong for Black, who is struggling merely to survive. The rook on the h-file and the knight on g5 dictate matters.

23 ... c4
24 ♕e2 cxd3
25 ♕xe6+ ♕xe6
26 ♘xe6 ♖fe8
27 ♖xd3

Whilst Black has admittedly managed to relieve the pressure, this has been achieved at a high cost, the ending is rather depressing for him as White has a clear extra pawn and the pair of bishops to support it.

27 ... ♗d6
28 ♘d4 ♘xd4
29 ♖xd4 ♗c5
30 ♖c4 1-0

Black did not wish to see the technical part of the game.

Index of Variations

1 e4 c5
2 ♘c3

2 g3 d5 (2 ... g6 *147*) 3 exd5 (3 ♗g2 *147*) 3 ... ♕xd5 4 ♘f3 ♗g4 5 ♗g2 (5 ♗e2 *147*) 5 ... ♕e6+ (5 ... ♘c6 *148*) 6 ♔f1 ♘c6 (6 ... ♗h3 *148*) 7 h3 (7 d3 *148*) 7 ... ♗h5 8 ♘c3 (8 d3 *148*) 8 ... ♘c6 9 d3 (9 ♘e2 *148*) 9 ... ♕d7 10 a4 (10 g4 *149*) 10 ... e6 *149*

2 ... ♘c6

2 ... e6 (2 ... g6 *95*; 2 ... b6 *95*) 3 g3 d5 4 exd5 (4 d3 *139*; 4 ♗g2 *139*) 4 ... exd5 5 ♗g2 (5 d4 *139*) 5 ... ♘f6 *135*

3 g3

3 d3 *88*; 3 g4 *95*; 3 ♘f3 *126–134*

3 ... g6

3 ... ♖b8 *96*; 3 ... e5 *96*; 3 ... ♘f6 *96*; 3 ... d6 *96*; 3 ... h5 *96*; 3 ... e6 *142*

4 ♗g2 ♗g7
5 d3

5 ♘ge2 d6 (5 ... ♖b8 *116*) 6 0–0 (6 d3 *see D*) 6 ... e5 7 f4 *119*

5 ... d6

5 ... e6 (5 ... b6 *88*; 5 ... ♖b8 *92*) 6 ♗e3 (6 ♘ge2 *106*; 6 ♘h3 *85*) 6 ... d6 (6 ... ♘d4 7 ♘ce2 b6 [7 ... ♘xe2 *14*; 7 ... ♘ge7 *14*; 7 ... d6 *16*] 8 ♗xd4 *15*) 7 ♕d2 ♘ge7 (7 ... h6 *19*; 7 ... ♕a5 *23*; 7 ... ♘d4 *23*; 7 ... ♖b8 *23*) 8 ♗h6 ♗xh6 (8 ... 0–0 *27*) 9 ♕xh6 ♘d4 10 0–0–0 *27*

A) 6 ♗e3
B) 6 f4
C) 6 ♘h3
D) 6 ♘ge2
6 ♗g5 *86*; 6 ♘f3 *122*

A)

6 ♗e3 e5

6 ... e6 *19–29*; 6 ... b6 *30*; 6 ... ♘f6 *33*; 6 ... ♘d4 *36*; 6 ... ♗d7 *36*; 6 ... ♘h6 *36*; 6 ... ♖b8 *36*; 6 ... b5 7 e5 ♕d7 (7 ... ♗b7 *37*) 8 exd6 *37*

7 ♕d2 ♘ge7
8 ♗h6 *30*

B)

6 f4

a) 6 ... ♘f6
b) 6 ... e5
c) 6 ... e6

a)

6 ... ♘f6

6 ... f5 *41*; 6 ... b6 *41*; 6 ... ♖b8 *92*

7 ♘f3 0–0

7 ... ♖b8 *42*; 7 ... ♗d7 *42*

8 0–0 ♖b8

8 ... a6 *42*; 8 ... d5 *42*; 8 ... ♘e8 *42*

9 h3

9 ♘h4 *42*

9 ... b5

9 ... ♘e8 *42*

10 a3 a5
11 ♗e3 b4
12 axb4 axb4
13 ♘e2 ♗b7

13 ... ♘e8 *45*; 13 ... ♗d7 *46*; 13 ... ♕c7 *46*

14 b3 *44*

b)

6 ... e5
7 ♘h3

7 ♘f3 *49*

7 ... ♘ge7

7 ... exf4 8 ♘xf4 *56*; 8 ♗xf4 *56*

8 0-0 0-0

8 ... ♘d4 9 f5 (9 ♖f2 *53*) 9 ... gxf5 10 ♕h5 (10 ♗g5 *53*; 10 ♘g5 *53*) 10 ... h6 *54*

9 f5 *50*

c)

6 ... e6
7 ♘f3 ♘ge7
8 0-0 0-0

8 ... ♗d7 *81*; 8 ... d5 *82*; 8 ... ♖b8 *82*

9 ♗e3

9 ♔h1 *60*; 9 ♕e2 *60*; 9 g4 *60*; 9 ♕e1 *75*; 9 ♗d2 *79*

9 ... ♘d4

9 ... b6 *75*; 9 ... ♖b8 *75*

10 e5

10 Ne2 *60*
10 Rb1 Nec6 (10 ... Bd7 *60*; 10 ... b6 *60*; 10 ... Rb8 *60*; 10 ... d5 *61*) 11 Ne2 *61*
10 Bf2 Nxf3+ (10 ... Nec6 *63*; 10 ... Rb8 *63*; 10 ... Bd7 *63*; 10 ... f5 *64*; 10 ... b6 *64*) 11 Bxf3 Nc6 12 Bg2 Nd4 (12 ... Rb8 *64*) 13 e5 *see below*

10 ... Nef5

10 ... Qb6 *67*

11 Bf2 Nxf3

11 ... d5 *70*

12 Qxf3 Nd4

12 ... Rb8 *70*; 12 ... Bd7 *70*

13 Qd1 f5

13 ... d5 *64*; 13 ... dxe5 *64*; 13 ... Rb8 *71*

14 exf6 *71*

C)

6 Nh3 h5

6 ... e5 7 f4 *53*; 6 ... Nf6 *86*; 6 ... e6 *86*

7 f4

7 Nd5 *86*

7 ... Bg4 *86*

D)

6 Nge2 e6

6 ... Qd7 *100*; 6 ... Nf6 *109*; 6 ... Rb8 *112*; 6 ... Bd7 *112*; 6 ...

♘d4 *119*; 6 ... e5 *119*

7	**0–0**	**♘ge7**
8	**♗g5**	**h6**

8 ... 0–0 *103*; 8 ... b6 *103*

9 **♗e3** *103*